FUROR and MYSTERY
& Other Writings

T0308595

FUROR and MYSTERY

& Other Writings

by RENÉ CHAR

Edited and translated by
MARY ANN CAWS
and NANCY KLINE

Introduction by
SANDRA BERMANN

Foreword by
MARIE-CLAUDE CHAR

Furor and Mystery & Other Writings
English translations ©2010 Mary Ann Caws and Nancy Kline. Black Widow Press edition and
arrangement ©2010. The French poems contained in this edition are reprinted by arrangment with
Editions Gallimard, Paris. All are ©2010 Editions GALLIMARD, Paris.

Black Widow Press thanks Florence Giry and Gallimard for working with us on this compilation.
Some of the English translations previously appeared in Selected Poems of René Char, New Direc-
tions, 1992, and are reprinted by permission. Appreciative thanks to New Directions Publishing
Corp. for allowing us to reprint these translations.

"Announcing One's Name" by René Char, translated by Gustaf Sobin, from Selected Poems,
©1990, 1992 by Gustaf Sobin. Reprinted by permission of New Directions Publishing Corp. Sales
territory: U.S., Canadian, & open market rights only. "A Trying Simplicity," "Allegiance," "Annals,"
"Argument," "Artine," "Convey," "Evadne," "Homage and Famine," "Invitation," "Joyous," "Long
Live...," "Madeleine with the Vigil Lamp," "Man Flees Suffocation," "Orion's Reception," "Penum-
bra," "Refusal Song," "Remanence," "Restore to Them...," "Shortcut," "The Absent," "The Ado-
lescent Chastised," "The Crystal Wheat-ear...," "The Extravagant One," "The First Moments," "The
Lichens," "The Nuptial Countenance," "The Swift," "Unbending Prayer," "Veterance," "Wrestlers,"
by René Char, translated by Mary Ann Caws, from Selected Poems, ©1992 by Mary Ann Caws.
Reprinted by permission of New Directions Publishing Corp. Sales territory: U.S., Canadian & open
market rights only. "Frequency," "From Moment to Moment," "In Love," "The Consequences," by
René Char, translated by Mary Ann Caws and Patricia Terry, from Selected Poems, ©1992 by
Mary Ann Caws and Patricia Terry. Reprinted by permission of New Directions Publishing Corp.
Sales territory: U.S., Canadian & open market rights only. "Anoukis and Later Jeanne," "Inebria-
tion," "The Meteor of August 13th," "The Windowpane," and "Why the Day Flies," by René Char,
translated by Nancy Kline, from Selected Poems, ©1992 by Nancy Kline. Reprinted by permission
of New Directions Publishing Corp. Sales territory: U.S., Canadian & open market rights only.

We wish to acknowledge and thank the Hemingway Grant Program for its support. This work re-
ceived support from the French Ministry of Foreign Affairs and the Cultural Services of the French
Embassy in the United States through their publishing assistance program.

Cet ouvrage publié dans le cadre du programme d'aide à la publication bénéficie du soutien du
Ministère des Affaires Etrangères et du Service Culturel de l'Ambassade de France représenté aux
Etats-Unis.

All rights reserved. This book, or parts thereof, may not be reproduced in any form or by any
means electronic, digital, or mechanical, including photocopy, scanning, recording, or any infor-
mation storage and retrieval system, without written permission from the publisher except in the
case of brief quotations embodied in critical articles and reviews. For information, contact Black
Widow Press, 9 Spring Lane, Boston, MA 02109.

Black Widow Press is an imprint of Commonwealth Books, Inc., Boston, MA. Distributed to the trade
by NBN (National Book Network) throughout North America, Canada, and the U.K. All Black
Widow Press books are printed on acid-free paper. Black Widow Press and its logo are registered
trademarks of Commonwealth Books, Inc.

Joseph S. Phillips and Susan J. Wood, PhD., Publishers
www.blackwidowpress.com

Text Design: Kerrie Kemperman

ISBN-13: 978-0-9842640-2-5
ISBN-10: 0-9842640-2-7

10 9 8 7 6 5 4 3 2

Printed in the U.S.A.

LA FONTAINE NARRATIVE / THE NARRATIVE FOUNTAIN

OTHER WRITINGS

LE MARTEAU SANS MAÎTRE / THE HAMMER WITH NO MASTER

LES MATINAUX / THE MORNING ONES

LA PAROLE EN ARCHIPEL / THE WORD AS ARCHIPELAGO

RECHERCHE DE LA BASE ET DU SOMMET /
SEARCH FOR THE BASE AND THE SUMMIT

A FAULX CONTENTE / TO YOUR HEART'S CONTENT

LES VOISINAGES DE VAN GOGH / IN THE VICINITY OF VAN GOGH

ACKNOWLEDGMENTS

Many thanks to the friends who have helped these translations and essays by their encouragement and suggestions.

First of all, of course, to Marie-Claude Char, our warmest gratitude; to Patricia Terry and to Sandra Bermann, for their participation in this project; to the audiences on whom we have tried out our ongoing efforts; to La Maison Française at NYU for sponsoring our first reading and discussion of this project, and especially to Francine Goldenhaar for her encouragement; to Ed Colker for his superb illustrations of some of these translations; to Brooklyn Rail for publishing excerpts and for offering us the opportunity to read at the Brooklyn Public Library; to Hilary and Jonathan Caws-Elwitt for their help in some thorny passages; to Rosanna Warren and her Translation Seminar at Boston University for their suggestions; to the Virginia Center for the Creative Arts, where the essay "Meeting René Char" and many of the translations in this book were originally written; to Rebecca Guy, Victoria Hallerman, Polly Howells, and Susan Sindall for being wonderful readers; and most of all, to Joe Phillips for his faith in poetry.

And to René Char, never really *in absentia* from this work, for his writing and his welcome.

Mary Ann Caws and Nancy Kline

PREFACE

A new translation of the poems of René Char is always an event. This time, it's a real banquet because it gathers around the poet not only translators, but friends.

Mary Ann Caws and Nancy Kline, through the testimonies they offer, bring alive the poet's words, evoking those moments so often shared under the Provençal sun, and, very surely, under that of friendship. As for Sandra Bermann, although she didn't know René Char himself, she explains, in a brilliant essay, the place he holds in history, as "le Capitaine Alexandre," head of the maquis and great *résistant* from 1940–1944, stressing how much all his poetry, from his surrealist adventure onwards, is at once action and a form of resistance, a perfect answer to René Char's words: "I have breathed aggressively, from the moment I was born." This anthology, by its wealth of witness illuminating the links of friendship forged throughout the years, will help Char to be still better known. Thanks to this warm evocation, a man stands upright among us.

How to speak of him today? A man with a magnetic gaze, a colossus with the look of a sportsman, who knew how to calm storms and to capture lightning with ease. As Saint-John Perse says of him: "Char, you have taken command of lightning in its very nest, and upon this lightning, you build." His poetry is love, but also revolt. Poetry has taken the place of the father, who has disappeared all too soon. He breaks with his family, throws himself into the surrealist adventure, leaving this movement once it has become, with André Breton, a "school." He is present, helpless, at the defeat of those fighting for the Spanish Republic and prepares himself for struggle. The war will compel him to take on heavy responsibilities. He becomes a rebel, a war leader, "le capitaine Alexandre," who will be in charge of seven départements or sectors from the Drôme to the Alpes Maritimes, with the greatest stock of weapons and explosives in the Southeastern part of France. He will not be forgotten, when France salutes its heroes.

He becomes the poet of the Resistance, admired and praised, when after the war he publishes *Les Feuillets d'Hypnos.* Then his collection of surrealist poems: *Le Marteau sans maître* is reprinted, and a long series of works follows, as friendships develop around him and regroup: Albert Camus, Georges Bataille, Raymond Queneau, Paul Eluard. He renews his friendships with painters he had known during the surrealist epoch: Henri Matisse, Georges Braque, Joan Miró, Nicolas de Staël. He writes prefaces for some of their exhibitions, and works in their studios, creating collaborative work. He continues his refusal to enroll in any political group. He takes the side of Albert Camus when he is condemned by Jean-Paul Sartre at the publication of *L'Homme révolté,* opposes the communist weekly *Les Lettres françaises* during the Kravchenko affair, militates against the implantation of missiles on the Plateau d'Albion and for the preservation of the banks of the Fontaine de Vaucluse, enlarges the circle of his painter friends with Maria Elena da Silva et Alexandre Galperine. He misses the Nobel prize, but is published in Gallimard's prestigious Pléiade collection.

In his last years, he preferred living in his house, les Busclats, completing there the poems of his last collection, *Eloge d'une Soupçonnée.* These years lived near him in which certain personal and fragmentary images arise, round out the journey of an "ungovernable man," who often quoted this sentence of Nietzsche as speaking for himself: "I have always put in my writings my whole life and my whole person. I don't know what purely intellectual problems might be."

The first image that comes to mind is that of his house, Les Busclats in l'Isle sur la Sorgue, so small for such a large man! He worked in a very dark room, across from a window facing the garden. On his work table the books formed high walls, and often one had to rise from the very low armchair, placed right against his desk, to glimpse his face and his hands continually in motion. In the winter a blazing fire burned always in the fireplace, and the smell of soup permeated the whole house. Placed right on the tile floor, an array of baskets of all sizes out of which spilled the mail, the journals, the newspapers, all adding to the disorder of the room. Over the fireplace, a reproduction of Georges de La Tour's *Prisoner*, some painted pebbles, a few stones and flints...

On my first visit to the Busclats, I left, my heart beating hard, with a treasure in the palm of my hand, a flint arrowhead. René Char had slipped it into an envelope on which he had written: "For Marie-Claude, I'm 8000 years old."

Together, we walked and crossed this land with long strides. The lark and the swift and the unquiet squirrel seemed to chant: "Long Live." On these paths, the cradle of a childhood ripped apart, we looked at the grace of the meadows, the ebullition of the waters, the Mont Ventoux "mirror of eagles," protecting with its wing the Dentelles de Montmirail.

In Lagnes, near the Fontaine de Vaucluse, René Char helped me acquire a cabanon, "le Rébanqué," where I would stay with my children. Situated up against the hills of the Vaucluse and facing the plain of Cavaillon, the house was completely isolated. You would get there on an earth path bordered with dry stones. In April, a field of flowering almond trees brightened the wild atmosphere of the place. We would walk along these paths where the voices of yesterday were murmuring. For it is in this cabanon that René used to receive his friends: Camus, de Staël, Christian et Yvonne Zervos, and where most of the poems in the collection *Les Matinaux* were written.

In Céreste, the village in the Basses Alpes (now called les Alpes de Haute Provence), which was his headquarters during the years of the Resistance, René Char told me of his refusing to return there. A page was turned, but the flame of memory was still burning. This moment, that lasted four long years, when he led his men to combat with "a lock in his jaw and a mountain in his gaze" still brought tears to his eyes.

Finally, a great project was born in the Busclats with the collaboration of the painter Alexandre Galperine. They had met in 1975, and Char had encouraged the artist to leave aside his large canvasses in order to illustrate and illuminate his poems with a brush stroke of delicacy and precision. Then René asked me to participate in the adventure, and incessant work got underway. The painter would seize the poems, eager to spread his colors out beside them, and when his drawing was barely dry, he would knock at the door of the Busclats, where René would be waiting for him impatiently. All three of us would spread out, assemble, discard, and set the leaves in order. Twenty-eight poems in manuscript were chosen and made luminous by Alexandre's vibrant palette. Published in April of 1987, *Le gisant mis en lumière,* this book of friendship and fraternity will have been the last "sovereign conversation" of the poet and the painter.

The dialogue was interrupted on February 19, 1988. A breath was extinguished, and yet a voice remains.

Marie-Claude Char

tr. MAC

RENÉ CHAR: POET AND RESISTANT

Sandra Bermann

"Place René Char (1907–1988): Poète et Résistant," reads a newly painted sign at the corner of boulevard Raspail and the rue du Bac in Paris. Not far from the rue de Chanaleilles, where Char had an apartment for years, and from hotels and cafes where he lived and wrote at other moments of his life, this intersection recalls, for the casual passerby as well as for the devoted reader, one of France's greatest twentieth century poets. An official 'lieu de mémoire' for this Poet and Resistant, it was dedicated in October 2007 at the centenary of his birth.

Unlike the translators of this volume, I never met René Char. I came to know him only through his poetry—from an early stage with the guidance of Mary Ann Caws and later through the generosity of Marie-Claude Char. For me, the texts of *Fureur et mystère,* and particularly their central group of prose poems, *Feuillets d'Hypnos,* themselves serve as lieux de mémoire.[i] They powerfully evoke Char's role as Resistant, in a France I did not know, but am learning, through his words, to remember. Yet they testify simultaneously to his extraordinary power as a poet. Inspired by historical events, his poems live for me, as for many of his twenty-first century readers, through their memorable as well as memorializing use of language—as dialogue, as aphorism and metaphor, as what he calls Imagination and Beauty. As such, they are a place to return to—a poetic memory site, as it were—a place to experience some of Char's most extraordinary work as Poet and Resistant.[ii]

Char and the Resistance
In one sense, René Char, the poet, was always a Resistant. From his earliest writings, and particularly during his association with Surrealism, he exemplified a style of poetry and of life that was an ongoing

challenge to, at times an outright refusal of bourgeois norms. He had long registered his vehement opposition to Nazism, to colonialism, and to the Franco regime in Spain. But the word 'Resistant' takes on particular resonance in the years 1938–47, the years when he composed most of the texts for what many believe is his greatest collection, *Fureur et mystère*. Writing in anticipation of the War, in its midst while actively fighting against the Nazi Occupation, and then in the often disillusioning aftermath, the poetry evokes years when suffering and death transformed the ordinary, raising new questions, without easy answers.

Though he had foreseen the War for years, alluding to it in poetry and prose,[iii] Char's direct experience of it began in 1939, when he was mobilized and sent to Alsace. At the time, he was thirty-two. Demobilized in 1940, after the Armistice, he returned briefly to his home in L'Isle-sur-la-Sorgue, in the Vaucluse region in southern France. But only briefly. Denounced there as a militant of the extreme left, he traveled east and north to Céreste, where friends gave him refuge. This was a village known to Char since his youth, whose situation and unprepossessing appearance made it an excellent choice for his Resistance activities. From here, Char soon began to create a network of partisans—men and women from Céreste and also from the nearby towns of Simiane, Forcalquier, Oraison, Digne, Manosque, as well as from L'Isle-sur-la-Sorgue, Aix-en Provence, and Avignon. In 1942, he was already actively involved in Resistance activities as part of the Armée Secrète, and as head of the section Durance-Sud, under the pseudonym, Alexandre. In 1943, when de Gaulle sent an envoy, Camille Rayon, to help organize the maquis for intensified action, Char was asked to head a division of Forces françaises combatants in the Basse-Alpes de Provence, and charged with region two of the S.A.P. (Section Atterrissage Parachutage Région 2), the section overseeing parachute landings of arms and munitions. He was also second in command in the broader organization Action (dedicated to combat missions) in this same region. As history tells us, allied parachute landings of arms and munitions found safety on the fields he and his partisans prepared. Not one was lost or discovered in Char's sector. In July of 1944, when De Gaulle and the allies prepared to invade France from the coasts of Provence, Char was called to Algeria to serve as liaison.[iv] Beloved by his men, known for his courage and strategic wisdom, he won the admiration of both French and American military leaders, with whom he worked in the landing in Provence. As he had agreed, he continued his wartime service for another three months after the end of hostilities before returning to civilian life. All the while he wrote.

Published in 1948, *Fureur et mystère* contains most, if not all, the poetry from this period. Much had not been published until the close of the war. For unlike other Resistance poets, Char had written—but purposely not published—his poetry during the Occupation. Only at the beginning of 1945 did texts appear in print that would later make up central portions of *Fureur et mystère*: "Seuls demeurent," the first part of the collection, was published in 1945 by Gallimard. (Raymond Queneau had presented the manuscript.) In 1946, "Feuillets d'Hypnos," Char's poetic war journal and the central section of *Fureur et mystère*, appeared in his friend Albert Camus' series, *L'Espoir.* A year later, in 1947, *Le Poème pulvérisé*, central to the third part of the collection, was published with an original engraving by Henri Matisse.[v]

From the collection as a whole emerge multiple traces of these times, appearing through an imagery evocative of the sights, sounds, odors of L'Isle-sur-la-Sorgue and the hills near Céreste, where most of Char's Resistance operations took place. Some texts concentrate purely on the natural world, appreciated during wartime with only heightened intensity. "The population of the meadows enchants me… The field-vole, the mole, somber children lost in the chimera of the grass, the blindworm, son of glass, the cricket, conformist as they come, the grasshopper who flaps and counts its linen…" he writes in 175. Others tell of love as well as nature, "Since the kiss on the mountain, time is guided by the golden summer of her hands and the oblique ivy" (176).

The poetry evokes Char's countryside concretely and lovingly. But it is as often tied to reflections on time—and to the historical moment in particular. It is a place/time that Hannah Arendt famously described in the preface to *Between Past and Future.* An image from Char's *Feuillets d'Hypnos* launches her discussion. "Our inheritance is preceded by no testament," (62) suggesting the loss of comforting continuities, and the breakdown of tradition that she finds characteristic of this moment and that makes it difficult to interpret in the usual ways.

If it is a time when continuities are suddenly severed, when history is beginning to re-think its possibilities, it is also a time when texts such as Char's, with their literary, symbolic evocations of specific times and places, reveal the importance of individual memory to the modern imagination. Though evident throughout the collection, it is particularly clear in the central section, *Feuillets d'Hypnos,* to which I will now turn briefly. Here, perhaps more consistently than anywhere else in his writing, we see the work of Char as Poet *and* Resistant.

Feuillets d'Hypnos: Memory
Feuillets d'Hypnos is presented by Char as a journal from the war years. His prologue makes clear the connection of his poetry with the empirical events of a lived history:

> These notes owe nothing to self-love, to the short story, the maxim, or the novel. A fire of dry herbs might just as well have been their editor. The sight of blood tortured led once to losing the thread, reduced their importance to nothing. They were written under stress, in anger, fear, emulation, disgust, guile, furtive meditation, the illusion of the future, friendship, love. Which is to say how much they are shaped by the event. Afterwards more skimmed than reread.

This notebook could have belonged to no one, so deep does the meaning of a man's life lie beneath his wanderings, so hard is it to tell apart from a sometimes extraordinary mimicry. Such tendencies were fought, however.

These notes record the resistance of a humanism conscious of its duties, cautious of its virtues, wanting to keep the inaccessible open to the imagination of its suns and determined to pay the price for that.

The very form of the collection, with its 237 numbered prose poems, first composed in 1943–44, then revised and poetically transformed, incarnates the pervasive sense of radical contingency, discontinuity, and loss which Char's individual poems so often address. We find texts of various lengths, organized in no clear chronology or thematic order. Juxtaposition rules, providing a sense of surprise and unevenness that appears through typography as well as the semantics of the text. Pauses in the rhythm of the poems, as well as discontinuities between them, evoke the contingencies in which life on the Maquis is lived. Within this collection of numbered prose poems, without telos, without chronology, action prevails—both military and linguistic. Each poem stands isolated—a query, a brief appeal, a memory, sometimes—merely—a hope.

Char's poetry often takes up his historical times quite specifically, engaging the poet's power to act as a witness and keeper, even a mirror of what he perceives: in 83, he writes, "The poet, keeper of the infinite faces of the living" or, in 156, "Accumulate, then distribute. Be the most compact, most useful, and least apparent part of the universe's mirror." And indeed, the variety of voices, perspectives and perceptions presented by the poet is one of its most striking qualities.[vi]

Some of Char's texts clearly elaborate upon lived historical events, as well as imagined actions, preserving them verbally, heightening them through plays of language and memory. From these we gather poetic traces of his times—some more narrative, some descriptive, many short and gnomic in form. So the reader is made privy to the ambush of a small division of German soldiers, the forest fire that erupts after a parachute drop of munitions, the search for Char in the town of Céreste by soldiers from the SS, and details of the daily life of his troops. Many poems explicitly recall and give value to the dead. The execution of Roger Bernard (138), a torture and death near Vachères (99), the remembered assassination of partisans such as Emile Cavagni, Roger Chaudon, Gustave Lefevre (157, 231, 94) deeply affect the collection. And the list could continue.

Such poems might be said to provide poetic renditions, or 'translations', of historical events. They are also, of course, actions in themselves. Difficult, at times almost impossible to write, they involve a creative remaking, of which Char was quite conscious:

> I do myself violence to preserve my voice in ink, despite my mood. Thus, it is with a pen whose nib is a battering ram—ceaselessly extinguished, ceaselessly relit, collected, tensed—and with one breath that I write this, and leave out that. Automaton of vanity? Sincerely not. The necessity is to examine the evidence, to turn it into a created entity (194).

There are, in fact, a number of astonishing things about Char's journal. One is its very self-reflectiveness, as suggested above. But another is the fact that the tragic history he describes has no prospect of an end. Without a sense of causality, or evident 'plotline', the tragic times of which Char writes will certainly not come to a peaceful conclusion: "Life should begin with an explosion and end with a peace agreement? Absurd." (140) If anything, the contingent, uncertain, changeful temporality he describes seems most likely to continue, as endemic to our human condition.

Yet another characteristic of Char's journal, and one of the most surprising, is its refusal to take a simple, patriotic stance. Char's poems from the Resistance, in contrast to many others of the time, powerfully resist the usual universalizing and nationalizing statements.[viii]

His poems deal decidedly with particulars, be they historical, imaginative or, as is almost always the case, combinations of both. They are not unequivocal in their depiction of 'good' and 'evil,' nor easy about what it costs to think in such terms. Though the Resistance itself is most often presented in a positive light—for the individual transformations it could create, for the unforgettable friendships it forged, and, above all for its moral necessity—it is also treated by Char, at times, with cynicism and questioning. Even the Liberation, which he believed would come, could not, he also knew, solve the problems—political and ethical—that he saw around him. In its 'mirroring,' Char's poetic journal takes events at unexpected angles that can sometimes be directed to the reader's, as well as the poet's, own times with prophetic force: "This war will stretch beyond platonic armistices. The implanting of political concepts will proceed contradictorily with the convulsive stealth of a hypocrisy certain of its rights. Don't smile. Thrust from you skepticism, resignation, and prepare your mortal soul to face, within the city walls, glacial demons similar to fiendish microbes" (7). The poet asks us to question, reread, rethink the historical past and its relation to the present anew.

It is in part because of the nature of the events, but in larger part because of Char's very particular address to them that his poems from the war years touch us so deeply even today. And this is not simply a matter of theme. It is, above all, the form and language of his poetry that make his distinctive sense of tragic temporality so palpable, a temporality with clear connections to both Nietzsche and Heraclitus[ix]—and that balance all of this with an aspiration toward freedom, hope, and what Char calls 'Beauty.'

Poet of the War Years

Though *Feuillets d'Hypnos* holds within it the memory of a lived history, it does not stop time, sealing it off in the past, in a world all its own. Rather, it engages the reader directly, through the challenge of language and form, asking us to reflect, to imagine differently, to see with new eyes.

The particular power Char ascribes to language and to art more generally emerges in one of his most often quoted texts, 178 of the *Feuillets d'Hypnos,* an appreciation of the painter, Georges de la Tour:

> The color reproduction of Georges de la Tour's "Prisoner," which I've stuck on the whitewashed wall of the room in which I work, seems over time to reflect its meaning into our circumstances. It wrings our hearts, but how deeply quenches our thirst! For two years now, not one resistance fighter who hasn't, coming through the door, burned his eyes on what that candle proves. The woman explains, the walled-in prisoner listens. The words that fall from this terrestrial silhouette of a red angel are essential words, words that immediately bring help. In the depths of the dark cell the minutes of the tallow's clarity lengthen and dilute the features of the seated man. His dry-nettle thinness—I see not one memory to make it shiver. His bowl is in ruins. But the swollen gown abruptly fills the dark cell. Better than any dawn, the Word of woman gives birth to the unhoped-for.
>
> My gratitude to Georges de la Tour who mastered the Hitlerian shadows with a dialogue between two human beings.

The saving power of language—as dialogue, but also as the site of imaginative birth and hope (or, as here, the 'unhoped-for')—is a leitmotif throughout the collection, one which plays on a number of registers. At times, it is a dialogue overheard between a leader and the partisans. (Hypnos writes, for instance, to his second in command on the maquis, with an entire list of life-saving admonitions and directions [87].) At other moments, we as readers are reminded of our own dialogical responsibilities to rethink and interpret the past: "The action that has a meaning to the living has value only for the dead, finds completion only in those consciousnesses that inherit and question it" (187). The poet sometimes poses a question directly: "How can you hear me? I'm speaking from so faraway..." (88). More often, the address is indirect. He writes, for instance, of the singularity of the moment and the act through a simple, gnomic sentence: "The act is virgin, even repeated" (46). Or he famously encourages the leap: "Be part of the leap. Do not be part of the banquet, its epilogue"(197). Here, the moment and its doing hold the spotlight. In the maquis, at a time and a place where action, not rational contemplation reigns, where cause has been radically severed from effect, action ought not linger to calculate its results. And, of course, the Resistance itself demanded the greatest leap, a leap of moral necessity, yet one whose practical results could not, at the time, be calculated. Though these short poems speak from, and to some extent to, their own historical cohort,[x] their continued use of the present tense or infinitive, with an indefinite addressee, also creates a complex dialogue with the reader in the present.

Such dialogic appeals—to partisans and/or to readers—are not the only sorts of linguistic openings to be found here. Char's poetry also offers imaginative gestures toward the 'unhoped-for,' the 'inaccessible,' of which he speaks in the poems above. Not, of course, visions of a happy ending. But poem after poem inscribes in language something even more important—a brief participation in the ongoing creativity and rebirth that inhabits life's changefulness and mortality—even during this most deadly historical moment. Char's sense of the poetic imagination is, in this way, consistent with the temporality of which it is a part. It prizes images of the everyday, of nature, and the material world from which it begins and to which it always returns, but also of something beyond it as well: the always unknown, the "unhoped-for," the "inaccessible." These last are regularly associated with imagination and hope.

At several points in the text, the poet reminds the reader directly of the importance of the imagination. He tells us, for instance, that though the Resistance is clearly physical and historical, the imagination can also play an active part. "Keep for later the imaginary part which is, itself too, capable of action," he writes in 18.

But what sort of action is this? Though such a question can never be fully answered, perhaps we could begin by saying that poetry can imagine and in some sense even *perform* an act of resistance, hope and freedom—by releasing the reader from the usual patterns of linguistic and mental patterning, while engaging in new acts of creation. Placing this in the historical context of Nazi propaganda, such linguistic novelty, such ruptures of the usual into strangeness, are all the more salient. In Char's *Feuillets d'Hypnos,* at least some of this imaginative action derives from his anti-generic form. Here we see the play of different kinds and lengths of texts and, especially, the prominence of the aphorism.

It is, in fact, in *Fureur et mystère* that the aphorism first becomes one of Char's dominant forms. Characteristic of two of his most beloved authors, Heraclitus and Nietzsche, the aphorism is a form that plays a pervasive, and purposely disruptive, role in the *Feuillets.* In its brief, syntactic frame, it can offer a surprising, and explosive resistance to semantic expectations. It puts language into movement, opening it to new possibilities. As Char writes in a preface to Battistini's French translation of Heraclitus, the aphorism, "strikes an opening and endows language with movement,"[xi] As he suggests in *Partage formel,* the originality of Heraclitus resides in images that are specific, tumultuous and that come together in an "exaltation of contraries." It is here that language can become something like an event, a present moment in its passing, one that allows neither foothold nor skyhook, only a passage of striking imagery.

In these short poems, where language becomes temporal event— novel metaphors and imagery arise. Char's metaphors themselves are far from ornamental, and do not often participate in a mimetic project. They are themselves often adventures—beyond the everyday and the referential. They are trans-port, separation from an original context and journey to an altogether new one. Essential to their quality is that force of contradiction Char associates with the aphorism as well, that refuses any sense of rest or of knowledge possessed. Their effect can shock and dismay: "Only the eyes are still capable of crying out" (104). Or provide a sense of deliverance: "The poem's line of flight. It should be *felt* by each" (98). Poems constructed in these ways turn away from conventional understandings and look expectantly to the future—a future of readerly dialogue and interpretation[xii].

Through his aphorisms and metaphors, Char often offers specific images of transformation and nascency. He writes, for instance, of the almond that "springs from its restive hardness and transposes your solitude" (191), or of "Imagination, my child" (101). At somewhat greater length, he writes, "At all the meals we take in common, we invite freedom to sit down. The chair remains empty, but the place continues to be set" (131). Such images offer brief visions of hope and new beginnings. But like life itself, like the desire and sometimes fearful contingency that starkly mark each day on the maquis, Char's language, presented in brief aphorisms or short prose poems, leaves its imagery incomplete, a journey begun, held in suspension.

Perhaps no poem better underscores the energetic power of poetic language than 56: "The poem is furious ascension; poetry, the play of arid riverbanks." In a diagram, referring to his poem and sent to Victor Brauner, Char shows the poem emerging from the present, but sweeping in its flight from the past into the future.[xiii] Here, the present is generative, revealing the juncture of past and future in the work of language.

Through their form and imagery, through their commitment to the power and creativity of language, Char's aphoristic prose poems disrupt the certainty of death with perceptions of new life, open imprisoning expectations with surprising juxtapositions, and find within the tragic pessimism of history moments of dialogue and hope. Such poetry, such imagination is, for Char, anything but a departure from the "real" work of the Resistance. Rather, it is an important addition to it. Some texts in fact make the connection Poetry–Resistance thematically explicit. Among them, one short text is particularly eloquent: "Resistance is only hope. Like the moon of Hypnos, full tonight in all its quarters, tomorrow vision over poems passing by" (168). Here, through a juxtaposition of images, the poet asks the reader to establish parallels between Resistance and the moon of Hypnos, hope and the passage of poems. And it is not without significance that hope is attached both to the idea of passage (with its implications of transience) and to poems. Hope inheres in poetry not because it offers an escape from the world. We know this from all the poems in the *Feuillets,* where the specificity of the everyday sights, sounds and actions is so vividly and continuously evoked. It is rather because language itself is a creative source, a site where action and beauty may be produced *within* this world.

Written in the Hitlerian shadows, in the keen awareness of death and loss, Char's poetry, with its aphorisms and metaphors, thus asserts an ongoing transformation and openness to the future. It can give rise to Beauty, the ever-renewable sign of human creativity in a world recognized not only as imperfect, but inevitably transient. It is also the sign of hope.

In the very last texts of *Feuillets d'Hypnos,* it is Beauty that is ultimately sought in the tragedy that is life—and that Char finds to be everywhere: "In our shadows, there is not one space alone for Beauty. The whole space is for Beauty" (237). And as the poet writes in the very last text, in a world of suffering, Beauty "joins with man determined to elude his destiny by means of its indomitable contrary: hope." The beauty language produces in poetry is, in this sense, an act of resistance in a world gone awry, and a necessary complement to the Dionysian temporality and loss that history—and life in history—seems to impose.

A Memory Site Revisited

In texts such as these from *Feuillets d'Hypnos,* Char's work as Poet and Resistant comes together in a particularly dramatic way. As such, they may be a good place to begin—or to return to—in the larger collection, *Fureur et mystère.* From their vantage point, for instance, references to the war, to Heraclitus and Georges de la Tour in *Partage formel* take on sudden resonance, and the aphoristic form as well as the role of the 'unknown' in the *Poème pulvérisé* gain a broader context. But as lieux de memoire, these texts tell us much about the particular moment in which they were written—if not always the specifics of history, then surely the deep logic of the times. Their imaginative power, belonging very deliberately to the world of language and art, is, at the same time, meant to inspire us with hope, even belief in the future. As such, this writing helps us to remember René Char, Poet *and* Resistant, and to appreciate his art as a place for Beauty and wisdom not only in his historical times, but also in our own.

---

[i] I use the term with reference to Pierre Nora's seminal essay, "Between Memory and History: Les Lieux de Mémoire," *Representations* 26, spring 1989, pp. 7–24.

[ii] Many texts in *Fureur et mystère* evoke the war years directly. There are also a number of others that speak to this period, the most important perhaps being the "Billets à Francis Curel" in René Char, *Oeuvres complètes,* Paris: Gallimard, 1983, pp. 632–639.

[iii] He does so particularly in *Seuls demeurent,* dated 1938–1944; this is the first section of *Fureur et mystère.*

[iv] See, for instance, Dominique Fourcade, "Chronologie" in, René Char, *Les Cahiers de l'Herne,* Paris: 1971, 2007, pp. 9–12; also, in much greater detail, Laurent Greilsamer, *L'éclair au front: la vie de René Char,* Paris: Fayard, 2004, pp. 135–225; Paul Veyne, *René Char en ses poèmes,* Paris: Gallimard, 1990, pp. 184–222; Laurent

Greilsamer et Paul Veyne, *René Char,* Paris: Culturesfrances, 2007; Daniel Leclair, *René Char: Là où brûle la poésie* (Paris: Aden, 2007), pp. 133–220.

ᵛ Dates of publication taken from René Char, *OC,* pp. LXXV–LXXVI.

ᵛⁱ See for intriguing observations on the historical and poetic complexity of voices, Carrie Noland, "Messages personnels: Radio, Cryptology, and the Resistance Poetry of René Char," in *Poetry at Stake: Lyric Aesthetics and the Challenge of Technology.* Princeton: Princeton University Press, 1999, pp. 142–62; also Van Kelly, "Passages Beyond the Resistance: René Char's Seuls demeurent and its Harmonics in Semprun and Foucault," *SubStance,* #102, Vol. 32, no. 3, 2003.

ᵛⁱⁱ Translation, history, and form are discussed at greater length in Sandra Bermann, "Translating History," in *Nation, Language, and the Ethics of Translation,* ed. Sandra Bermann and Michael Wood (Princeton: Princeton University Press), pp. 257–73. For superb historical notes on each text and close analysis as well, see Jean-Claude Mathieu, *La poésie de René Char ou le sel de la splendeur,* Vol II. Paris: José Corti, 1995.

ᵛⁱⁱⁱ See Eric Marty, "Feuillets d'Hypnos, Le pouvoir au poétique," in *René Char: Le géant magnétique, centenaire.* Télérama hors série, (Paris, 2007), pp. 52–55; also Bermann, op. cit.

ⁱˣ For connections to Nietzsche and Heraclitus, see Veyne, pp. 302–332.

ˣ See Noland, pp. 142–162.

ˣⁱ René Char, "Héraclite d'Ephèse," in *René Char: Dans l'atelier du poète,* ed. Marie-Claude Char. Paris: Gallimard, 1996, p. 547. Translation mine.

ˣⁱⁱ See Van Kelly's discussion of Char's effects on Semprun and Foucault, op. cit.

ˣⁱⁱⁱ "Hommage à Victor Brauner. L'Ascension furieuse," in *René Char: sous la direction d'Antoine Coran,* Bibliothèque nationale de France (Paris: Gallimard, 2007), p. 82.

FUREUR ET MYSTÈRE

FUROR AND MYSTERY

BANDEAU DE FUREUR ET MYSTÈRE

Le poète, on le sait, mêle le manque et l'excès, le but et le passé. D'où l'insolvabilité de son poème. Il est dans la malédiction, c'est-à-dire qu'il assume de perpétuels et renaissants périls, autant qu'il refuse, les yeux ouverts, ce que d'autres acceptent, les yeux fermés : le profit d'être poète. Il ne saurait exister de poète sans appréhension pas plus qu'il n'existe de poèmes sans provocation. Le poète passé par tous les degrés solitaires d'une gloire dont il est, de bonne guerre, exclu. C'est la condition pour sentir et dire juste. Quand il parvient génialement à l'incandescence et à l'inaltéré (Eschyle, Lao-Tseu, les présocratiques grecs, Thérèse d'Avila, Shakespeare, Saint-Just, Rimbaud, Hölderlin, Nietzsche, Van Gogh, Melville), il obtient le résultat que l'on connaît. Il ajoute de la noblesse à son cas lorsqu'il est hésitant dans son diagnostic et le traitement des maux de l'homme de son temps, lorsqu'il formule des réserves sur la meilleure façon d'appliquer la connaissance et la justice dans le labyrinthe du politique et du social. Il doit accepter le risque que sa lucidité soit jugée dangereuse. Le poète est la partie de l'homme réfractaire aux projets calculés. Il peut être appelé à payer n'importe quel prix ce privilège ou ce boulet. Il doit savoir que mal vient toujours de plus loin qu'on ne croit, et ne meurt pas forcément sur la barricade qu'on lui a choisie.

Fureur et mystère est, les temps le veulent, un recueil de poèmes, et, sur la vague du drame et du revers inéluctable d'où résurgit la tentation, un dire de notre affection ténue pour le nuage et pour l'oiseau.

Furor and Mystery

ABOUT FUROR AND MYSTERY

The poet, we know, mingles lack and excess, the goal and the past. From this, the insolubility of his poem. He is under a curse, that is to say he assumes perils both perpetual and renascent, insofar as he refuses, with his eyes open, what others accept, with their eyes closed: the profit of being a poet. There could not be an unapprehensive poet any more than there could be a poem without provocation. The poet passes through all the solitary stages of a collective glory from which he is, quite fairly, excluded. It's the condition for feeling and speaking with justice. When he arrives, brilliantly, at the incandescent and the unchanged (Aeschylus, Lao-Tse, the Greek presocratics, Thérèse d'Avila, Shakespeare, Saint-Just, Rimbaud, Hölderlin, Nietzsche, Van Gogh, Melville), he attains the result we know. He adds nobility to his case when he hesitates in his diagnosis and the treatment of the evils of man in his own time, when he makes some reservations about the best way to apply knowledge and justice in the social and political labyrinth. He must accept the risk of having his lucidity deemed dangerous. The poet is that part of man rebellious to calculated projects. He may be called to pay no matter what price for this privilege or this ball and chain. He must know that evil always comes from further off than we think, and doesn't necessarily die on the barricade chosen for him.

Fureur et mystère is, the times would have it so, a collection of poems, and, about the wave of drama and of the ineluctable reversal from which temptation surges forth once more, a statement of our sustained affection for the cloud and the bird.

1948

—MAC

René Char

SEULS DEMEURENT
(1938–1944)

THEY ALONE REMAIN
(1938–1944)

ARGUMENT

1938

L'homme fuit l'asphyxie.

L'homme dont l'appétit hors de l'imagination se calfeutre sans finir de s'approvisionner, se délivrera par les mains, rivières soudainement grossies.

L'homme qui s'épointe dans la prémonition, qui déboise son silence intérieur et le répartit en théâtres, ce second c'est le faiseur de pain.

Aux uns la prison et la mort. Aux autres la transhumance du Verbe.

Déborder l'économie de la création, agrandir le sang des gestes, devoir de toute lumière.

Nous tenons l'anneau où sont enchaînés côte à côte, d'une part le rossignol diabolique, d'autre part la clé angélique.

Sur les arêtes de notre amertume, l'aurore de la conscience s'avance et dépose son limon.

Aoûtement. Une dimension franchit le fruit de l'autre. Dimensions adversaires. Déporté de l'attelage et des noces, je bats le fer des fermoirs invisibles.

ARGUMENT

1938

Man flees suffocation.

Man, whose appetite beyond imagination shuts himself up in laying supplies, will find freedom by his hands, rivers suddenly swollen.

Man who grows blunt through premonitions, who deforests his inner silence and divides it into stages, the latter one is the maker of bread.

To the former, prison and death. To the latter, the repasturing of the Word.

To exceed the economy of creation, to increase the blood of gestures, task of all light.

We hold the ring where the devilish nightingale and the angelic key are chained together, side by side.

Over the ridge of our bitterness, the dawn of conscience comes forth to deposit its loam.

August ripening. One dimension traverses the fruit of the other. Warring dimensions. Deported from the yoke and from the nuptials, I strike the iron of invisible hinges.

—MAC

René Char

39

CONGÉ AU VENT

A flancs de coteau du village bivouaquent des champs fournis de mimosas. A l'époque de la cueillette, il arrive que, loin de leur endroit, on fasse la rencontre extrêmement odorante d'une fille dont les bras se sont occupés durant la journée aux fragiles branches. Pareille à une lampe dont l'auréole de clarté serait de parfum, elle s'en va, le dos tourné au soleil couchant.

Il serait sacrilège de lui adresser la parole.

L'espadrille foulant l'herbe, cédez-lui le pas du chemin.

Peut-être aurez-vous la chance de distinguer sur ses lèvres la chimère de l'humidité de la Nuit?

VIOLENCES

La lanterne s'allumait. Aussitôt une cour de prison l'étreignait. Des pêcheurs d'anguilles venaient là fouiller de leur fer les rares herbes dans l'espoir d'en extraire de quoi amorcer leurs lignes. Toute la pègre des écumes se mettait à l'abri du besoin dans ce lieu. Et chaque nuit le même manège se répétait dont j'étais le témoin sans nom et la victime. J'optai pour l'obscurité et la réclusion.

Étoile du destiné. J'entr'ouvre la porte du jardin des morts. Des fleurs serviles se recueillent. Compagnes de l'homme. Oreilles du Créateur.

IN THE ABSENCE OF WIND

On flanks of the village hillside bivouac fields that are deep in mimosa. Far away from the harvest of the flowers, you may fragrantly come face to face with a girl whose arms have been occupied all day long in the fragile branches. Like a lamp whose halo of brightness would be a perfume, she goes her way, her back to the setting sun.

It would be sacrilege to speak to her.

Your sandals crushing the grass, yield her the path.

Won't you, perhaps, have the luck to perceive on her lips a shimmer of humid night?

—PT

VIOLENT MOMENTS

Light from the lantern. A prison courtyard embraced it instantly. Eel fishermen were arriving to search the sparse grass in the hope of finding something to put on their hooks. All the underworlds of foam took refuge from need in this place. And every night the same thing went on, of which I was the nameless witness and the victim. I opted for being insignificant and a recluse.

Star of the destined one. I partly opened the door of the garden of the dead. Servile flowers were taking their ease. Keeping men company. Ears of the Creator.

—MAC & PT

René Char

LA COMPAGNE DU VANNIER

Je t'aimais. J'aimais ton visage de source raviné par l'orage et le chiffre de ton domaine enserrant mon baiser. Certains se confient à une imagination toute ronde. Aller me suffit. J'ai rapporté du désespoir un panier si petit, mon amour, qu'on a pu le tresser en osier.

FRÉQUENCE

Tout le jour, assistant l'homme, le fer a appliqué son torse sur la boue enflammée de la forge. À la longue, leurs jarrets jumeaux ont fait éclater la mince nuit du métal à l'étroit sous la terre.

L'homme sans se hâter quitte le travail. Il plonge une dernière fois ses bras dans le flanc assombri de la rivière. Saura-t-il enfin saisir le bourdon glacé des algues?

THE BASKET-WEAVER'S LOVE

I loved you. I loved your face, a spring furrowed by storm, and the emblem of your domain enclosing my kiss. Some put their trust in a round imagination. Just going is enough for me. I brought back from despair so small a basket, my love, they wove it of willow.

—MAC & PT

FREQUENCY

All day long, helping out, the iron leaned its torso against the flaming mire of the forge. Finally, their twin hocks shattered the thin night of the metal so tightly confined in the earth.

The man without haste leaves his work. One last time his arms plunge into the darkened flank of the river. Will he finally grasp the icy bell-shaped algae?

—MAC & PT

ENVOÛTEMENT À LA RENARDIÈRE

Vous qui m'avez connu, grenade dissidente, point du jour déployant le plaisir comme exemple, votre visage,—tel est-il, qu'il soit toujours,—si libre qu'à son contact le cerne infini de l'air se plissait, s'entr'ouvrant à ma rencontre, me vêtait des beaux quartiers de votre imagination. Je demeurais là, entièrement inconnu de moi-même, dans votre moulin à soleil, exultant à la succession des richesses d'un cœur qui avait rompu son étau. Sur notre plaisir s'allongeait l'influente douceur de la grande roue consumable du mouvement, au terme de ses classes.

À ce visage,—personne ne l'aperçut jamais,—simplifier la beauté n'apparaissait pas comme une atroce économie. Nous étions exacts dans l'exceptionnel qui seul sait se soustraire au caractère alternatif du mystère de vivre.

Dès lors que les routes de la mémoire se sont couvertes de la lèpre infaillible des monstres, je trouve refuge dans une innocence où l'homme qui rêve ne peut vieillir. Mais ai-je qualité pour m'imposer de vous survivre, moi qui dans ce Chant de Vous me considère comme le plus éloigné de mes sosies?

BEWITCHMENT AT THE REFINERY

You who have known me, dissentient pomegranate, daybreak unfurling joy for an example, your face—as it is, may it always be—so free that at its touch air's infinite ring crumpled, half-opening as I met it, clothing me with the fine streets of your imagination. I remained there, entirely unknown to myself, in your sun mill, exulting at the successive riches of a heart which had snapped open its vice. Over our joy there stretched out the influential gentleness of motion's great consumable wheel, at the end of its classes.

For this face—no one ever perceived it—to simplify beauty never seemed a terrible diminishing. We were exact in the exceptional, alone exempt from the alternate nature of the mystery of living.

Since memory's roads have cloaked themselves in the unfailing leprosy of monsters, I have taken refuge in an innocence where the man who dreams cannot grow old. But am I the one to assume the task of surviving you, I who in this Song of You find myself the most distant of my counterparts?

—MAC

LA JEUNESSE

Loin de l'embuscade des tuiles et de l'aumône des calvaires, vous vous donnez naissance, otages des oiseaux, fontaines. La pente de l'homme faite de la nausée de ses cendres, de l'homme en lutte avec sa providence vindicative, ne suffit pas à vous désenchanter.

Éloge, nous nous sommes acceptés.

« Si j'avais été muette comme la marche de pierre fidèle au soleil et qui ignore sa blessure cousue de lierre, si j'avais été enfant comme l'arbre blanc qui accueille les frayeurs des abeilles, si les collines avaient vécu jusqu'à l'été, si l'éclair m'avait ouvert sa grille, si tes nuits m'avaient pardonnée... »

Regard, verger d'étoiles, les genêts, la solitude sont distincts de vous! Le chant finit l'exil. La brise des agneaux ramène la vie neuve.

A YOUTH

Far from the ambush of tiles and the alms of calvaries, you bring yourselves to being, fountains, birds' hostage. Man's inclination, made from the nausea of his ashes, man struggling with his vindictive fate, isn't enough to disenchant you.

Praise, we have accepted ourselves.

"Had I been mute like the stone step faithful to the sun, paying no attention to its wound sewn from ivy, had I been a child like the white tree welcoming the frights of bees, had the hills lived until summer, had the lightning opened its grill for me, had your nights pardoned me..."

Glance, star orchard, broom, aloneness, are separate from you! Song ends exile. The breeze of lambs restores new life.

—MAC

René Char

CALENDRIER

J'ai lié les unes aux autres mes convictions et agrandi ta Présence. J'ai octroyé un cours nouveau à mes jours en les adossant à cette force spacieuse. J'ai congédié la violence qui limitait mon ascendant. J'ai pris sans éclat le poignet de l'équinoxe. L'oracle ne me vassalise plus. J'entre : j'éprouve ou non la grâce.

La menace s'est polie. La plage qui chaque hiver s'encombrait de régressives légendes, de sibylles aux bras lourds d'orties, se prépare aux êtres à secourir. Je sais que la conscience qui se risque n'a rien à redouter de la plane.

MAISON DOYENNE

Entre le couvre-feu de l'année et le tressaillement d'un arbre à la fenêtre. Vous avez interrompu vos donations. La fleur d'eau de l'herbe rôde autour d'un visage. Au seuil de la nuit l'insistance de votre illusion reçoit la forêt.

CALENDAR

I have bound my convictions one to another and amplified
your Presence. I have granted a new course to my days by pressing
them back against this spacious force. I have dismissed the vio-
lence that was limiting my ascendancy. I have quietly taken the
wrist of the equinox. The oracle no longer subjugates me. I enter:
I do or do not receive grace.

The threat has been refined. The beach that was encumbered
every winter with regressive legends, sybils whose arms were
heavy with nettles, prepares itself for creatures in need of help. I
know the consciousness that risks itself has nothing to fear from
the plane.

—NK

ELDEST HOUSE

Between the year's curfew and the quiver of a tree at the
window. You have interrupted your giving. The water-flower of
the grass prowls around a face. On the threshold of the night, your
illusion's perseverance welcomes in the forest.

—NK

René Char   49

ALLÈGEMENT

« J'errais dans l'or du vent, déclinant le refuge des villages où m'avaient connu des crève-coeur extrêmes. Du torrent épars de la vie arrêtée j'avais extrait la signification loyale d'Irène. La beauté déferlait de sa gaine fantasque, donnait des roses aux fontaines. »

La neige le surprit. Il se pencha sur le visage anéanti, en but à longs traits la superstition. Puis il s'éloigna, porté par la persévérance de cette houle, de cette laine.

ANNIVERSAIRE

Maintenant que tu as uni un printemps sans verglas aux embruns d'un massacre entré dans l'odyssée de sa cendre, fauche la moisson accumulée à l'horizon peu sûr, restitue-la aux espoirs qui l'entourèrent à sa naissance.

Que le jour te maintienne sur l'enclume de sa fureur blanche! Ta bouche crie l'extinction des couteaux respirés. Tes filtres chauds-entrouverts s'élancent aux libertés.

Rien que l'âme d'une saison sépare ton approche de l'amande de l'innocence.

ALLEVIATION

"I wandered in the gold of the wind, declining to take refuge in villages where I had suffered extreme heartbreak. From the sparse torrent of halted life, I had extracted the loyal meaning of Irene. Beauty spilled out of her odd corset, bestowed roses on the fountains."

Snow surprised him. He leaned over the face blotted out, drank superstition from it in long draughts. Then he went off, borne along by the perseverance of this surge, this strand.

—MAC

ANNIVERSARY

Now that you've joined a spring with no silver thaw to the mists of a massacre entered into the odyssey of its ash, scythe down the harvest built up on the unsure horizon, return it to the hopes surrounding it from birth.

May the day hold you on the forge of its white fury!

Your mouth cries the extinction of the knives breathed in. Your hot and half-opened filters fly towards freedoms.

Only the soul of a season separates your coming from the almond of innocence.

—MAC

René Char

MÉDAILLON

Eaux de verte foudre qui sonnent l'extase du visage aimé, eaux cousues de vieux crimes, eaux amorphes, eaux saccagées d'un proche sacre… Dût-il subir les semonces de sa mémoire éliminée, le fontainier salue des lèvres l'amour absolu de l'automne.

Identique sagesse, toi qui composes l'avenir sans croire au poids qui décourage, qu'il sente s'élancer dans son corps l'électricité du voyage.

MEDALLION

Waters of green lightning that peal the ecstasy of the beloved face, waters stitched with old crimes, amorphous waters, waters pillaged by a consecration close at hand... Though he must undergo the summons of his eliminated memory, still the well-digger greets with his lips the absolute love of autumn.

Identical wisdom, you who compose the future without believing in disheartening weight, may he feel his body throb with the electricity of the voyage.

—NK

René Char

AFIN QU'IL N'Y SOIT RIEN CHANGÉ

1

Tiens mes mains intendantes, gravis l'échelle noire, ô Dévouée;
la volupté des graines fume, les villes sont fer et causerie lointaine.

2

Notre désir retirait à la mer sa robe chaude avant de nager sur
son cœur.

3

Dans la luzerne de ta voix tournois d'oiseaux chassent soucis
de sécheresse.

4

Quand deviendront guides les sables balafrés issus des lents
charrois de la terre, le calme approchera de notre espace clos.

5

La quantité de fragments me déchire. Et debout se tient la
torture.

6

Le ciel n'est plus aussi jaune, le soleil aussi bleu. L'étoile furtive
de la pluie s'annonce. Frère, silex fidèle, ton joug s'est fendu. L'en-
tente a jailli de tes épaules.

SO THAT NOTHING IS CHANGED

1

Take these hands that steward you, climb up the black ladder, oh Devoted One; the voluptuous pleasure of seeds is smoking, the cities are of iron and distant chatter.

2

Our desire stripped off the sea's hot dress before swimming on its heart.

3

In the alfalfa of your voice swirling birds disperse fears of drought.

4

When the sands gashed by earth's slow wagon-trains begin to guide us, calm will come to our closed space.

5

The quantity of fragments tears me apart. And the torture is endured standing.

6

The sky is no longer as yellow, nor the sun as blue. The rain's furtive star looms. Brother, faithful flint, your yoke has split. Understanding flashed from your shoulders.

7

Beauté, je me porte à ta rencontre dans la solitude du froid. Ta lampe est rose, le vent brille. Le seuil du soir se creuse.

8

J'ai, captif, épousé le ralenti du lierre à l'assaut de la pierre de l'éternité.

9

« Je t'aime », répète le vent à tout ce qu'il fait vivre.
Je t'aime et tu vis en moi.

7

Beauty, I move toward your encounter in the solitude of the cold. Your lamp is pink, the wind shines. The threshold of the evening widens.

8

In my captivity, I have conjoined the ivy's slow motion to the assault of eternity's rock.

9

"I love you," repeats the wind to all it quickens. I love you and you live in me.

.

—NK

LE LORIOT

Le loriot entra dans la capitale de l'aube. L'épée de son chant ferma le lit triste.

Tout à jamais prit fin.

THE ORIOLE

September 3, 1939

The oriole entered the capital of dawn. The sword of his song closed the sad bed.

Everything forever ended.

—MAC

René Char   59

ÉLÉMENTS

Au souvenir de Roger Bonon,
tué en mai 1940 (mer du Nord).

Cette femme à l'écart de l'affluence de la rue tenait son enfant dans ses bras comme un volcan à demi consumé tient son cratère. Les mots qu'elle lui confiait parcouraient lentement sa tête avant de trouer la léthargie de sa bouche. Il émanait de ces deux êtres, dont l'un ne pesait guère moins que la coque d'une étoile, un épuisement obscur qui bientôt ne se raidirait plus et glisserait dans la dissolution, cette terminaison précoce des misérables.

Au ras du sol la nuit entrait légère dans leur chair qui titubait. A leurs yeux les mondes avaient cessé de s'affronter, s'ils l'avaient jamais fait.

Dans cette femme encore jeune un homme devait avoir racine, mais il demeurait invisible comme si l'horreur, à bout de forces, s'en était tenue là.

L'entrain égoïste, congé des idiots et des tyrans, qui flâne toujours dans les mêmes parties éclairées de son quartier est apostume; la vulnérabilité qui ose se découvrir nous engage étroitement.

J'entrevois le jour où quelques hommes qui ne se croiront pas généreux et acquittés parce qu'ils auront réussi à chasser l'accablement et la soumission au mal des abords de leurs semblables en même temps qu'ils auront atteint et maîtrisé les puissances de chantage qui de toutes parts les bravaient, j'entrevois le jour où quelques hommes entreprendront sans ruse le voyage de l'énergie de l'univers. Et comme la fragilité et l'inquiétude s'alimentent de poésie, au retour il sera demandé à ces hauts voyageurs de vouloir bien se souvenir.

Furor and Mystery

ELEMENTS

*To the memory of Roger Bonon,
killed in May 1940 (the North Sea).*

This woman, to one side of the swarming street, held her child in her arms as a volcano half consumed holds its crater. The words she confided to him drifted slowly through her head before penetrating the lethargy of her mouth. From these two beings, one of them as light as the shell of a star, there emanated a faint exhaustion that would soon not stiffen, rather slide into dissolution, this precocious end of the poor.

At ground level, night would enter lightly into their flesh which was lurching about. In their eyes, worlds had ceased colliding, if they had ever done so.

In this woman still young, a man must have taken root, but he remained invisible as if horror, itself exhausted, had stopped at that point.

Egoistic spirit, in which idiots and tyrants take their leave, which always hangs about in the same lit-up parts of her quarters is posthumous, vulnerability daring to show itself takes hold of us immediately.

I foresee the day when some who will not believe themselves especially generous and excused because they will have managed to chase away the dejection and the depression of their fellow humans, as they will have overcome the powers of blackmail which assailed them from all sides, I foresee the day when some will take upon themselves without any ruse the ongoing energy of the universe. And as fragility and disquiet nourish themselves on poetry, on the way back these high voyageurs will be asked please to remember.

—MAC

René Char

FORCE CLÉMENTE

Je sais où m'entravent mes insuffisances, vitrail si la fleur se détache du sang du jeune été. Le cœur d'eau noire au soleil a pris la place du soleil, a pris la place de mon cœur. Ce soir, la grande roue errante si grave du désir peut bien être de moi seul visible…
Ferai-je ailleurs jamais naufrage?

LÉONIDES

Es-tu ma femme? Ma femme faite pour atteindre la rencontre du présent? L'hypnose du phénix convoite ta jeunesse. La pierre des heures l'investit de son lierre.

Es-tu ma femme? L'an du vent où guerroie un vieux nuage donne naissance à la rose, à la rose de violence.
Ma femme faite pour atteindre la rencontre du présent.

Le combat s'éloigne et nous laisse un cœur d'abeille sur nos terres, l'ombre éveillée, le pain naïf. La veillée file lentement vers l'immunité de la Fête.

Ma femme faite pour atteindre la rencontre du présent.

MERCIFUL STRENGTH

I know where my shortcomings hem me in, a stained-glass window if the flower detaches itself from the blood of the so young summer. The blackwater heart of the sun has taken the place of the sun, the place of my heart. Tonight, the great wandering wheel of desire may well be visible to me alone... Shall I ever be ship-wrecked somewhere else?

—MAC

LEONIDES

Are you my woman? My woman fated to fulfill the encounter with the present? The hypnotic trance of the phoenix covets your youth. The stone of the hours clothes it with ivy.

Are you my woman? The year of wind in which an old cloud wages war is giving birth to the rose, the rose of violence.
My woman fated to fulfill the encounter with the present.

The fighting grows distant and leaves to us a bee-heart on our land, the shadow awakened, the bread ingenuous. Evening moves slowly toward the Feast's immunity.

My woman fated to fulfill the encounter with the present.

—NK

René Char

FENAISON

O nuit, je n'ai rapporté de ta félicité que l'apparence parfumée d'ellipses d'oiseaux insaisissables! Rien n'imposait le mouvement que ta main de pollen qui fondait sur mon front aux moulinets d'une lampe d'anémone. Aux approches du désir les meules bleu de ciel s'étaient l'une après l'autre soulevées, car mort là-bas était le Faneur, vieillard masqué, acteur félon, chimiste du maudit voyage.

Je m'appuie un moment sur la pelle du déluge et chantourne sa langue. Mes sueurs d'agneau noir provoquent le sarcasme. Ma nausée se grossit de soudains consentements dont je n'arrive pas à maintenir le cours. Anneau tard venu, enclavé dans la chevalerie pythienne saturée de feu et de vieillesse, quel compagnon engagerais-je? Je prends place inaperçu sur le tirant de l'étrave jusqu'à la date fleurie où rougeoiera ma cendre.

O nuit, je n'ai pu traduire en galaxie son Apparition que j'épousai étroitement dans les temps purs de la fugue! Cette Sœur immédiate tournait le cœur du jour.

Salut à celui qui marche en sûreté à mes côtés, au terme du poème. Il passera demain DEBOUT sous le vent.

Furor and Mystery

HAYMAKING

Oh night, I have brought back from your happiness only the fragrant appearance of the ellipses of unattainable birds! Nothing imposed motion but your hand of pollen which melted on my forehead in the whirls of an anemone lamp. At the approach of desire, the blue stacks of the sky had risen one after another, for over there, dead, was the Haymaker, an old masked man, a treacherous actor, the chemist of the cursed voyage.

I lean for a moment on the spade of the deluge and turn its tongue around. My black sheep sweat provokes sarcasm. My nausea increases with sudden consents whose course I can't contain. Late-come ring, dovetailed in the pythian chivalry imbued with fire and age, what companion should I engage? I take my place unperceived on the waterline of the ship's stem until the beflowered time when my ashes will catch flame.

Oh night, I have not been able to render in a galaxy its Apparition which I wed narrowly in the pure time of the flight! This immediate Sister turned the heart of the day.

Greetings to the one who walks in certainty by my side, to the end of the poem. Who will tomorrow pass STANDING under the wind.

—MAC

L'ABSENT

Ce frère brutal mais dont la parole était sûre, patient au sacrifice, diamant et sanglier, ingénieux et secourable, se tenait au centre de tous les malentendus tel un arbre de résine dans le froid inalliable. Au bestiaire de mensonges qui le tourmentait de ses gobelins et de ses trombes il opposait son dos perdu dans le temps. Il venait à vous par des sentiers invisibles, favorisait l'audace écarlate, ne vous contrariait pas, savait sourire. Comme l'abeille quitte le verger pour le fruit déjà noir, les femmes soutenaient sans le trahir le paradoxe de ce visage qui n'avait pas des traits d'otage.

J'ai essayé de vous décrire ce compère indélébile que nous sommes quelques-uns à avoir fréquenté. Nous dormirons dans l'espérance, nous dormirons en son absence, puisque la raison ne soupçonne pas que ce qu'elle nomme, à la légère, absence, occupe le fourneau dans l'unité.

THE ABSENT ONE

This brutal brother but whose word was true, steadfast in the face of sacrifice, diamond and wild boar, ingenious and helpful, held himself in the center of all misunderstandings like a resinous tree in the cold admitting of no alloy. Against the bestiary of lies tormenting him with its goblins and its whirlwinds, he set his back, lost in time. He came to you by invisible paths, preferred a scarlet forwardness, did not thwart you, knew how to smile. As the bee leaves the orchard for the fruit already black, women withstood without betraying it the paradox of this face which had none of the lineaments of a hostage.

I have tried to describe for you this indelible companion whose friendship some of us have kept. We shall sleep in hope, we shall sleep in his absence, reason not suspecting that what it names, thoughtlessly, absence, dwells within the crucible of unity.

—MAC

L'ÉPI DE CRISTAL ÉGRÈNE DANS LES HERBES
SA MOISSON TRANSPARENTE

La ville n'était pas défaite. Dans la chambre devenue légère le donneur de liberté couvrait son amour de cet immense effort du corps, semblable à celui de la création d'un fluide par le jour. L'alchimie du désir rendait essentiel leur génie récent à l'univers de ce matin. Loin derrière eux leur mère ne les trahirait plus, leur mère si immobile. Maintenant ils précédaient le pays de leur avenir qui ne contenait encore que la flèche de leur bouche dont le chant venait de naître. Leur avidité rencontrait immédiatement son objet. Ils douaient d'omniprésence un temps qu'on n'interrogeait pas.

Il lui disait comment jadis dans des forêts persécutées il interpellait les animaux auxquels il apportait leur chance, son serment aux monts internés qui l'avait conduit à la reconnaissance de son exemplaire destin et quel boucher secret il avait dû vaincre pour acquérir à ses yeux la tolérance de son semblable.

Dans la chambre devenue légère et qui peu à peu développait les grands espaces du voyage, le donneur de liberté s'apprêtait à disparaître, à se confondre avec d'autres naissances, une nouvelle fois.

THE CRYSTAL WHEAT-EAR SHEDS IN THE GRASSES
ITS TRANSPARENT HARVEST

The town was not undone. In the room become weightless, the bestower of freedom covered his beloved with this immense effort of the body, akin to a fluid's creation by the day. Desire in its alchemy rendered their recent genius essential to that morning's universe. Far behind them, their mother would betray them no more, their mother so unmoving. Now they preceded the country of their future which contained as yet only the arrow of their mouth whose song had just been born. Their avidity met its object straightaway. They endowed with omnipresence a time free of questioning.

He told her how in days gone by, in the persecuted forests, he would summon animals to whom he brought their good fortune, how his oath to the imprisoned mountains had made him recognize his exemplary fate and what secret butcher he'd had to conquer before winning in his own eyes his fellow-man's tolerance.

In the room become weightless and gradually unfurling vast expanses of voyage, the bestower of freedom readied himself to disappear, to mingle with other births, once again.

—MAC

LOUIS CUREL DE LA SORGUE

Sorgue qui t'avances derrière un rideau de papillons qui pétillent, ta faucille de doyen loyal à la main, la crémaillère du supplice en collier à ton cou, pour accomplir ta journée d'homme, quand pourrai-je m'éveiller et me sentir heureux au rythme modelé de ton seigle irréprochable? Le sang et la sueur ont engagé leur combat qui se poursuivra jusqu'au soir, jusqu'à ton retour, solitude aux marges de plus en plus grandes. L'arme de tes maîtres, l'horloge des marées, achève de pourrir. La création et la risée se dissocient. L'air-roi s'annonce. Sorgue, tes épaules comme un livre ouvert propagent leur lecture. Tu as été, enfant, le fiancé de cette fleur au chemin tracé dans le rocher, qui s'évadait par un frelon… Courbé, tu observes aujourd'hui l'agonie du persécuteur qui arracha à l'aimant de la terre la cruauté d'innombrables fourmis pour la jeter en millions de meurtriers contre les tiens et ton espoir. Écrase donc encore une fois cet œuf cancéreux qui résiste…

Il y a un homme à présent debout, un homme dans un champ de seigle, un champ pareil à un chœur mitraillé, un champ sauvé.

LOUIS CUREL DE LA SORGUE

Sorgue advancing behind a curtain of flickering butterflies, holding your sickle of loyal elder, the torture rack worn as a necklace, to fulfill your man-long day, when may I waken joyous at the graven rhythm of your irreproachable rye? Blood and sweat have joined their combat which will last until evening, until your return, solitude with ever greater margins. All but rotted now, the weapon of your master, the clock of tides. Creation and mockery separate. The air-king proclaims his coming. Sorgue, your shoulders propagate their reading like an open book. As a child, you were betrothed to the flower whose path was traced in rock, who escaped by a hornet... Stooping, you observe today the agony of the persecutor who wrenched from the terrestrial magnet the cruelty of innumerable ants to hurl it in murderous millions against your people and your hope. Crush then once more this cancerous egg resisting...

There is a man now standing, a man in a field of rye, a field like a machine-gunned chorus, a field redeemed.

—MAC

NE S'ENTEND PAS

Au cours de la lutte si noire et de l'immobilité si noire, la terreur aveuglant mon royaume, je m'élevai des lions ailés de la moisson jusqu'au cri froid de l'anémone. Je vins au monde dans la difformité des chaînes de chaque être. Nous nous faisions libres tous deux. Je tirai d'une morale compatible les secours irréprochables. Malgré la soif de disparaître, je fus prodigue dans l'attente, la foi vaillante. Sans renoncer.

LE DEVOIR

L'enfant que, la nuit venue, l'hiver descendait avec précaution de la charrette de la lune, une fois à l'intérieur de la maison balsamique, plongeait d'un seul trait ses yeux dans le foyer de fonte rouge. Derrière l'étroit vitrail incendié l'espace ardent le tenait entièrement captif. Le buste incliné vers la chaleur, ses jeunes mains scellées à l'envolée de feuilles sèches du bien-être, l'enfant épelait la rêverie du ciel glacé :

« Bouche, ma confidente, que vois-tu ?

— Cigale, je vois un pauvre champignon au cœur de pierre, en amitié avec la mort. Son venin est si vieux que tu peux le tourner en chanson.

— Maîtresse, où vont mes lignes?

— Belle, ta place est marquée sur le banc du parc où le cœur a sa couronne.

— Suis-je le présent de l'amour? »

Dans la constellation des Pléiades, au vent d'un fleuve adolescent, l'impatient Minotaure s'éveillait.

UNHEARD

In the course of struggle so dark and immobility so dark, terror blinding my kingdom, I rose from the harvest's winged lions to the anenome's cold cry. I came to the world in the deformity of each being's chains. We both freed ourselves. From a compatible morality I drew an irreproachable help. Despite a thirst to disappear, I was prodigal in waiting, in valiant faith. No renouncing.

—MAC

SCHOOLWORK

Once inside the aromatic house, the child whom after dark the winter lifted down with caution from the wagon of the moon abruptly plunged her gaze into the fireplace of melting red. Behind the narrow burning stained-glass window, blazing space held her entirely captive. Torso leaning toward the heat, young hands soldered to the flight of leaves dry with contentedness, the child spelled out the revery of the icy sky:

"Mouth, my confidante, what do you see?"

"Cicada, I can see a poor mushroom whose heart is stone befriending death. Its venom is so old that you can turn it into song."

"Mistress, where do my lines go?"

"Beautiful, your place is marked out on the garden bench where the heart's crown is kept."

"Am I the present of love?"

In the constellation of the Pleiades, in the wind above an adolescent river, the impatient Minotaur was waking.

—NK

René Char

PAR LA BOUCHE DE L'ENGOULEVENT

Enfants qui cribliez d'olives le soleil enfoncé dans le bois de la mer, enfants, ô frondes de froment, de vous l'étranger se détourne, se détourne de votre sang martyrisé, se détourne de cette eau trop pure, enfants aux yeux de limon, enfants qui faisiez chanter le sel à votre oreille, comment se résoudre à ne plus s'éblouir de votre amitié? Le ciel dont vous disiez le duvet, la Femme dont vous trahissiez le désir, la foudre les a glacés.

Châtiments! Châtiments!

VIVRE AVEC DE TELS HOMMES

Tellement j'ai faim, je dors sous la canicule des preuves. J'ai voyagé jusqu'à l'épuisement, le front sur le séchoir noueux. Afin que le mal demeure sans relève, j'ai étouffé ses engagements. J'ai effacé son chiffre de la gaucherie de mon étrave. J'ai répliqué aux coups. On tuait de si près que le monde s'est voulu meilleur. Brumaire de mon âme jamais escaladé, qui fait feu dans la bergerie déserte? Ce n'est plus la volonté elliptique de la scrupuleuse solitude. Aile double des cris d'un million de crimes se levant soudain dans des yeux jadis négligents, montrez-nous vos desseins et cette large abdication du remords!

Montre-toi; nous n'en avions jamais fini avec le sublime bien-être des très maigres hirondelles. Avides de s'approcher de l'ample allégement. Incertains dans le temps que l'amour grandissait. Incertains, eux seuls, au sommet du cœur.

Tellement j'ai faim.

1939

THROUGH THE NIGHTJAR'S MOUTH

Children who riddled the sun with olives, the sun driven into the woods of the sea, children, oh fronds of wheat, the stranger turns away from you, turns from your martyred blood, turns from that too-pure water, children with eyes of silt, children who made the salt sing in your ears, how to accept no longer being dazzled by your friendship? The sky whose feathery down you spoke, the Woman whose desire you revealed, the lightning has iced them over.

Chastisement! Chastisement!

—NK

LIVING WITH SUCH MEN

So hungry am I that I sleep under the dog-days of proofs. I've traveled to exhaustion, my forehead pressed against the knotted drying-rack. Lest evil be perpetuated, I have stifled its commitments, removed its sign from the awkwardness of my bowsprit. I answered volley with volley. Killing came so near that the world willed itself a better one. Brumaire of my soul, never scaled, who is firing in the deserted sheep pen? No longer is it the elliptical desire of a scrupulous solitude. Double wing of cries of a million crimes looming up suddenly in eyes once negligent, show us your purpose and this wide abdication from remorse!

Show us your presence, we had not done with the sublime well-being of the thinnest swallows. Avid to move toward an ample assuaging. Irresolute within the time of love's growing. Irresolute, they only, at the heart's summit.

So hungry am I.

—MAC

L'ÉCLAIRAGE DU PÉNITENCIER

Ta nuit je l'ai voulue si courte que ta marâtre taciturne fut vieille avant d'en avoir conçu les pouvoirs.

J'ai rêvé d'être à ton côté ce fugitif harmonieux à la personne à peine indiquée, au bénéfice provenant de route triste et d'angélique. Nul n'ose le retarder.

Le jour s'est soudain resserré. Perdant tous les morts que j'aimais, je congédie ce chien la rose, dernier vivant, distrait été.

Je suis l'exclu et le comblé. Achevez-moi, beauté planeuse, ivres paupières mal fermées. Chaque plaie met à la fenêtre ses yeux de phénix éveillé. La satisfaction de résoudre chante et gémit dans l'or du mur.

Ce n'est encore que le vent du joug.

PRISONHOUSE LIGHTING

I wished your night so brief that your close-mouthed stepmother would grow old before she understood its powers.

I dreamed of being that harmonious fugitive at your side, his person scarcely sketched out, his advantage coming from a sad road, and from the angelical. None dares to delay him.

The day has suddenly contracted. Losing all the dead I loved, I dismiss this dog of a rose, last living thing, absent-minded summer.

I am the excluded one, and filled to overflowing. Finish me off, sharp-bladed beauty, drunken eyelids badly closed. Every wound lifts to the window its wakened-phoenix eyes. The pleasure of resolution sings and moans in the wall's gold.

It is still no more than the wind of the yoke.

—NK

René Char

LE BOUGE DE L'HISTORIEN

La pyramide des martyrs obsède la terre.

Onze hivers tu auras renoncé au quantième de l'espérance,
à la respiration de ton fer rouge, en d'atroces performances
psychiques. Comète tuée net, tu auras barré sanglant la nuit de
ton époque. Interdiction de croire tienne cette page d'où tu prenais
élan pour te soustraire à la géante torpeur d'épine du Monstre, à
son contentieux de massacreurs.

Miroir de la murène! Miroir du vomito! Purin d'un feu plat
tendu par l'ennemi!

Dure, afin de pouvoir encore mieux aimer un jour ce que tes
mains d'autrefois n'avaient fait qu'effleurer sous l'olivier trop
jeune.

HISTORIAN'S HOVEL

The martyrs' pyramid obsesses the earth.

Eleven winters you will have renounced so very much hope,
the breath of your crimson sword, in atrocious psychic acts.
A comet slain sharp, you will have scratched out bleeding the night
of your epoch. May the refusal to believe hold this page from
which you sprang to escape the gigantic sloth of the Monster's
thorn, its contentious murderers.

Mirror of the muraena! Mirror of vomit! Manure slop of an
insipid dish held out by the enemy!

Endure, so that you can one day increase your love for that
which your erstwhile hands had only grazed under the olive tree,
too young.

—MAC

CHANT DU REFUS

Début du partisan

Le poète est retourné pour de longues années dans le néant du père. Ne l'appelez pas, vous tous qui l'aimez. S'il vous semble que l'aile de l'hirondelle n'a plus de miroir sur terre, oubliez ce bonheur. Celui qui panifiait la souffrance n'est pas visible dans sa léthargie rougeoyante.

Ah! beauté et vérité fassent que vous soyez *présents* nombreux aux salves de la délivrance!

CARTE DU 8 NOVEMBRE

Les clous dans notre poitrine, la cécité transissant nos os, qui s'offre à les subjuguer? Pionniers de la vieille église, affluence du Christ, vous occupez moins de place dans la prison de notre douleur que le trait d'un oiseau sur la corniche de l'air. La foi! Son baiser s'est détourné avec horreur de ce nouveau calvaire. Comment son bras tiendrait-il démurée notre tête, lui qui vit, retranché des fruits de son prochain, de la charité d'une serrure inexacte? Le suprême écœurement, celui à qui la mort même refuse son ultime fumée, se retire, déguisé en seigneur.

Notre maison vieillira à l'écart de nous, épargnant le souvenir de notre amour couché intact dans la tranchée de sa seule reconnaissance.

Tribunal implicite, cyclone vulnéraire, que tu nous rends tard le but et la table où la faim entrait la première! Je suis aujourd'hui pareil à un chien enragé enchaîné à un arbre plein de rires et de feuilles.

Furor and Mystery

REFUSAL SONG

Beginning of the Partisan

The poet has returned for a long span of years into the naught of the father. Do not call him, all you who love him. If it seems to you that the swallow's wing has no longer a mirror on earth, forget that happiness. He who worked suffering into bread is not visible in his glowing lethargy.

Ah! may beauty and truth ensure your numerous *presence* at the salvos of liberation!

—MAC

NOTE OF NOVEMBER 8 [1942]

Nails in our breast, blindness chilling our bones, who can offer to overcome them? Pioneers of the old church, affluence of Christ, you take up less space in the prison of our pain than the trace of a bird on the ledge of air. Faith! Its embrace has turned away with horror from this new calvary. How could its arm hold our head in place, its arm that lives cut off from the fruits of its neighbor, from the charity of a faulty lock? Supreme disgust, to which even death refuses its ultimate smoke, draws back, disguised as a lord.

Our house will grow old apart from us, sparing the memory of our love laid intact in the ditch of its only recognition.

Implicit tribunal, woundwort cyclone, how late you hold out to us the goal and the table where hunger entered first! I am today like a mad dog chained to a tree full of laughter and leaves.

—MAC

René Char

PLISSEMENT

Qu'il était pur, mon frère, le prête-nom de ta faillite —
j'entends tes sanglots, tes jurons —. O vie transcrite du large sel
maternel! L'homme aux dents de furet abreuvait son zénith dans
la terre des caves, l'homme au teint de mouchard tuméfiait partout
la beauté bien-aimée. Vieux sang voûté, mon gouverneur, nous
avons guetté jusqu'à la terreur le dégel lunaire de la nausée. Nous
nous sommes étourdis de patience sauvage; une lampe inconnue
de nous, inaccessible à nous, à la pointe du monde, tenait éveillés
le courage et le silence.

Vers ta frontière, ô vie humiliée, je marche maintenant au pas
des certitudes, averti que la vérité ne précède pas obligatoirement
l'action. Folle sœur de ma phrase, ma maîtresse scellée, je te sauve
d'un hôtel de décombres.

Le sabre bubonique tombe des mains du Monstre au terme de
l'exode du temps de s'exprimer.

PLEATING

How pure he was, my brother, the figurehead of your failure—
I hear your sobs, your swearing. Oh life transcribed from the wide
maternal salt! The man with ferret teeth quenched his zenith in
the earth of caves, the man color of the informer made a tumor
of all beloved beauty. Old vaulted blood, my governor, we have
watched terrified. We have been stunned with wild patience; a
lamp unknown to us, inaccessible to us, at the point of the world,
kept courage and silence awake.

Towards your frontier, oh humiliated life, I walk now in step
with certainties, warned that truth does not necessarily precede
action. Mad sister of my sentence, my confirmed mistress, I save
you from a hotel of ruins.

The bubonic sabre falls from the hands of the Monster as the
exodus from the time of expression comes to an end.

—MAC

René Char

HOMMAGE ET FAMINE

Femme qui vous accordez avec la bouche du poète, ce torrent au limon serein, qui lui avez appris, alors qu'il n'était encore qu'une graine captive de loup anxieux, la tendresse des hauts murs polis par votre nom (hectares de Paris, entrailles de beauté, mon feu monte sous vos robes de fugue), Femme qui dormez dans le pollen des fleurs, déposez sur son orgueil votre givre de médium il-limité, afin qu'il demeure jusqu'à l'heure de la bruyère d'ossements l'homme qui pour mieux vous adorer reculait indéfiniment en vous la diane de sa naissance, le poing de sa douleur, l'horizon de sa victoire.

(Il faisait nuit. Nous nous étions serrés sous le grand chêne de larmes. Le grillon chanta. Comment savait-il, solitaire, que la terre n'allait pas mourir, que nous, les enfants sans clarté, allions bientôt parler?)

LA LIBERTÉ

Elle est venue par cette ligne blanche pouvant tout aussi bien signifier l'issue de l'aube que le bougeoir du crépuscule.

Elle passa les grèves machinales; elle passa les cimes éventrées.

Prenaient fin la renonciation à visage de lâche, la sainteté du mensonge, l'alcool du bourreau.

Son verbe ne fut pas un aveugle bélier mais la toile où s'inscrivit mon souffle.

D'un pas à ne se mal guider que derrière l'absence, elle est venue, cygne sur la blessure, par cette ligne blanche.

HOMAGE AND FAMINE

Woman atune to the mouth of the poet, this torrent with serene alluvium, who taught him, when he was only a captive seed of anxious wolf, the tenderness of high walls burnished by your name (acres of Paris, entrails of beauty, my fire rises under your dresses of fugue), Woman sleeping in flower pollen, lay lightly on his pride your frost of limitless medium, that he remain until the hour of the heather of bones the man who the better to adore you thrust back unendingly in you the clarion of his birth, the fist of his suffering, the horizon of his victory.

(It was night. We were huddled under the great oak of tears. The cricket chirped. How did he know, solitary, that the earth was not to die, that we, children without clarity, were soon to speak?)

—MAC

FREEDOM

It came along this white line that might as easily mean dawn's release as the candlestick of twilight.

It passed beyond the unconscious shores; it passed beyond the eviscerated summits.

Ending now were the renunciation with a coward's face, the sanctity of lies, the executioner's alcohol.

Its word was not a blind battering-ram, but the canvas on which my breath was inscribed.

With a step that could lose its way only behind absence, it came, swan on the wound, along this white line.

—MAC & NK

René Char

LE VISAGE NUPTIAL

THE NUPTIAL COUNTENANCE

CONDUITE

Passe.
La bêche sidérale
autrefois là s'est engouffrée.
Ce soir un village d'oiseaux
très haut exulte et passe.

Écoute aux tempes rocheuses
des présences dispersées
le mot qui fera ton sommeil
chaud comme un arbre de septembre.

Vois bouger l'entrelacement
des certitudes arrivées
près de nous à leur quintessence,
ô ma Fourche, ma Soif anxieuse!

La rigueur de vivre se rode
sans cesse à convoiter l'exil.
Par une fine pluie d'amande,
mêlée de liberté docile,
ta gardienne alchimie s'est produite,
ô Bien-aimée!

CONVEY

Pass.
The sidereal spade
Long ago struck in there.
Tonight a high village of birds
Exults and passes.

Listen at the stony temples
of presences dispersed
to the word making your sleep
warm as a September tree.

Mark the moving of the interwoven certainties
that beside us have attained
their quintessence,
o my Cleaving, my anxious Thirst!

The rigor of living ceaselessly
Wears down, coveting exile.
Through a fine rain of almond,
mingled with gentle liberty,
your guardian alchemy has done its work,
o Beloved!

—MAC

René Char

GRAVITÉ

L'emmuré

S'il respire il pense à l'encoche
Dans la tendre chaux confidente
Où ses mains du soir étendent ton corps.

Le laurier l'épuise,
La privation le consolide.

O toi, la monotone absente,
La fileuse de salpêtre,
Derrière des épaisseurs fixes
Une échelle sans âge déploie ton voile!

Tu vas nue, constellée d'échardes,
Secrète, tiède et disponible,
Attachée au sol indolent,
Mais l'intime de l'homme abrupt dans sa prison.

A te mordre les jours grandissent,
Plus arides, plus imprenables que les nuages qui se déchirent au
    fond des os.

*

J'ai pesé de tout mon désir
Sur ta beauté matinale
Pour qu'elle éclate et se sauve.

GRAVITY

Walled-in

Each breath reminds him of the hollow
In the tender limestone confidant
Where his evening hands stretch out your body.

The laurel tree exhausts him,
he is strengthened by privation.

You, the absent single-toned,
Weaver of saltpeter,
Behind thickness set in stone
An ageless ladder unfurls your veil!

You go naked, spangled with shards
Secret, warm, easy
Attached to indolent earth,
Yet the intimate of the brusque man imprisoned.

The days feed on you, growing fatter,
Drier, more impregnable than clouds torn in the depth of bones.

*

With all my desire I weighed
Upon your morning beauty
For it to burst open and break free.

René Char

L'ont suivie l'alcool sans rois mages,
Le battement de ton triangle,
La main-d'œuvre de tes yeux
Et le gravier debout sur l'algue.

Un parfum d'insolation
Protège ce qui va éclore.

In its wake, alcohol with no magi,
Your triangle beating,
The labor of your eyes
And gravel astride the algae.

A sunstruck fragrance
Shelters what will be born.

—MAC & NK

LE VISAGE NUPTIAL

A présent disparais, mon escorte, debout dans la distance;
La douceur du nombre vient de se détruire.
Congé à vous, mes alliés, mes violents, mes indices.
Tout vous entraîne, tristesse obséquieuse.
J'aime.

L'eau est lourde à un jour de la source.
La parcelle vermeille franchit ses lentes branches à ton front,
    dimension rassurée.
Et moi semblable à toi,
Avec la paille en fleur au bord du ciel criant ton nom,
J'abats les vestiges,
Atteint, sain de clarté.

Ceinture de vapeur, multitude assouplie, diviseurs de la crainte,
    touchez ma renaissance.
Parois de ma durée, je renonce à l'assistance de ma largeur
    vénielle;
Je boise l'expédient du gîte, j'entrave la primeur des survies.
Embrasé de solitude foraine,
J'évoque la nage sur l'ombre de sa Présence.

Le corps désert, hostile à son mélange, hier, était revenu parlant
    noir.
Déclin, ne te ravise pas, tombe ta massue de transes, aigre
    sommeil.
Le décolleté diminue les ossements de ton exil, de ton escrime;
Tu rends fraîche la servitude qui se dévore le dos;
Risée de la nuit, arrête ce charroi lugubre
De voix vitreuses, de départs lapidés.

Furor and Mystery

THE NUPTIAL COUNTENANCE

Now let my escort disappear, standing in the distance;
numbers have just lost their sweetness.
I give you leave, my allies, my violent ones, my indices.
Everything summons you away, fawning sorrow.
I am in love.

Water is heavy at a day's flow from the spring.
The crimson foliage crosses its slow branches at your forehead,
    dimension reassured.
And I, like you,
with the straw in flower at the edge of the sky crying your name,
I cut down the traces,
stricken, strong in clarity.

Ring of vapor, many made supple, dividers of fear, touch my
    renewal.
Walls of my enduring, I renounce the succor of my venial breadth;
I timber the device of the dwelling, I thwart the first fruits of
    survivals.
Afire with itinerant solitude,
I evoke the swimming on the shade of her Presence.

The desert body hostile to an alloyage, had returned yesterday,
    speaking darkly.
Decline, do not halt your movement, drop your bludgeon of
    seizures, acrid sleep.
Indentation diminishes the bones of your exile, of your sparring;
you freshen constraint self-devouring;
gust of the night, halt this grim cartage
of glazed voices, stone-pelted departures.

René Char   95

Tôt soustrait au flux des lésions inventives
(La pioche de l'aigle lance haut le sang évasé)
Sur un destin présent j'ai mené mes franchises
Vers l'azur multivalve, la granitique dissidence.

Ô voûte d'effusion sur la couronne de son ventre,
Murmure de dot noire!
Ô mouvement tari de sa diction!
Nativité, guidez les insoumis, qu'ils découvrent leur base,
L'amande croyable au lendemain neuf.
Le soir a fermé sa plaie de corsaire où voyageaient les fusées vagues
    parmi la peur soutenue des chiens.
Au passé les micas du deuil sur ton visage.

Vitre inextinguible: mon souffle affleurait déjà l'amitié de ta
    blessure,
Armait ta royauté inapparente.
Et des lèvres du brouillard descendit notre plaisir au seuil de dune,
    au toit d'acier.
La conscience augmentait l'appareil frémissant de ta permanence;
La simplicité fidèle s'étendit partout.

Timbre de la devise matinale, morte-saison de l'étoile précoce,
Je cours au terme de mon cintre, colisée fossoyé.
Assez baisé le crin nubile des céréales:
La cardeuse, l'opiniâtre, nos confins la soumettent.
Assez maudit le havre des simulacres nuptiaux:
Je touche le fond d'un retour compact.

Ruisseaux, neume des morts anfractueux,
Vous qui suivez le ciel aride,
Mêlez votre acheminement aux orages de qui sut guérir de la
    désertion,
Donnant contre vos études salubres.

Furor and Mystery

Soon subtracted from the flux of contriving lesions
(the eagle's pickaxe flings high the flaring blood)
across a present destiny I have led my exemptions
toward an azure multivalved, granite dissidence.

O vaulted effusion upon the crown of her belly,
murmurings of dark dowry!
O the exhausted motion of her diction!
Nativity, guide the unyielding, may they find their foundations,
the almond believable in the fresh day to come.
Evening has closed its corsair's gash where the rockets soared
    aimlessly amid a dogged fear.
Past now the micas of mourning on your face.

Unquenchable pane: my breath was already grazing the friendship
    of your wound,
arming your hidden royalty.
And from the lips of the fog descended our joy with its threshold
    of dune, its roof of steel.
Awareness increased the quivering array of your permanence;
faithful simplicity spread everywhere.

Tone of morning's adage, slack season of the early star,
I rush to the term of my arch, coliseum interred.
Long enough embraced the nubile hair of grain:
O stubborn one, carder, our reaches force its submission.
Long enough condemned the haven of nuptial semblances:
I touch the depths of a compact return.

Streams, neuma of the craggy dead,
you who follow the arid sky,
mingle your going with his storms, who could heal desertion,
striking against your saving studies.

Au sein du toit le pain suffoque à porter coeur et lueur.
Prends, ma Pensée, la fleur de ma main pénétrable,
Sens s'éveiller l'obscure plantation.

Je ne verrai pas tes flancs, ces essaims de faim, se dessécher,
    s'emplir de ronces;
Je ne verrai pas l'empuse te succéder dans ta serre;
Je ne verrai pas l'approche des baladins inquiéter le jour renaissant;
Je ne verrai pas la race de notre liberté servilement se suffire.

Chimères, nous sommes montés au plateau.
Le silex frissonnait sous les sarments de l'espace;
La parole, lasse de défoncer, buvait au débarcadère angélique.
Nulle farouche survivance:
L'horizon des routes jusqu'à l'afflux de rosée,
L'intime dénouement de l'irréparable.

Voici le sable mort, voici le corps sauvé:
La Femme respire, l'Homme se tient debout.

At the roof's center bread suffocates carrying heart and light.
Take, oh my Thought, the flower of my penetrable hand,
Feel the dark planting waken.

I shall not see your sides, those swarms of hunger, dry up, fill with
brambles;
I shall not see the mantis replace you in your greenhouse;
I shall not see the minstrels approach, disquieting the reborn day;
I shall not see our freedom's lineage servile in self-sufficiency.

Chimeras, we have climbed upland.
Flint quivered beneath vine-shoots of space;
the word, tired of battering, drank at the angelic wharf.
No savage survival:
the horizon of roads to the abounding dew,
intimate unfolding of the irreparable.

This is the sand dead, this the body saved:
Woman breathes, Man stands upright.

—MAC

ÉVADNÉ

L'été et notre vie étions d'un seul tenant
La campagne mangeait la couleur de ta jupe odorante
Avidité et contrainte s'étaient réconciliées
Le château de Maubec s'enfonçait dans l'argile
Bientôt s'effondrerait le roulis de sa lyre
La violence des plantes nous faisait vaciller
Un corbeau rameur sombre déviant de l'escadre
Sur le muet silex de midi écartelé
Accompagnait notre entente aux mouvements tendres
La faucille partout devait se reposer
Notre rareté commençait un règne
(Le vent insomnieux qui nous ride la paupière
En tournant chaque nuit la page consentie
Veut que chaque part de toi que je retienne
Soit étendue à un pays d'âge affamé et de larmier géant)

C'était au début d'adorables années
La terre nous aimait un peu je me souviens.

EVADNE

Summer and our life, we were continuous
The country devoured the color of your sweet-smelling skirt
Avidity and constraint had been reconciled
Maubec Castle was settling in the clay
Soon the rolling of its lyre would cease
The violence of plants made us reel
A crow somber rower swerving from the fleet
On the mute flint of quartered noon
Accompanied our understanding with tender movements
Everywhere the sickle must have been at rest
Our rarity began a reign
(The sleepless wind rippling our eyelids
Turning each night the page consented
Wishes any part of you I retain
To extend in a land of famished age and high tear-stone)

This was at the outset of adorable years
The earth loved us a little I remember.

—MAC

POST-SCRIPTUM

Écartez-vous de moi qui patiente sans bouche;
A vos pieds je suis né, mais vous m'avez perdu;
Mes feux ont trop précisé leur royaume;
Mon trésor a coulé contre votre billot.

Le désert comme asile au seul tison suave
Jamais ne m'a nommé, jamais ne m'a rendu.

Écartez-vous de moi qui patiente sans bouche :
Le trèfle de la passion est de fer dans ma main.

Dans la stupeur de l'air où s'ouvrent mes allées,
Le temps émondera peu à peu mon visage,
Comme un cheval sans fin dans un labour aigri.

POST-SCRIPTUM

Go from me now in my mouthless waiting;
At your feet I was born, but you've lost me;
My desires have made their reign too precise;
My treasure has run out against your block.

The desert refuge for the sole sweet fire-brand
Named me never, never restored me.

Go from me now in my mouthless waiting.
The trefoil of passion is iron in my hand.

In the air's amazement where my ventures open,
Time will prune away my face bit by bit,
Like a horse ceaseless in embittered ploughing.

—MAC

René Char

PARTAGE FORMEL

FORMAL SHARE

PARTAGE FORMEL

Mes soeurs, voici l'eau du sacre qui
pénètre toujours plus étroite au mur de l'été.

I

L'imagination consiste à expulser de la réalité plusieurs
personnes incomplètes pour, mettant contribution les puissances
magiques et subversives du désir, obtenir leur retour sous la forme
d'une présence entièrement satisfaisante. C'est alors l'inextinguible
réel incréé.

II

Ce dont le poète souffre le plus dans ses rapports avec le
monde, c'est du manque de justice interne. La vitre-cloaque de
Caliban derrière laquelle les yeux tout-puissants et sensibles
d'Ariel s'irritent.

III

Le poète transforme indifféremment la défaite en victoire,
la victoire en défaite, empereur prénatal seulement soucieux du
recueil de l'azur.

IV

Quelquefois sa réalité n'aurait aucun sens pour lui, si le poète
n'influençait pas en secret le récit des exploits de celle des autres.

V

Magicien de l'insécurité, le poète n'a que des satisfactions
adoptives. Cendre toujours inachevée.

VI

Derrière l'œil fermé d'une de ces Lois préfixes qui ont pour
notre désir des obstacles sans solution, parfois se dissimule
un soleil arriéré dont la sensibilité de fenouil à notre contact

FORMAL SHARE

My sisters, here is the water of consecration which
plunges always more deeply to the heart of summer.

I

Imagination consists in dismissing from reality several
incomplete persons, using the magical and subversive powers
of desire, in order to have them return as a presence entirely
satisfying. It is then the uncreated real, impossible to extinguish.

II

What the poet suffers from most in relations with the world, is
the lack of *internal* justice. Caliban's cesspool windowpane, behind
which Ariel's all-powerful and sensitive eyes grow irritated.

III

The poet transforms indifferently defeat into victory, victory
into defeat, a prebirth emperor caring only for what the azure
gathers.

IV

At times his own reality would have no meaning for him, if
the poet didn't secretly influence the tale of its exploits by others.

V

Magician of uncertainty, the poet has only makeshift
satisfactions. Embers always unfinished.

VI

Behind the closed eye of one of the prefixed Laws which have
for our desire obstacles without solution, sometimes there hides a
backwards sun whose fennel sensitivity gushes forth violently at

violemment s'épanche et nous embaume. L'obscurité de sa tendresse, son entente avec l'inespéré, noblesse lourde qui suffit au poète.

VII

Le poète doit tenir la balance égale entre le monde physique de la veille et l'aisance redoutable du sommeil, les lignes de la connaissance dans lesquelles il couche le corps subtil du poème, allant indistinctement de l'un à l'autre de ces états différents de la vie.

VIII

Chacun vit jusqu'au soir qui complète l'amour. Sous l'autorité harmonieuse d'un prodige commun à tous, la destinée particulière s'accomplit jusqu'à la solitude, jusqu'à l'oracle.

IX

A DEUX MÉRITES. – Héraclite, Georges de La Tour, je vous sais gré d'avoir de longs moments poussé dehors de chaque pli de mon corps singulier ce leurre : la condition humaine incohérente, d'avoir tourné l'anneau dévêtu de la femme d'après le regard du visage de l'homme, d'avoir rendu agile et recevable ma dislocation, d'avoir dépensé vos forces à la couronne de cette conséquence sans mesure de la lumière absolument impérative l'action contre le réel, par tradition signifiée, simulacre et miniature.

X

Il convient que la poésie soit inséparable du prévisible, mais non encore formulé.

XI

Peut-être la guerre civile, nid d'aigle de la mort enchantée? O rayonnant buveur d'avenir mort!

Furor and Mystery

our contact to embalm us. The obscurity of its tenderness, its understanding with the unexpected, a weighty nobility sufficient for the poet.

VII

The poet must keep an equal balance between the physical world of waking and the fearful ease of sleep, the lines of knowledge where he lays down the subtle body of the poem, moving between these different states of life.

VIII

Each one lives until the evening which completes love. Under the harmonious authority of a miracle common to all, the particular destiny is fulfilled until solitude, until the oracle.

IX

TWO MERITS. – Heraclitus, Georges de La Tour, I am grateful to you for having for long moments thrust out from each fold of my singular body this enticement: the incoherent human condition, for having turned the unclothed ring of woman relative to the look on man's face, for having rendered agile and admissible my displacement, for having spent your strength at the crown of this immeasurable consequence of absolutely imperative light: the action against the real, signified by tradition, simulacra and miniature.

X

It is fitting that poetry be inseparable from the foreseeable, but not yet formulated.

XI

Perhaps civil war, eagle nest of enchanted death? Oh radiant drinker of dead future!

XII

Disposer en terrasses successives des valeurs poétiques tenables en rapports prémédités avec la pyramide du Chant à l'instant de se révéler, pour obtenir cet absolu inextinguible, ce rameau du premier soleil : le feu non vu, indécomposable.

XIII

Fureur et mystère tour à tour le séduisirent et le consumèrent. Puis vint l'année qui acheva son agonie de saxifrage.

XIV

Gravitaient autour de son pain aigre les circonstances des rebondissements, des renaissances, des foudroiements et des nages incrustantes dans la fontaine de Saint-Allyre.

XV

En poésie, combien d'initiés engagent encore de nos jours, sur un hippodrome situé dans l'été luxueux, parmi les nobles bêtes sélectionnées, un cheval de corrida dont les entrailles fraîchement recousues palpitent de poussières répugnantes! Jusqu'à ce que l'embolie dialectique qui frappe tout poème frauduleusement élaboré fasse justice dans la personne de son auteur de cette impropriété inadmissible.

XVI

Le poème est toujours marié à quelqu'un.

XVII

Héraclite met l'accent sur l'exaltante alliance des contraires. Il voit en premier lieu en eux la condition parfaite et le moteur indispensable à produire l'harmonie. En poésie il est advenu qu'au moment de la fusion de ces contraires surgissait un impact sans origine définie dont l'action dissolvante et solitaire provoquait le glissement des abîmes qui portent de façon si antiphysique le poème. Il appartient au poète de couper court à ce danger en

Furor and Mystery

XII

To dispose poetic values in successive tenable terraces in premeditated relations with the pyramid of the Song at the moment of revealing itself, to obtain this inextinguishable absolute, this branch of the first sun: fire not seen, not to be decomposed.

XIII

Furor and mystery one then the other seduced and consumed him. After that, the year that ended his agony of saxifrage.

XIV

There gravitated around his bitter bread the circumstances of surges, rebirths, lightning flashes, and petrifying baths in the fountain of Saint-Allyre.

XV

In poetry, how many of the initiated are still engaged nowadays, on a hippodrome situated in the luxurious summer, among the choice noble beasts, a bullfight horse whose freshly sewn-together entrails pulse with repugnant dust! Until the dialectic embolism that strikes every poem fraudulently elaborated metes out justice to the person of the author of this inadmissible impropriety.

XVI

The poem is always married to someone.

XVII

Heraclitus stresses the exalting alliance of contraries. He sees first of all in them the perfect condition and the indispensable motor for producing harmony. In poetry it is a given that at the moment of fusion of these contraries there emerged an impact without any definite origin whose dissolving and unique action encouraged the slide of those abysses that carry the poem along in such an anti-physical fashion. It's up to the poet to cut short this

faisant intervenir, soit un élément traditionnel à raison éprouvée, soit le feu d'une démiurgie si miraculeuse qu'elle annule le trajet de cause à effet. Le poète peut alors voir les contraires — ces mirages ponctuels et tumultueux — aboutir, leur lignée immanente *se personnifier,* poésie et vérité, comme nous savons, étant synonymes.

XVIII
Adoucis ta patience, mère du Prince. Telle jadis tu aidais à nourrir le lion de l'opprimé.

XIX
Homme de la pluie et enfant du beau temps, vos mains de défaite et de progrès me sont également nécessaires.

XX
De ta fenêtre ardente, reconnais dans les traits de ce bûcher subtil le' poète, tombereau de roseaux qui brûlent et que l'inespéré escorte.

XXI
En poésie c'est seulement à partir de la communication et de la libre-disposition de la totalité des choses entre elles à travers nous que nous nous trouvons engagés et définis, à même d'obtenir notre forme originale et nos propriétés probatoires.

XXII
A l'âge d'homme j'ai vu s'élever et grandir sur le mur mitoyen de la vie et de la mort une échelle de plus en plus nue, investie d'un pouvoir d'évulsion unique : le rêve. Ses barreaux, à partir d'un certain progrès, ne soutenaient plus les lisses épargnants du sommeil. Après a brouillonne vacance de la profondeur injectée dont les figures chaotiques servirent de champ à l'inquisition d'hommes bien' doués mais incapables dé toiser l'universalité du drame, voici que l'obscurité s'écarte et que VIVRE devient, sous la forme d'un âpre ascétisme allégorique, la conquête des pouvoirs extraordinaires

danger by the intervention either of a traditional element well proven, or the fire of a demiurge sufficiently miraculous to annul the trajectory from cause to effect. The poet can then see the final result of these contraries—these punctual and tumultuous mirages—their immanent lineage *personified,* poetry and truth being, as we know, synonymous.

XVIII

Gentle your patience, mother of the Prince. That way you used to help nourish the lion of the oppressed.

XIX

Man of rain and child of good weather, your hands of defeat and of progress are equally necessary.

XX

From your burning window, recognize in the traits of this subtle funeral-pyre the poet, the tipcart of burning reeds, escorted by the unexpected.

XXI

In poetry, only after the communication and free disposition of all things between themselves through us do we find ourselves involved and defined, able to obtain our original form and our probative properties.

XXII

As a grownup I saw there rising and growing larger on the wall between life and death a ladder increasingly bare, invested with a unique power of evulsion: the dream. Its rungs, starting with a certain progress, no longer held up the smooth economisers of sleep. After the confusing vacancy of congested depth, whose chaotic figures served as a field for the inquisition of men gifted but incapable of sizing up the universality of the drama, now darkness draws aside and L I V I N G becomes, in the form of a harsh

dont nous nous sentons profusément traversés mais que nous n'exprimons qu'incomplètement faute de loyauté, de discernement cruel et de persévérance.

Compagnons pathétiques qui murmurez à peine, allez la lampe éteinte et rendez les bijoux. Un mystère nouveau chante dans vos os. Développez votre étrangeté légitime.

XXIII

Je suis le poète, meneur de puits tari que tes lointains, ô mon amour, approvisionnent.

XXIV

Par un travail physique intense on se maintient au niveau du froid extérieur et, ce faisant, on supprime le risque d'être annexé par lui; ainsi, à l'heure du retour au réel non suscité par notre désir, lorsque le temps est venu de confier à son destin le vaisseau du poème, nous nous trouvons dans une situation analogue. Les roues — ces gravats — de notre moulin pétrifié s'élancent, raclant des eaux basses et difficiles. Notre effort réapprend des sueurs proportionnelles. Et nous allons, lutteurs à terre mais jamais mourants, au milieu de témoins qui nous exaspèrent et de vertus indifférentes.

XXV

Refuser la goutte d'imagination qui manque au néant, c'est se vouer à la patience de rendre à l'éternel le mal qu'il nous fait.

O urne de laurier dans un ventre d'aspic!

XXVI

Mourir, ce n'est jamais que contraindre sa conscience, au moment même où elle s'abolit, à prendre congé de quelques quartiers physiques actifs ou somnolents d'un corps qui nous fut passablement étranger puisque sa connaissance ne nous vint qu'au travers

allegorical asceticism, the conquest of extraordinary powers we feel profusely traversing us, but which we express only incompletely, through a lack of loyalty, cruel distinction, and perseverance.

Pathetic companions scarcely murmuring, go on with your lamp extinguished and give back the jewels. A new mystery sings in your bones. Develop your legitimate strangeness.

XXIII

I am the poet, in charge of the dried-up well which your distances, oh my love, nourish.

XXIV

Through an intense physical labor we keep ourselves at the level of exterior cold, and so doing, avoid the risk of being annexed by it; thus, when it is time for the return to the real not aroused by our desire, time to turn over the vessel of the poem to its fate, we find ourselves in an analogous situation. The wheels—this plaster rubbish—of our petrified mill rush forward, sweeping over low-lying and difficult waters. Our effort has to relearn the sweat required. And we go on, fighters earth-bound but never dying amidst exasperating witnesses and indifferent virtues.

XXV

Refusing the drop of imagination lacking to nothingness, is to devote ourselves patiently to riposting to the eternal the harm it does us.

Oh urn of laurel in a stomach of aspic!

XXVI

To die is never anything but constraining our conscience, at the very moment when it wipes itself out, to take leave of some physical elements of a body, active or somnolent, which was rather a stranger to us because any knowledge of it came only through

d'expédients mesquins et sporadiques. Gros bourg sans grâce au brouhaha duquel s'employaient des habitants modérés... Et au-dessus de cet atroce hermétisme s'élançait une colonne d'ombre à face voûtée, endolorie et à demi aveugle, de loin en loin — ô bonheur — scalpée par la foudre.

XXVII

Terre mouvante, horrible, exquise et condition humaine hétérogène se saisissent et se qualifient mutuellement. La poésie se tire de la somme exaltée de leur moire.

XXVIII

Le poète est l'homme de la stabilité unilatérale.

XXIX

Le poème émerge d'une imposition subjective et d'un choix objectif.

Le poème est une assemblée en mouvement de valeurs origi-nales déterminantes en relations contemporaines avec *quelqu'un que celte circonstance fait premier.*

XXX

Le poème est l'amour réalisé du désir demeuré désir.

XXXI

Certains réclament pour elle le sursis de l'armure; leur blessure a le spleen d'une éternité de tenailles. Mais la poésie qui va nue sur ses pieds de roseau, sur ses pieds de caillou, ne se laisse réduire nulle part. Femme, nous baisons le temps fou sur sa bouche, où côte à côte avec le grillon zénithal, elle chante la nuit de l'hiver dans la pauvre boulangerie, sous la mie d'un pain de lumière.

trivial and sporadic expedients. Big graceless city whose moderate inhabitants lent themselves to the brouhaha... And above this atrocious hermetics there rose a column of shadow with a vaulted face, pained and half blind, now and then—oh happiness—scalped by lightning.

XXVII

Moving, horrible, exquisite earth and the heterogeneous human condition take hold of each other and are mutually qualified. Poetry extracts itself from the exalted sum of their moire.

XXVIII

The poet is the person of onesided stability.

XXIX

The poem emerges from a subjective imposition and an objective choice.

The poem is an assemblage of original determining values always in motion and in present relations with *someone whom this circumstance puts first.*

XXX

The poem is the realized love of desire remaining desire.

XXXI

Some claim for it the reprieve of armor; their wound has the spleen of an eternity of pincers. But poetry going naked on its feet of reed, on its feet of pebble, does not let itself be lessened anywhere. Woman, we kiss crazed time on its mouth, where side by side with the cricket at its zenith, it sings the winter night in the poor bakery, deep inside a bread of light.

XXXII

Le poète ne s'irrite pas de l'extinction hideuse de la mort, mais confiant en son toucher particulier transforme toute chose en laines prolongées.

XXXIII

Au cours de son action parmi les essarts de l'universalité du Verbe, le poète intègre, avide, impressionnable et téméraire se gardera de sympathiser avec les entreprises qui aliènent le prodige de la liberté en poésie, c'est-à-dire de l'intelligence dans la vie.

XXXIV

Un être qu'on ignore est un être infini, susceptible, en intervenant, de changer notre angoisse et notre fardeau en aurore artérielle.

Entre innocence et connaissance, amour et néant, le poète étend sa santé chaque jour.

XXXV

Le poète en traduisant l'intention en acte inspiré, en convertissant un cycle de fatigues en fret de résurrection, fait entrer l'oasis du froid par tous les pores de la vitre de l'accablement et crée le prisme, hydre de l'effort, du merveilleux, de la rigueur et du déluge, ayant tes lèvres pour sagesse et mon sang pour retable.

XXXVI

Le logement du poète est des plus vagues; le gouffre d'un feu triste soumissionne sa table de bois blanc.

La vitalité du poète n'est pas une vitalité de l'au-delà mais un point diamanté *actuel* de présences transcendantes et d'orages pèlerins.

XXXII

The poet is not irritated at the hideous extinction of death, but confident in his particular touch transforms everything into enduring strands.

XXXIII

In the course of his action, among the clearing of the universality of the Word, the poet, integral, avid, impressionable and rash, restrains himself from sympathizing with endeavors dismissive of the wonder of freedom in poetry, that is, of intelligence in life.

XXXIV

A being you don't notice is a being infinite, likely by his intervention to change our anguish and our burden into an arterial dawn.

Between innocence and knowledge, love and nothingness, the poet extends his health each day.

XXXV

By translating intention into an inspired act, converting a cycle of fatigues into a cargo of resurrection, the poet has the oasis of cold enter through all the pores of the glass of dejection and creates the prism, hydra of effort, of the marvelous, of rigor and the flood, having your lips for wisdom and my blood for altarpiece.

XXXVI

The dwelling of the poet is the vaguest possible; the gulf of a sad fire underwrites his white wood table.

The vitality of the poet is not a vitality of the beyond, but an *actual* diamantine point of transcendent presences and pilgrim storms.

XXXVII

Il ne dépend que de la nécessité et de votre volupté qui me créditent que j'aie ou non le Visage de l'échange.

XXXVIII

Les dés aux minutes comptées, les dés inaptes à étreindre, parce qu'ils sont naissance et vieillesse.

XXXIX

Au seuil de la pesanteur, le poète comme l'araignée construit sa route dans le ciel. En partie caché à lui-même, il apparaît aux autres, dans les rayons de sa ruse inouïe, mortellement visible.

XL

Traverser avec le poème la pastorale des déserts, le don de soi aux furies, le feu moisissant des larmes. Courir sur ses talons, le prier, l'injurier. L'identifier comme étant l'expression de son génie ou encore l'ovaire écrasé de son appauvrissement. Par une nuit, faire irruption à sa suite, enfin, dans les noces de la grenade cosmique.

XLI

Dans le poète deux évidences sont incluses : la première livre d'emblée tout son sens sous la variété des formes dont le réel extérieur dispose; elle est rarement creusante, est seulement pertinente; la seconde se trouve insérée dans le poème, elle dit le commandement et l'exégèse des dieux puissants et fantasques qui habitent le poète, évidence indurée qui ne se flétrit ni ne s'éteint. Son hégémonie est attributive. Prononcée, elle occupe une étendue considérable.

XLII

Être poète, c'est avoir de l'appétit pour un malaise dont la consommation, parmi les tourbillons de la totalité des choses existantes et pressenties, provoque, au moment de se clore, la félicité.

XXXVII

It only depends on necessity and your voluptuousness which credit me that I have or not the Face of exchange.

XXXVIII

Dice with minutes measured, dice inapt to embrace, because they are birth and age.

XXXIX

At the threshold of gravity, the poet like the spider constructs his path in the sky. Partially hidden from himself, he appears to others, in the light beams of his unbelievable ruse, mortally visible.

XL

To cross with the poem the pastoral of deserts, the gift of self to the furies, the mouldy fire of tears. To run after its heels, to beseech it, to insult it. To identify it as the expression of genius or again the smashed ovary of impoverishment. One night, to irrupt after it, finally, in the nuptials of the cosmic pomegranate.

XLI

In the poet are included two evidences: the first delivers straight off all its meaning under the variety of forms available to the exterior real; it is rarely deepening, is only pertinent; the second finds itself inserted in the poem, it tells the order and the exegesis of the powerful and whimsical gods who inhabit the poet, a hardened evidence neither withers nor fades. Its hegemony is predictive. Declared, it takes up a considerable space.

XLII

To be a poet is to have an appetite for discomfort whose consummation, among the whirlwinds of all things existing and foreseen, stirs up, at the moment of closure, happiness.

XLIII

Le poème donne et reçoit de sa multitude l'entière démarche du poète s'expatriant de son huis clos. Derrière cette persienne de sang brûle le cri d'une force qui se détruira elle seule parce qu'elle a horreur de la force, sa sœur subjective et stérile.

XLIV

Le poète tourmente à l'aide d'injaugeables secrets la forme et la voix de ses fontaines.

XLV

Le poète est a genèse d'un être qui projette et d'un être qui retient. A l'amant il emprunte le vide, à la bien-aimée, la lumière. Ce couple formel, cette double sentinelle lui donnent pathétiquement sa voix.

XLVI

Inexpugnable sous sa tente de cyprès, le poète, pour se convaincre et se guider, ne doit pas craindre de se servir de toutes les clefs accourues dans sa main. Cependant il ne doit pas confondre une animation de frontières avec un horizon révolutionnaire.

XLVII

Reconnaître deux sortes de possible : le possible *diurne* et le possible *prohibé*. Rendre, s'il se peut, le premier l'égal du second; les mettre sur la voie royale du fascinant impossible, degré le plus haut du compréhensible.

XLVIII

Le poète recommande : « Penchez-vous, penchez-vous davantage. » Il ne sort pas toujours indemne de sa page, mais comme le pauvre il sait tirer parti de l'éternité d'une olive.

Furor and Mystery

XLIII

The poem gives and receives from its multitude the entire bearing of the poet leaving behind his closed door. Behind this shutter of blood burns the cry of one strength self-destructive because it has a horror of force, its subjective and sterile sister.

XLIV

The poet torments with the help of immeasurable secrets the form and the voice of his fountains.

XLV

The poet is the genesis of a being who projects and a being who retains. From the lover he borrows emptiness, from the beloved, light. This formal couple, this double sentinel, gives him pathetically its voice.

XL

Impregnable under his tent of cypress, the poet, to convince and guide himself, should not fear using all the keys piled up in his hand. However he must not confuse a border animation with a revolutionary horizon.

XLVII

To recognize two sorts of possibles: the *daily* possible and the *prohibited* possible. To make the first the equal of the second if this can be; to place them on the royal path of the impossible *fascinant,* the highest degree of the understandable.

XLVIII

The poet recommends: "Bend over, bend over more." He does not always emerge unscathed from his page, but, like the poor man, he knows how to use the eternity of an olive.

XLIX

A chaque effondrement des preuves le poète répond par une salve d'avenir.

L

Toute respiration propose un règne la tâche de persécuter, la décision de maintenir, la fougue de rendre libre. Le poète partage dans l'innocence et dans la pauvreté la condition des uns, condamne et rejette l'arbitraire des autres.

Toute respiration propose un règne : jusqu'à ce que soit rempli le destin de cette tête monotype qui pleure, s'obstine et se dégage pour se briser dans l'infini, hure de l'imaginaire.

LI

Certaines époques de la condition de l'homme subissent l'assaut glacé d'un mal qui prend appui sur les points les plus déshonorés de la nature humaine. Au centre de cet ouragan, le poète complétera par le refus de soi le sens de son message, puis se joindra au parti de ceux qui, ayant ôté à la souffrance son masque de légitimité, assurent le retour éternel de l'entêté portefaix, passeur de justice.

LII

Cette forteresse épanchant la liberté par toutes ses poternes, cette fourche de vapeur qui tient dans l'air un corps d'une envergure prométhéenne que la foudre illumine et évite, c'est le poème, aux caprices exorbitants, qui dans l'instant nous obtient puis s'efface.

LIII

Après la remise de ses trésors (tournoyant entre deux ponts) et l'abandon de ses sueurs, le poète, la moitié du corps, le sommet du souffle dans l'inconnu, le poète n'est plus le reflet d'un fait accompli. Plus rien ne le mesure, ne le lie. La ville sereine, la ville imperforée est devant lui.

XLIX

To each collapse of proofs the poet responds by a salvo of the future.

L

Every breath proposes a reign: the duty of persecution, the decision of keeping on, the spirit of setting free. The poet shares in innocence and in poverty the condition of some, condemns and rejects the arbitrary of others.

Every breath proposes a reign: until the fate is settled of this monotype head weeping, persevering, and breaking off to shatter in the infinite, head of the imaginary.

LI

Certain epochs of the human condition undergo the frozen assault of an evil that is supported by the most dishonorable elements of human nature. At the center of this hurricane, the poet will fill in, by the refusal of himself, the meaning of his message, then will join on the side of those who, having removed from suffering its mask of legitimacy, assure the eternal return of the stubborn porter, the ferryman of justice.

LII

This fortress, spreading out freedom through all its gates, this fork of vapor that holds in the air a body of a promethean breadth that lightning lights up and avoids, is the poem, with its exorbitant caprices, which in the moment seizes us and then vanishes.

LIII

After conferring his treasures (spinning about between two bridges) and abandoning his perspiration, the poet, half of the body, the summit of breath in the unknown, the poet is no longer the reflection of an accomplished fact. Nothing measures him any longer, nor binds him. The serene city, unperforated, lies in front of him.

LIV

Debout, croissant dans la durée, le poème, mystère qui intronise. A l'écart, suivant l'allée de la vigne commune, le poète, grand Commenceur, le poète intransitif, quelconque en ses splendeurs intraveineuses, le poète tirant le malheur de son propre abîme, avec la Femme à son côté s'informant du raisin rare.

LV

Sans doute appartient-il à cet homme, de fond en comble aux prises avec le Mal dont il connaît le visage vorace et médullaire, de transformer le fait fabuleuX en fait historique. Notre conviction inquiète ne doit pas le dénigrer mais l'interroger, nous, fervents tueurs d'êtres réels dans la personne successive de notre chimère. Magie médiate, imposture, il fait encore nuit, j'ai mal, mais tout fonctionne à nouveau.

L'évasion dans son semblable, avec d'immenses perspectives de poésie, sera peut-être un jour possible.

LIV

Standing, growing larger as it lasts, the poem, mystery that enthrones. To the side, following the path of the common vine the poet, great Beginner, the intransitive poet, just anyone in his intravenous splendors, the poet drawing unhappiness from his own abyss, with Woman at his side getting the news of the rare grape.

LV

Doubtless it pertains to this man, quite entirely struggling with Evil whose voracious historical and medullary face he knows, to transform fabulous fact into historical fact. Our unquiet talk must not denigrate him but interrogate him, we, fervent murderers of real beings in the successive person of our chimera. Mediated magic, imposture, it is still night, I am unwell, but everything is working again.

Evasion into his equal, with immense perspectives of poetry, will someday perhaps be possible.

—MAC

MISSION ET RÉVOCATION

Devant les précaires perspectives d'alchimie du dieu détruit — inaccompli dans l'expérience — je vous regarde, formes douées de vie, chosees inouïies, chosees quelconques, et j'interroge : « Commandement interne? Sommation du dehors? » La terre s'éjecte de ses parenthèses illettrées. Solei! et nuit dans un or identique parcourent et négocient l'espace-esprit, Ia chair-muraille. Le coeur s'évanouit... Ta réponse, connaissance, ce n'est plus Ia mort, université suspensive.

MISSION AND REVOCATION

Before the precarious alchemical perspectives of the god destroyed—unaccomplished in experience—I gaze at you, forms endowed with life, unheard of things, ordinary things, and I ask: "Internal commandment? Summons from outside?" The earth bursts out from between its illiterate parentheses. Sun and night in an identical gold traverse and negotiate the space-spirit, the flesh-barrier. The heart is fainting... Your response, knowledge, is no longer death, that suspensive university.

—MAC

FEUILLETS D'HYPNOS
(1943–1944)

LEAVES OF HYPNOS
(1943–1944)

FEUILLETS D'HYPNOS

A Albert Camus

*Hypnos saisit l'hiver et le vêtit de granit.
L'hiver se fit sommeil et Hypnos devint feu. La
suite appartient aux hommes.*

*Ces notes n'empruntent rien à l'amour de soi, à la nouvelle, à la maxime
ou au roman. Un feu d'herbes sèches eût tout aussi bien été leur éditeur. La
vue du sang supplicié en a fait une fois perdre le fil, a réduit à néant leur
importance. Elles furent écrites dans la tension, la colère, la peur, l'émula-
tion, le dégoût, la ruse, le recueillement furtif, l'illusion de l'avenir, l'amitié,
l'amour. C'est dire combien elles sont affectées par l'événement. Ensuite plus
souvent survolées que relues.*

*Ce carnet pourrait n'avoir appartenu à personne tant le sens de la vie
d'un homme est sous-jacent a ses pérégrinations, et difficilement séparable
d'un mimétisme parfois hallucinant. De telles tendances furent néanmoins
combattues.*

*Ces notes marquent la résistance d'un humanisme conscient de ses de-
voirs, discret sur ses vertus, désirant réserver l'inaccessible champ libre à la
fantaisie de ses soleils, et décidé à payer le prix pour cela.*

1

Autant que se peut, enseigne à devenir efficace, pour le but à
atteindre mais pas au delà. Au delà est fumée. Où il y a fumée il y a
changement.

2

Ne t'attarde pas à l'ornière des résultats.

3

Conduire le réel jusqu'à l'action comme une fleur glissée à
la bouche acide des petits enfants. Connaissance ineffable du
diamant désespéré (la vie).

LEAVES OF HYPNOS

To Albert Camus

> *Hypnos seized hold of winter and clothed it in granite. Winter turned into sleep and Hypnos became fire. What happened next belongs to men.*

These notes owe nothing to self-love, to the short story, the maxim, or the novel. A fire of dry herbs might just as well have been their editor. The sight of blood tortured led once to losing the thread, reduced their importance to nothing. They were written under stress, in anger, fear, emulation, disgust, guile, furtive meditation, the illusion of the future, friendship, love. Which is to say how much they are shaped by the event. Afterwards more often skimmed than reread.

This notebook could have belonged to no one, so deep does the meaning of a man's life lie beneath his wanderings, so hard is it to tell apart from a sometimes extraordinary mimicry. Such tendencies were fought, however.

These notes record the resistance of a humanism conscious of its duties, cautious of its virtues, wanting to keep the inaccessible *open to the imagination of its suns, and determined to pay the* price *for that.*

1

As much as possible, teach how to become effective only as far as the goal, but no farther. Farther is smoke. Where there is smoke there is unpredictability.

2

Do not linger in the rut of results.

3

Guide the real into action like a flower slipped into the tart mouths of infants. Ineffable knowledge of the desperate diamond (life).

René Char

4

Être stoïque, c'est se figer, avec les beaux yeux de Narcisse. Nous avons recensé toute la douleur qu'éventuellement le bourreau pouvait prélever sur chaque pouce de notre corps; puis le cœur serré, nous sommes allés et avons fait face.

5

Nous n'appartenons à personne sinon au point d'or de cette lampe inconnue de nous, inaccessible à nous qui tient éveillés le courage et le silence.

6

L'effort du poète vise à transformer *vieux ennemis* en *loyaux adversaires,* tout lendemain fertile étant fonction de la réussite de ce projet, surtout là où s'élance, s'enlace, décline, est décimée toute la gamme des voiles où le vent des continents rend son cœur au vent des abîmes.

7

Cette guerre se prolongera au delà des armistices platoniques. L'implantation des concepts politiques se poursuivra contradictoirement, dans les convulsions et sous le couvert d'une hypocrisie sûre de ses droits. Ne souriez pas. Écartez le scepticisme et la résignation, et préparez votre âme mortelle en vue d'affronter intramuros des démons glacés analogues aux génies microbiens.

8

Des êtres raisonnables perdent jusqu'à la notion de la durée probable de leur vie et leur équilibre quotidien lorsque l'instinct de conservation s'effondre en eux sous les exigences de l'instinct de propriété. Ils deviennent hostiles aux frissons de l'atmosphère et se soumettent sans retenue aux instances du mensonge et du mal. C'est sous une chute de grêle maléfique que s'effrite leur misérable condition.

4

To be stoic is to congeal, with the beautiful gaze of Narcissus. We calculated every suffering the torturer could possibly extract from every inch of our bodies; then, sick at heart, we went and faced him.

5

We belong to no one except the golden point of light from that lamp unknown to us, inaccessible to us that keeps awake courage and silence.

6

The poet's effort strives to transform *old enemies* into *loyal adversaries,* every fertile tomorrow hinging on the project's success, especially when the whole gamut of sails bellies out, intertwines, declines, is decimated, where the wind of the continents gives up its heart to the wind of the abyss.

7

This war will stretch beyond platonic armistices. The implanting of political concepts will proceed contradictorily with the convulsive stealth of a hypocrisy certain of its rights. Don't smile. Thrust from you skepticism, resignation, and prepare your mortal soul to face, within the city walls, glacial demons analogous to fiendish microbes.

8

Reasonable beings entirely lose sight of their probable life span and their daily equilibrium when the instinct for self-preservation caves in to the property instinct. They become hostile to the slightest quivering of the atmosphere and give themselves wholeheartedly to being wooed by lies and evil. Their miserable condition crumbles under a malevolent hailstorm.

Arthur le Fol, après les tâtonnements du début, participe maintenant, de toute sa forte nature décidée, à nos jeux de hasard. Sa fringale d'action doit se satisfaire de la tâche précise que je lui assigne. Il obéit et se limite, par crainte d'être tancé! Sans cela, Dieu sait dans quel guêpier final sa bravoure le ferait glisser! Fidèle Arthur, comme un soldat de l'ancien temps!

10

Toute l'autorité, la tactique et l'ingéniosité ne remplacent pas une parcelle de conviction au service de la vérité. Ce lieu commun, je crois l'avoir amélioré.

11

Mon frère l'Élagueur, dont je suis sans nouvelles, se disait plaisamment un familier des chats de Pompéi. Quand nous apprîmes la déportation de cet être généreux, sa prison ne pouvait plus s'entr'ouvrir; des chaînes défiaient son courage, l'Autriche le tenait.

12

Ce qui m'a mis au monde et qui m'en chassera n'intervient qu'aux heures où je suis trop faible pour lui résister. Vieille personne quand je suis né. Jeune inconnue quand je mourrai.

La seule et même Passante.

13

Le temps vu à travers l'image est un temps perdu de vue. L'être et le temps sont bien différents. L'image scintille éternelle, quand elle a dépassé l'être et le temps.

9

After initial fumblings, Crazy Arthur [Arthur le Fol] now participates with the full force of his resolute nature in our games of chance. His keen appetite for action must be satisfied with the precise task I assign him. He obeys and controls himself, for fear of being scolded! Without that, God only knows in what final hornets' nest his bravery would land him! Loyal Arthur, like a soldier in ancient times!

10

All the authority, tactics and ingenuity in the world cannot replace one particle of conviction in the service of truth. I think I've improved this commonplace.

11

My brother The Pruner, of whom I have no news, used jokingly to call himself a cousin to the cats of Pompeii. By the time we learned of this generous creature's deportation, his prison could no longer open; chains defied his courage, Austria had him in its clutches.

12

What brought me into the world and will chase me from it only intrudes at moments when I am too weak to resist. Old when I was born. When I die she will be young, unknown.

One and the same Passerby.

13

Time seen through the image is time lost from view. Being and time are quite different. The image shimmers eternal, when it has outstripped being and time.

14

Je puis aisément me convaincre, après deux essais concluants, que le voleur qui s'est glissé à notre insu parmi nous est irrécupérable. Souteneur (il s'en vante), d'une méchanceté de vermine, flancheur devant l'ennemi, s'ébrouant dans le compte rendu de l'horreur comme porc dans la fange; rien à espérer, sinon les ennuis les plus graves, de la part de cet affranchi. Susceptible en outre d'introduire un vilain fluide ici.

Je ferai la chose moi-même.

15

Les enfants s'ennuient le dimanche. Passereau propose une semaine de vingt-quatre jours pour dépecer le dimanche. Soit une heure de dimanche s'ajoutant à chaque jour, de préférence, l'heure des repas, puisqu'il n'y a plus de pain sec.

Mais qu'on ne lui parle plus du dimanche.

16

L'intelligence avec l'ange, notre primordial souci.

(Ange, ce qui, à l'intérieur de l'homme, tient à l'écart du compromis religieux, la parole du plus haut silence, la signification qui ne s'évalue pas. Accordeur de poumons qui dore les grappes vitaminées de l'impossible. Connaît le sang, ignore le céleste. Ange: la bougie qui se penche au nord du cœur.)

17

J'ai toujours le cœur content de m'arrêter à Forcalquier, de prendre un repas chez les Bardouin,[1] de serrer les mains de Marius l'imprimeur et de Figuière. Ce rocher de braves gens est la citadelle de l'amitié. Tout ce qui entrave la lucidité et ralentit la confiance est banni d'ici. Nous nous sommes épousés une fois pour toutes devant l'essentiel.

---

[1] Les personnes citées le sont sous leur vrai nom, rétabli au mois de septembre 1944.

14

I am quite convinced, after two conclusive tests, that the thug who slipped into our midst, without our knowledge, is irredeemable. A bully (he boasts of it), malicious as vermin, flinching before the enemy, wallowing in reports of horror like a pig in mud; nothing to be hoped for, except the gravest trouble, from this unscrupulous scoundrel. Capable, in addition, of introducing a fluid villainy here.

I'll do the thing myself.

15

Children are bored on Sunday. Sparrow [Passereau] proposes a twenty-four-day week in order to carve Sunday up. Why not an hour of Sunday added to each day, at mealtimes preferably, since there are no more breadcrumbs.

But just don't mention Sunday to him anymore.

16

Communicating with the angel, our primordial care.

(Angel, that part of man which safeguards from religious compromise the language of highest silence, whose meaning is not measured out. Tuner of lungs who gilds the nutritious grapes of the impossible. Know the blood, ignore the celestial. Angel: the candle that leans to the heart's north.)

17

My heart is always content to stop at Forcalquier, to have a meal at the Bardouin's[1], to shake hands with Marius the printer and Figuière. This rock of worthy people is the citadel of friendship. All that shackles lucidity and slows down trust is banished here. We have married each other, once and for all, in the presence of the essential.

---

[1] Persons cited under their real names, restored in the month of September 1944.

18

Remettre à plus tard la part imaginaire qui, elle aussi, est susceptible d'action.

19

Le poète ne peut pas longtemps demeurer dans la stratosphère du Verbe. Il doit se lover dans de nouvelles larmes et pousser plus avant dans son ordre.

20

Je songe à cette armée de fuyards aux appétits de dictature que reverront peut-être au pouvoir, dans cet oublieux pays, ceux qui survivront à ce temps d'algèbre damnée.

21

Amer avenir, amer avenir, bal parmi les rosiers…

22

AUX PRUDENTS: Il neige sur le maquis et c'est contre nous chasse perpétuelle. Vous dont la maison ne pleure pas, chez qui l'avarice écrase l'amour, dans la succession des journées chaudes, votre feu n'est qu'un garde-malade. Trop tard. Votre cancer a parlé. Le pays natal n'a plus de pouvoirs.

23

Présent crénelé…

24

La France a des réactions d'épave dérangée dans sa sieste. Pourvu que les caréniers et les charpentiers qui s'affairent dans le camp allié ne soient pas de nouveaux naufrageurs!

18

Keep for later the imaginary part, which is, itself too, capable of action.

19

The poet cannot remain for long in the stratosphere of the Word. He must coil up in new tears and push further into his own order.

20

I think about that army of deserters with an appetite for dictatorship whom the survivors of this era of accursed algebra may well see in power again, in this forgetful country.

21

Bitter future, bitter future, dancing amidst the rosebushes…

22

TO THE PRUDENT: It is snowing on the maquis, and hunting us down is perpetually in season. You whose house does not weep, within whom greed is crushing love, in the succession of these hot days your fire is nothing but a sick-nurse. Too late. Your cancer has spoken. The native land has lost its powers.

23

This crenelated present…

24

France reacts like floating wreckage whose nap has been disturbed. If only the hull workers and carpenters bustling around in the allied camp aren't new shipwreckers!

25

Midi séparé du jour. Minuit retranché des hommes. Minuit au glas pourri, qu'une, deux, trois, quatre heures ne parviennent pas à bâillonner…

26

Le temps n'est plus secondé par les horloges dont les aiguilles s'entre-dévorent aujourd'hui sur le cadran de l'homme. Le temps, c'est du chiendent, et l'homme deviendra du sperme de chiendent.

27

Léon affirme que les chiens enragés sont beaux. Je le crois.

28

Il existe une sorte d'homme toujours en avance sur ses excréments.

29

Ce temps, par son allaitement très spécial, accélère la prospérité des canailles qui franchissent en se jouant les barrages dressés autrefois par la société contre elles. La même mécanique qui les stimule, les brisera-t-elle en se brisant, lorsque ses provisions hideuses seront épuisées?

(Et le moins possible de rescapés du haut mal.)

30

Archiduc me confie qu'il a découvert sa vérité quand il a épousé la Résistance. Jusque-là il était un acteur de sa vie frondeur et soupçonneux. L'insincérité l'empoisonnait. Une tristesse stérile peu à peu le recouvrait. Aujourd'hui *il aime,* il se dépense, il est engagé, il va nu, il provoque. J'apprécie beaucoup cet alchimiste.

25

Noon separated from day. Midnight cut off from men. Midnight with its putrid knell, which one o'clock, two o'clock, three o'clock, four o'clock do not succeed in muzzling...

26

Time is no longer assisted by clocks, whose hands today devour each other on man's face. Time is crabgrass, and man will become crabgrass sperm.

27

Leon avers that mad dogs are beautiful. I believe him.

28

There exists one kind of man who is always ahead on his excrements.

29

By virtue of its very special breast-feeding, this era fosters the prosperity of those riffraff who make child's play of leaping the barriers society set up against them in the past. Will the mechanism stimulating them break them as it breaks down, when its hideous supplies are gone?

(And the fewest possible survivors of this high evil.)

30

Archduke [Archiduc] confides he found his truth when he adopted the Resistance. Up to then, he was a player in his irreverent suspicious life. Insincerity was poisoning him. Bit by bit he was enveloped in a sterile sadness. Today *he loves,* he gives of himself, he is engaged, he goes naked, he provokes. I do appreciate this alchemist.

31

J'écris brièvement. Je ne puis guère m'absenter longtemps. S'étaler conduirait à l'obsession. L'adoration des bergers n'est plus utile à la planète.

32

Un homme sans défauts est une montagne sans crevasses. Il ne m'intéresse pas.

(Règle de sourcier et d'inquiet.)

33

Rouge-gorge, mon ami, qui arriviez quand le parc était désert, cet automne votre chant fait s'ébouler des souvenirs que les ogres voudraient bien entendre.

34

Épouse et n'épouse pas ta maison.

35

Vous serez une part de la saveur du fruit.

36

Temps où le ciel recru pénètre dans la terre, où l'homme agonise entre deux mépris.

37

Révolution et contre-révolution se masquent pour à nouveau s'affronter.

Franchise de courte durée! Au combat des aigles succède le combat des pieuvres. Le génie de l'homme, qui pense avoir découvert les vérités formelles, accommode les vérités qui tuent en vérités qui *autorisent* à tuer. Parade des grands inspirés à rebours sur le front de l'univers cuirassé et pantelant! Cependant que les névroses collectives s'accusent dans l'œil des mythes et des symboles, l'homme psychique met la vie au supplice sans qu'il paraisse

31

I write briefly. I can hardly absent myself for long. Self-display would lead to obsessing. The adoration of the shepherds is no longer useful to the planet.

32

A man without shortcomings is a mountain without crevasses. He doesn't interest me.

(Dowser's rule of thumb, and worrier's.)

33

Redbreast, my friend, who used to arrive when the grounds were deserted, this fall your song sets off a landslide of memories that the ogres would very much like to hear.

34

Marry and do not marry your house.

35

You will be part of the fruit's flavor.

36

Era when the dead-tired sky penetrates the earth, when man lies dying between two contempts.

37

Revolution and counterrevolution mask themselves to confront each other once again.

Short-lived candor! To the combat of eagles now succeeds the combat of octopuses. The genius of man, who thinks he has discovered categorical truths, accomodates truths that kill in truths that *authorize* killing. The grandiose aberrant mystics on parade at the front lines of this armored panting universe! Whereas collective neuroses indict themselves in the eye of myth and symbol, psychic man submits life to torture, apparently without its causing him the

lui en coûter le moindre remords. La fleur *tracée,* la fleur hideuse, tourne ses pétales noirs dans la chair folle du soleil. Où êtes-vous source? Où êtes-vous remède? Économie vas-tu enfin changer?

38

Ils se laissent choir de toute la masse de leurs préjugés ou ivres de l'ardeur de leurs faux principes. Les associer, les exorciser, les alléger, les muscler, les assouplir, puis les convaincre qu'à partir d'un certain point l'importance des idées reçues est extrêmement relative et qu'en fin de compte « l'affaire » est une affaire de vie et de mort et non de nuances à faire prévaloir au sein d'une civilisation dont le naufrage risque de ne pas laisser de trace sur l'océan de la destinée, c'est ce que je m'efforce de faire approuver autour de moi.

39

Nous sommes écartelés entre l'avidité de connaître et le désespoir d'avoir connu. L'aiguillon ne renonce pas à sa cuisson et nous à notre espoir.

40

Discipline, comme tu saignes!

41

S'il n'y avait pas parfois l'étanchéité de l'ennui, le cœur s'arrêterait de battre.

42

Entre les deux coups de feu qui décidèrent de son destin, il eut le temps d'appeler une mouche: « Madame ».

43

Bouche qui décidiez si ceci était hymen ou deuil, poison ou breuvage, beauté ou maladie, que sont devenues l'amertume et son aurore la douceur?

Tête hideuse qui s'exaspère et se corrompt!

least remorse. The tracked flower, the hideous flower, turns its black petals toward the mad flesh of the sun. Where are you, fountainhead? Where are you, remedy? System, will you change at last?

38

They flop down with the full weight of their prejudices or inebriated by the heat of their false principles. To include them, exorcise them, unburden them, strengthen them, relax them, then convince them that, after a certain point, the importance of received ideas is extremely relative and that ultimately this "business" is a business of life or death, it is not about the triumph of nuances at the heart of a civilization whose shipwreck threatens to leave not a trace on the ocean of destiny—it is for this that I struggle to gain approval around me.

39

We are torn between the craving to know and the despair of having known. The goad does not give up its sting nor we our hope.

40

Discipline, how you bleed!

41

If at times there were no watertight boredom, the heart would stop beating.

42

Between the two shots that decided his destiny, he had time to call a fly "Madame."

43

Mouth that used to decide if this were marriage or mourning, poison or libation, beauty or disease, what has become of bitterness and its dawn, sweetness?

Hideous head that worsens and spoils!

44

Amis, la neige attend la neige pour un travail simple et pur, à la limite de l'air et de la terre.

45

Je rêve d'un pays festonné, bienveillant, irrité soudain par les travaux des sages en même temps qu'ému par le zèle de quelques dieux, aux abords des femmes.

46

L'acte est vierge, même répété.

47

Martin de Reillanne nous appelle: les catamini.

48

Je n'ai pas peur. J'ai seulement le vertige. Il me faut réduire la distance entre l'ennemi et moi. L'affronter *horizontalement*.

49

Ce qui peut séduire dans le néant éternel c'est que le plus beau jour y soit indifféremment celui-ci ou tel autre.

(Coupons cette branche. Aucun essaim ne viendra s'y pendre.)

50

Face à tout, À TOUT CELA, un colt, promesse de soleil levant!

51

L'arracher à sa terre d'origine. Le replanter dans le sol présumé harmonieux de l'avenir, compte tenu d'un succès inachevé. Lui faire toucher le progrès sensoriellement. Voilà le secret de mon *habileté*.

44

Friends, the snow awaits the snow for work simple and pure, at the outer limit of the air and earth.

45

I dream of a country festooned, benevolent, suddenly irritated by the labors of the sensible, and moved, too, by the ardor of a few gods, when women are around.

46

The act is virgin, even repeated.

47

Martin de Reillanne calls us: the on-the-sly.

48

I am not afraid. I am only dizzy. I must reduce the distance between the enemy and me. Confront him *horizontally*.

49

What can seduce us about eternal nothingness is that there the loveliest of days might just as easily be this one or that one.
(Let's lop this branch. No hive will come to dangle here.)

50

In the face of everything, ALL THAT, a Colt, promise of the rising sun!

51

Uproot him from his land of origin. Replant him in the presumably harmonious soil of the future, with the possibility of only partial success. Give him the feel of progress through the senses. That is the secret of my *skill*.

52

"Les souris de l'enclume." Cette image m'aurait paru charmante autrefois. Elle suggère un essaim d'étincelles décimé en son éclair. (L'enclume est froide, le fer pas rouge, l'imagination dévastée.)

53

Le mistral qui s'était levé ne facilitait pas les choses. À mesure que les heures s'écoulaient, ma crainte augmentait, à peine raffermie par la présence de Cabot guettant sur la route le passage des convois et leur arrêt éventuel pour développer une attaque contre nous. La première caisse explosa en touchant le sol. Le feu activé par le vent se communiqua au bois et fit rapidement tache sur l'horizon. L'avion modifia légèrement son cap et effectua un second passage. Les cylindres au bout des soies multicolores s'égaillèrent sur une vaste étendue. Des heures nous luttâmes au milieu d'une infernale clarté, notre groupe scindé en trois: une partie face au feu, pelles et haches s'affairant, la seconde, lancée à découvrir armes et explosifs épars, les amenant à port de camion, la troisième constituée en équipe de protection. Des écureuils affolés, de la cime des pins, sautaient dans le brasier, comètes minuscules.

L'ennemi nous l'évitâmes de justesse. L'aurore nous surprit plus tôt que lui.

(Prends garde à l'anecdote. C'est une gare où le chef de gare déteste l'aiguilleur!)

54

Étoiles du mois de mai…

Chaque fois que je lève les yeux vers le ciel, la nausée écroule ma mâchoire. Je n'entends plus, montant de la fraîcheur de mes souterrains *le gémir du plaisir*, murmure de la femme entrouverte. Une cendre de cactus préhistoriques fait voler mon désert en éclats! Je ne suis plus *capable* de mourir…

Cyclone, cyclone, cyclone…

Furor and Mystery

52

"Mice in the anvil." This image would have charmed me in the past. It suggests a swarm of sparks dispersed as lightning. (The anvil is cold, the iron no longer glowing, the imagination ravaged.)

53

The mistral that had risen didn't make things any easier. As the hours wore on, my fear increased, scarcely reassured by Cabot's watching for any convoys passing along the road that might stop to attack us. The first crate exploded as it touched the ground. The fire, accelerated by the wind, spread to the woods and rapidly became conspicuous on the horizon. The plane modified its course a little and carried out a second drop. The cylinders at the ends of multicolored silks scattered over a vast expanse. For hours we struggled in the midst of hellish brightness, our group divided in three: one part confronting the fire, busy with shovels and axes; the second sent out to locate scattered arms and explosives, bringing them within reach of trucks; the third constituting a defense squad. Panic-stricken squirrels leapt from the tops of the pines into the blaze, miniscule comets.

We just managed to elude the enemy. Dawn caught us earlier than he did.

(Beware of the anecdote. It's a railroad station where the stationmaster hates the switchman!)

54

Stars in the month of May...

Each time I raise my eyes toward the sky, my jaw is overcome with nausea. I no longer hear, mounting from the freshness of my depths, *the groan of pleasure,* murmur of woman opened. A cinder of prehistoric cactuses shatters my desert! I am no longer *capable* of dying...

Cyclone, cyclone, cyclone...

55

N'étant jamais définitivement modelé, l'homme est receleur de son contraire. Ses cycles dessinent des orbes différents selon qu'il est en butte à telle sollicitation ou non. Et les dépressions mystérieuses, les inspirations absurdes, surgies du grand externat crématoire, comment se contraindre à les ignorer? Ah! circuler généreusement sur les saisons de l'écorce, tandis que l'amande palpite, libre...

56

Le poème est ascension furieuse; la poésie, le jeu des berges arides.

57

La source est roc et la langue est tranchée.

58

Parole, orage, glace et sang finiront par former un givre commun.

59

Si l'homme parfois ne fermait pas souverainement les yeux, il finirait par ne plus voir ce qui vaut d'être regardé.

60

Ensoleiller l'imagination de ceux qui bégaient au lieu de parler, qui rougissent à l'instant d'affirmer. Ce sont de fermes partisans.

61

Un officier, venu d'Afrique du Nord, s'étonne que mes « bougres de maquisards », comme il les appelle, s'expriment dans une langue dont le sens lui échappe, son oreille étant rebelle « au parler des images ». Je lui fais remarquer que l'argot n'est que pittoresque alors que a langue qui est ici en usage est due à l'émerveillement communiqué par les êtres et les choses dans l'intimité desquels nous vivons continuellement.

55

Never definitively molded, man harbors his contrary. His cycles design different spheres, depending on which attraction he's exposed to. And the mysterious depressions, the absurd inspirations, risen from the huge outpatient crematorium—how to force oneself to ignore them? Ah! To circulate generously through the seasons of the bark, while the almond palpitates, free…

56

The poem is furious ascension; poetry, the play of arid riverbanks.

57

The spring is rock and the tongue is sliced off.

58

Word, storm, ice and blood will ultimately form a common frost.

59

If man did not sometimes supremely close his eyes, he would end up no longer seeing what's worth looking at.

60

Flood with sunlight the imagination of those who stammer instead of speaking, who blush in the instant of assertion. They are steadfast partisans.

61

An officer, up from North Africa, is astonished that my "resistance guys," as he calls them, express themselves in a language whose meaning escapes him, his ear rebelling at "talk in images." I point out to him that slang is merely picturesque, whereas the language used here springs from the wonder communicated by the beings and things in whose intimacy we live continuously.

René Char

62

Notre héritage n'est précédé d'aucun testament.

63

On ne se bat bien que pour les causes qu'on modèle soi-même et avec lesquelles on se brûle en s'identifiant.

64

« Que fera-t-on de nous, *après?* » C'est la question qui préoccupe Minot dont les dix-sept ans ajoutent : « Moi, je redeviendrai peut-être le mauvais sujet que j'étais à quinze ans… » Cet enfant trop uniment porté par l'exemple de ses camarades, dont la bonne volonté est trop impersonnellement identique à la leur, ne se penche jamais sur lui-même. Actuellement c'est ce qui le sauve. Je crains *qu'après* il ne retourne à ses charmants lézards dont l'insouci est guetté par les chats…

65

La qualité des résistants n'est pas, hélas, partout la même! A côté d'un Joseph Fontaine, d'une rectitude et d'une teneur de sillon, d'un François Cuzin, d'un Claude Dechavannes, d'un André Grillet, d'un Marius Bardouin, d'un Gabriel Besson, d'un docteur Jean Roux, d'un Roger Chaudon aménageant le silo à blé d'Oraison en forteresse des périls, combien d'insaisissables saltimbanques plus soucieux de jouir que de produire! A prévoir que ces coqs du néant nous timbreront aux oreilles, la Libération venue…

66

Si je consens à cette appréhension qui commande à la vie sa lâcheté, je mets aussitôt au monde une foule d'amitiés formelles qui volent à mon secours.

67

Armand, le météo, définit sa fonction : le service énigmatique.

62

Our inheritance is preceded by no testament.

63

You only fight well for causes you yourself have shaped, with which you identify—and burn.

64

"What will they do with us *afterwards*?" That's the question preoccupying Minot, whose seventeen years add, "Me, maybe I'll go back to being the slacker I was at fifteen..." This child too easily swayed by the example of his comrades, whose good will is too impersonally identical with theirs, never looks into himself. Right now this saves him. I fear that *afterwards* he will return to his charming lizards, for whose insouciance cats lie in wait...

65

The quality of resistance fighters is not, alas, always the same! Next to Joseph Fontaine, as straight and sure as a furrow, Francis Cuzin, Claude Dechavannes, Andre Grillet, Marius Bardouin, Gabriel Besson, Doctor Jean Roux, Roger Chaudon turning the grain silo at Oraison into a fortress of dangers, how many slippery charlatans, more interested in pleasuring themselves than in pro-ducing! It is to be expected that these cocks of nothingness will crow our ears off, once the Liberation comes...

66

If I yield to that fear which controls life's cowardice, immediately I bring forth a crowd of unequivocal friendships that fly to my aid.

67

Armand, the weatherman, defines his role: the enigmatic service.

68

Lie dans le cerveau : à l'est du Rhin. Gabegie morale : de ce côté-ci.

69

Je vois l'homme perdu de perversions politiques, confondant action et expiation, nommant conquête son anéantissement.

70

L'alcool silencieux des démons.

71

Nuit, de toute la vitesse du boomerang taillé dans nos os, et qui siffle, siffle…

72

Agir en primitif et prévoir en stratège.

73

A en croire le sous-sol de l'herbe où chantait un couple de grillons cette nuit, la vie prénatale devait être très douce.

74

Solitaire et multiple. Veille et sommeil comme une épée dans son fourreau. Estomac aux aliments séparés. Altitude de cierge.

75

Assez déprimé par cette ondée (Londres) éveillant tout juste la nostalgie du secours.

76

A Carlate qui divaguait, j'ai dit : « Quand vous serez mort, vous vous occuperez des choses de la mort. Nous ne serons plus avec vous. Nous n'avons déjà pas assez de toutes nos ressources pour régler notre ouvrage et percevoir ses faibles résultats. Je ne

68

Dregs in the brain: to the east of the Rhine. Moral mismanagement: on this side.

69

I see man lost to political perversions, confusing action with expiation, naming his annihilation conquest.

70

The demons' silent alcohol.

71

Night, swift as the boomerang carved of our bones, and whistling, whistling...

72

Act as a primitive, foresee as a strategist.

73

If we're to believe the subsoil of the grass, where a pair of crickets sang tonight, prenatal life must have been very sweet.

74

Solitary and multiple. Vigil and sleep like a sword in its scabbard. Stomach for distinct foods. Altar candle's altitude.

75

Quite depressed by that transmission (London), awakening, precisely, the nostalgia for help...

76

I said to Carlate, who was wandering: "When you're dead, you'll occupy yourself with the things of death. We will no longer be with you. We're already lacking enough resources to do our work and gather in its feeble results. I don't want mist to weigh on

veux pas que de la brume pèse sur nos chemins parce que les nuées étouffent vos sommets. L'heure est propice aux métamorphoses. Mettez-la à profit ou allez-vous-en. »

(Carlate est sensible à la rhétorique solennelle. C'est un désespéré sonore, un infrarouge gras.)

77

Comment se cacher de ce qui *doit* s'unir à vous? (Déviation de la modernité.)

78

Ce qui importe le plus dans certaines situations c'est de maîtriser à temps l'euphorie.

79

Je remercie la chance qui a permis que les braconniers de Provence se battent dans notre camp. La mémoire sylvestre de ces primitifs, leur aptitude pour le calcul, leur flair aigu par tous les temps, je serais surpris qu'une défaillance survînt de ce côté. Je veillerai à ce qu'ils soient chaussés comme des dieux!

80

Nous sommes des malades sidéraux incurables auxquels la vie sataniquement donne l'illusion de la santé. Pourquoi? Pour dépenser la vie et railler la santé?

(Je dois combattre mon penchant pour ce genre de pessimisme atonique, héritage intellectuel…)

81

L'acquiescement éclaire le visage. Le refus lui donne la beauté.

82

Sobres amandiers, oliviers batailleurs et rêveurs, sur l'éventail du crépuscule, postez notre étrange santé.

our roads because clouds choke your summits. The hour is ripe for metamorphoses. Put it to good use or get out."

(Carlate is sensitive to solemn rhetoric. He's a sonorous defeatist, a fat infrared.)

77

How to hide from what *must* join with you? (A deviation of modernity.)

78

What matters most in certain situations is to curb euphoria in time.

79

I thank chance, which has granted that the poachers of Provence are fighting in our camp. The memory of the woods that these primitives possess, their aptitude for calculation, their sharp sense of smell in any weather—I would be surprised at a failing in this quarter. I will see to it that they are shod like gods!

80

We are chronic sidereal invalids to whom, satanically, life lends the illusion of health. Why? To consume life and mock health?

(I must fight my penchant for this kind of limp pessimism, an intellectual heritage...)

81

Acquiescence lights up the face. Refusal gives it beauty.

82

Sober almond trees, dreamy and pugnacious olive trees: against the outspread fan of dusk, post our strange health...

83

Le poète, conservateur des infinis visages du vivant.

84

C'est mettre à vif son âme que de rebrousser chemin dans son intimité avec un être, en même temps qu'on assume sa perfection. Ligoté, involontaire, j'éprouve cette fatalité et demande pardon à cet être.

85

Curiosité glacée. Evaluation sans objet.

86

Les plus pures récoltes sont semées dans un sol qui n'existe pas. Elles éliminent la gratitude et ne doivent qu'au printemps.

87

LS*, je vous remercie pour l'homodépôt Durance 12. Il entre en fonction dès cette nuit. Vous veillerez à ce que la jeune équipe affectée au terrain ne se laisse pas entraîner à apparaître trop souvent dans les rues de Duranceville. Filles et cafés dangereux plus d'une minute. Cependant ne tirez pas trop sur la bride. Je ne veux pas de mouchard dans l'équipe. Hors du réseau, qu'on ne communique pas. Stoppez vantardise. Vérifiez à deux sources corps renseignements. Tenez compte cinquante pour cent romanesque dans la plupart des cas. Apprenez à vos hommes à prêter attention, à rendre compte exactement, à savoir poser l'arithmétique des situations. Rassemblez les rumeurs et faites synthèse. Point de chute et boîte à lettres chez l'ami des blés. Éventualité opération Waffen, camp des étrangers, les Mées, avec débordement sur Juifs et Résistance. Républicains espagnols très en danger. Urgent que vous les préveniez. Quant à vous, évitez le combat. Homo-dépôt sacré. Si alerte, dispersez-vous. Sauf pour délivrer camarade capturé, ne

* Léon Zyngerman, alias Léon Saingermain.

The poet, keeper of the infinite faces of the living.

It skins the soul alive to step back from your intimacy with someone, in the very moment when you take responsibility for his training. Tied hand and foot, involuntarily, I experience this fate and ask forgiveness of this being.

Icy curiosity. Appraisal with no object.

The purest harvests are sown in earth that does not exist. They eliminate gratitude and are indebted only to spring.

LS*, I thank you for the Durance 12 base. It begins functioning tonight. You will make sure that the young cohort assigned to the area doesn't get drawn into appearing too often in the streets of Duranceville. Girls and cafes dangerous for more than a minute. Don't, however, pull too hard on the reins. I do not want an informer in the unit. Out of network no communication. Put a stop to boasting. Verify information with two sources. Be aware fifty percent fiction in most cases. Teach your men to pay attention, report with exactitude, know how to lay out the arithmetic of situations. Gather rumors and synthesize. Drop-point and mailbox with the friend of grains. Possibility Waffen operation, foreigners' camp, les Mées, spreading to Jews and Resistance. Spanish Republicans very much in danger. Urgent you forewarn them. As for you, avoid combat. Base sacred. If an alert, disperse. Except to free a captured comrade, never give the enemy any sign of your existence. Intercept suspects. I trust your judgment. The camp will

* Léon Zyngerman, alias Léon Saingermain.

donnez jamais l'ennemi signe d'existence. Interceptez suspects. Je fais confiance à votre discernement. Le camp ne sera jamais montré. Il n'existe pas de camp, mais des charbonnières qui ne fument pas. Aucun linge d'étendu au passage des avions, et tous les hommes sous les arbres et dans le taillis. Personne ne viendra vous voir de ma part, l'ami des blés et le Nageur exceptés. Avec les hommes de l'équipe soyez rigoureux et attentionné. Amitié ouate discipline. Dans le travail, faites toujours quelques kilos de plus que chacun, sans en tirer orgueil. Mangez et fumez visiblement moins qu'eux. N'en préférez aucun à un autre. N'admettez qu'un mensonge improvisé et gratuit. Qu'ils ne s'appellent pas de loin. Qu'ils tiennent leur corps et leur literie propres. Qu'ils apprennent à chanter bas et à ne pas siffler d'air obsédant, à dire telle qu'elle s'offre la vérité. La nuit, qu'ils marchent en bordure des sentiers. Suggérez les précautions; laissez-leur le mérite de les découvrir. Émulation excellente. Contrariez les habitudes monotones. Inspirez celles que vous ne voulez pas trop tôt voir mourir. Enfin, aimez au même moment qu'eux les êtres qu'ils aiment. Additionnez, ne divisez pas. Tout va bien ici. Affections. HYPNOS.

88
Comment m'entendez-vous? Je parle de si loin…

89
François exténué par cinq nuits d'alertes successives, me dit : «J'échangerais bien mon sabre contre un café! » François a vingt ans.

90
On donnait jadis un nom aux diverses tranches de la durée : ceci était un jour, cela un mois, cette église vide, une année. Nous voici abordant la seconde où la mort est la plus violente et la vie la mieux définie.

Furor and Mystery

never be exposed. No camp exists, just charcoal-burners that do not smoke. No clothes drying when planes fly over, and all the men under trees and in the brush. Nobody will come to see you on my behalf, except for the friend of grains and the Swimmer. With the men of the unit be rigorous and attentive. Friendship cushions discipline. At work, always carry a few kilos more than everyone else, without being proud of it. Eat and smoke visibly less than they do. Do not play favorites. Allow only off-the-cuff and inessential lies. No calling out to each other from faraway. Their bodies and bedding to be kept clean. Let them learn to sing low and not to whistle obsessively, to tell the bare-faced truth. At night, they should walk along the edges of paths. Suggest precautions; give them credit for the idea. Emulation excellent. Discourage monotonous habits. Applaud those you'd like to see continue. Finally, love those they love, in the same moment that they do. Add, do not divide. All goes well here. Fondly. HYPNOS.

88
How can you hear me? I'm speaking from so faraway...

89
François, exhausted by five successive nights on high alert, says to me: "I'd give my saber for a cup of coffee!" François is twenty years old.

90
Once, names were given to the different slices of duration: this was a day, that a month, this empty church a year. Now we are colliding with that second when death is most violent, life most clear-cut.

91

Nous errons auprès de margelles dont on a soustrait les puits.

92

Tout ce qui a le visage de la colère et n'élève pas la voix.

93

Le combat de la persévérance.

La symphonie qui nous portait s'est tue. Il faut croire à l'alternance. Tant de mystères n'ont pas été pénétrés ni détruits.

94

Ce matin, comme j'examinais un tout petit serpent qui se glissait entre deux pierres : « L'orvet du deuil », s'est écrié Félix. La disparition de Lefèvre, tué la semaine passée, affleure superstitieusement en image.

95

Les ténèbres du Verbe m'engourdissent et m'immunisent. Je ne participe pas à l'agonie féerique. D'une sobriété de pierre, je demeure la mère de lointains berceaux.

96

Tu ne peux pas te relire mais tu peux signer.

97

L'avion déboule. Les pilotes invisibles se délestent de leur jardin nocturne puis pressent un feu bref sous l'aisselle de l'appareil pour avertir que c'est fini. Il ne reste plus qu'à rassembler le trésor éparpillé. De même le poète…

91

We are wandering around well stones from which they have removed the wells.

92

Everything that has the face of anger and does not raise its voice.

93

The battle of perseverance.

The symphony that carried us is silenced. We must believe in alternation. So many mysteries have not been penetrated or destroyed.

94

This morning, while I was examining a tiny snake as it slipped between two stones, Felix cried out, "The blindworm of grief!" The disappearance of Lefèvre, killed last week, crops up superstitiously as an image.

95

The shadows of the Word benumb and immunize me. I do not participate in the enchanting death throes. Of a stone sobriety, I remain the mother of distant cradles.

96

You can't reread yourself, but you can sign your name.

97

The plane swerves down. Invisible pilots discharge their nocturnal garden, then press a brief light under the wing to signal that it's finished. All that remains is to gather in the scattered treasure. Just so, the poet…

98

La ligne de vol du poème. Elle devrait être *sensible* à chacun.

99

Tel un perdreau mort, m'est apparu ce pauvre infirme que les Miliciens ont assassiné à Vachères après l'avoir dépouillé des hardes qu'il possédait, l'accusant d'héberger des réfractaires. Les bandits avant de l'achever jouèrent longtemps avec une fille qui prenait part à leur expédition. Un oeil arraché, le thorax défoncé, l'innocent absorba cet enfer et LEURS RIRES.

(Nous avons capturé la fille.)

100

Nous devons surmonter notre rage et notre dégoût, nous devons les faire partager, afin d'élever et d'élargir notre action comme notre morale.

101

Imagination, mon enfant.

102

La mémoire est sans action sur le souvenir. Le souvenir est sans force contre la mémoire. Le bonheur ne *monte* plus.

103

Un mètre d'entrailles pour mesurer nos chances.

104

Les yeux seuls sont encore capables de pousser un cri.

105

L'esprit, de long en large, comme cet insecte qui aussitôt la lampe éteinte gratte la cuisine, bouscule le silence, triture les saletés.

Furor and Mystery

98

The poem's line of flight. It should be *felt* by each.

99

He looked to me like a dead partridge, that poor cripple the Militians murdered at Vachères, after having stripped him of what little he possessed, accusing him of harboring rebels. Before they killed him, the thugs played around a long time, with a girl who took part in their expedition. A torn-out eye, a crushed thorax, the innocent fellow took the brunt of this inferno and THEIR LAUGHTER.

(We captured the girl.)

100

We must overcome our rage and our disgust, we must insure that they are shared, to elevate and extend our action, our morale.

101

Imagination, my child.

102

Memory cannot affect recollections. Recollections are power-less over memory. Happiness no longer *mounts*.

103

A meter of guts to measure our chances.

104

Only the eyes are still capable of crying out.

105

The mind, back and forth, like that insect who as soon as the light goes out scratches in the kitchen, jostles the silence, crunches up filth.

106

Devoirs infernaux.

107

On ne fit pas un lit aux larmes comme à un visiteur de passage.

108

Pouvoirs passionnés et règles d'action.

109

Toute la masse d'arôme de ces fleurs pour rendre sereine la nuit qui tombe sur nos larmes.

110

L'éternité n'est guère plus longue que la vie.

111

La lumière a été chassée de nos yeux. Elle est enfouie quelque part dans nos os. A notre tour nous la chassons pour lui restituer sa couronne.

112

Le timbre paradisiaque de l'autorisation cosmique.
(Au plus étroit de ma nuit, que cette grâce me soit accordée, ́ bouleversante et significative plus encore que ces signes perçus d'une telle hauteur qu'il n'est nul besoin de les conjecturer.)

113

Être le familier de ce qui ne se produira pas, dans une religion, une insensée solitude, mais dans cette suite d'impasses sans *nourriture* où tend à se perdre le visage aimé.

114

Je n'écrirai pas de poème d'acquiescement.

106

Diabolical duties.

107

You do not offer a bed to tears as you would to a passing guest.

108

Passionate powers and rules of action.

109

All the massive fragrance of these flowers, to soothe the night falling on our tears.

110

Eternity is scarcely longer than life.

111

The light has been hunted from our eyes. It lies buried somewhere in our bones. We in our turn hunt for it, to restore its crown.

112

The paradisiac stamp of cosmic authorization.
(Confined in my narrowest night, may this grace be accorded me, overwhelming, even more meaningful than those signs glimpsed from such a height that there is no need to guess at them.)

113

Be an intimate friend to that which will not happen—religiously, in mad solitude, in that series of impasses without *nourishment* where the beloved face begins to disappear.

114

I will write no poem of acquiescence.

115

Au jardin des Oliviers, qui était en surnombre?

116

Ne pas tenir compte outre mesure de la duplicité qui se mani-feste dans les êtres. En réalité, le filon est sectionné en de multiples endroits. Que ceci soit stimulant plus que sujet d'irritation.

117

Claude me dit : « Les femmes sont les reines de l'absurde. Plus un homme s'engage avec elles, plus elles compliquent cet engage-ment. Du jour où je suis devenu "partisan," je n'ai plus été mal-heureux ni déçu… »

Il sera toujours temps d'apprendre à Claude qu'on ne taille pas dans sa vie sans se couper.

118

Femme de punition.

Femme de résurrection.

119

Je pense à la femme que j'aime. Son visage soudain s'est masqué. Le vide est à son tour malade.

120

Vous tendez une allumette à votre lampe et ce qui s'allume n'éclaire pas. C'est loin, très loin de vous, que le cercle illumine.

121

J'ai visé le lieutenant et Esclabesang le colonel. Les genêts en fleurs nous dissimulaient derrière leur vapeur jaune flamboyante. Jean et Robert ont lancé les gammons. La petite colonne ennemie a immédiatement battu en retraite. Excepté le mitrailleur, mais il n'a

115

In the Garden of Olives, who was extra?

116

Don't keep track too closely of the duplicity that people demonstrate. In reality, the lode is severed in many places. Let this be stimulating rather than a subject of irritation.

117

Claude said to me: "Women are queens of the absurd. The more a man gets involved with them, the more they complicate the involvement. From the day I became a 'partisan,' I've no longer been unhappy or disappointed..."

There is plenty of time to teach Claude that you don't carve up your life without cutting yourself.

118

Woman of punishment.
Woman of resurrection.

119

I am thinking of the woman I love. Suddenly her face is masked. The void in its turn sickens.

120

You hold a match to your lamp and what ignites casts no light. It is far, very far from you, that the circle illuminates.

121

I took aim at the lieutenant and the colonel, Esclabesang. Flowering broom hid us behind its flamboyant yellow vapor. Jean and Robert threw grenades. The small enemy column immediately retreated. Except for the machine-gunner—but he did not have

pas eu le temps de devenir dangereux : son ventre a éclaté. Les deux voitures nous ont servi à filer. La serviette du colonel était pleine d'intérêt.

122

Fontaine-la-pauvre, fontaine somptueuse.
(La marche nous a scié les reins, excavé la bouche.)

123

Dans ces jeunes hommes, un émouvant appétit de conscience. Nulle trace des étages montés et descendus si souvent par leurs pères. Ah! pouvoir les mettre dans le droit chemin de la condition humaine, celle dont on ne craindra pas qu'il faille un jour la réhabiliter. Mais Dieu se tenant à l'écart de nos querelles et l'étau des origines sentant ses pouvoirs lui échapper, il faudra exiger des experts nouveaux une ampleur de pensée et une minutie d'application dont je ne saisis pas les présages.

124

LA FRANCE-DES-CAVERNES

125

Mettre en route l'intelligence sans le secours des cartes d'état-major.

126

Entre la réalité et son exposé, il y a ta vie qui magnifie la réalité, et cette abjection nazie qui ruine son exposé.

127

Viendra le temps où les nations sur la marelle de l'univers seront aussi étroitement dépendantes les unes des autres que les organes d'un même corps, solidaires en son économie.
Le cerveau, plein à craquer de machines, pourra-t-il encore

time to get dangerous: his belly exploded. The two cars served as our escape. The colonel's briefcase was full of interest.

122

Fountain-of-the-Poor, sumptuous fountain.
(The march was backbreaking, mouth-dredging.)

123

In these young men, a moving appetite for conscience. No trace of their fathers' frequent ups and downs. Ah! to be able to set them on the right road through the human condition, the one you needn't fear will someday need repair. But since God stays out of our quarrels and the vise of origins is weakening, we will have to demand from new experts an amplitude of thought and a minute attention to detail whose early signs I do not discern.

124

FRANCE-OF-THE-CAVES

125

Start the intelligence on its way without the aid of ordnance maps.

126

Between reality and its narrative, there is your life, which magnifies reality, and the Nazi degradation, which blights the narrative.

127

The time will come when nations on the hopscotch board of the universe will depend as closely on each other as the organs of one body, unified in its structure.
Filled to bursting with machines, will the brain still be able to

garantir l'existence du mince ruisselet de rêve et d'évasion? L'homme, d'un pas de somnambule, marche vers les mines meurtrières, conduit par le chant des inventeurs…

128

Le boulanger n'avait pas encore dégrafé les rideaux de fer de sa boutique que déjà le village était assiégé, bâillonné, hypnotisé, mis dans l'impossibilité de bouger. Deux compagnies de SS et un détachement de miliciens le tenaient sous la gueule de leurs mitrailleuses et de leurs mortiers. Alors commença l'épreuve.

Les habitants furent jetés hors des maisons et sommés de se rassembler sur la place centrale. Les clés sur les portes. Un vieux, dur d'oreille, qui ne tenait pas compte assez vite de l'ordre, vit les quatre murs et le toit de sa grange voler en morceaux sous l'effet d'une bombe. Depuis quatre heures j'étais éveillé. Marcelle était venue à mon volet me chuchoter l'alerte. J'avais reconnu immédiatement l'inutilité d'essayer de franchir le cordon de surveillance et de gagner la campagne. Je changeai rapidement de logis. La maison inhabitée où je me réfugiai autorisait, à toute extrémité, une résistance armée efficace. Je pouvais suivre de la fenêtre, derrière les rideaux jaunis, les allées et venues nerveuses des occupants. Pas un des miens n'était présent au village. Cette pensée me rassura. A quelques kilomètres de là, ils suivraient mes consignes et resteraient tapis. Des coups me parvenaient, ponctués d'injures. Les SS avaient surpris un jeune maçon qui revenait de relever des collets. Sa frayeur le désigna à leurs tortures. Une voix se penchait hurlante sur le corps tuméfié : « Où est-il ? Conduis-nous. », suivie de silence. Et coups de pieds et coups de crosses de pleuvoir. Une rage insensée s'empara de moi, chassa mon angoisse. Mes mains communiquaient à mon arme leur sueur crispée, exaltaient sa puissance contenue. Je calculais que le malheureux se tairait encore cinq minutes, puis, fatalement, il *parlerait.* J'eus honte de souhaiter sa mort avant cette échéance. Alors apparut jaillissant de chaque rue la marée des femmes, des enfants, des vieillards, se rendant au lieu de rassemblement, suivant un *plan concerté.* Ils

safeguard the existence of our thin rivulet of dream and escape? Man marches at a sleepwalker's pace toward murderous mines, led on by the inventors' song...

128

The baker had not yet unfastened the metal curtains of his shop when already the village was besieged, gagged, hypnotized, suspended in utter immobility. Two SS companies and a detachment of militia held it beneath the muzzles of their machine guns and their mortars. Then the ordeal began.

The inhabitants were thrown out of their houses and ordered to assemble in the central square. Keys in all the locks. One old man, hard of hearing, who didn't respond quickly enough to the order, saw the four walls and roof of his barn shattered by a bomb. For four hours I had been awake. Marcelle had come to whisper the alert through my shutters. I immediately saw the futility of trying to get past the cordon of surveillance to reach the countryside. Quickly I changed dwellings. The uninhabited house where I took refuge would make effective armed resistance possible, in my last moments. Through the window I could follow, from behind yellowed curtains, the nervous comings and goings of the occupiers. None of my people were present in the village. This thought cheered me. Several kilometers away, they would follow my instructions and remain undercover. The sound of blows reached me, punctuated by curses. The SS had caught a young mason as he returned from setting traps. His fright destined him for their torture. A voice leaned screaming over the swollen body: 'Where is he? Take us,' followed by silence. And kicks and rifle butts rained down. An insane rage took hold of me, banished my anguish. My hands communicated their clenched sweat to my weapon, exalted its controlled power. I calculated that the poor fellow would be quiet for five more minutes, then, inevitably, he *would talk*. It shamed me to wish for his death before he could deliver. At that moment there appeared, gushing from every street, a tide of women, children, old people, who were reporting to the assembly point, according to an

se hâtaient sans hâte, ruisselant littéralement sur les SS, les paralysant « en toute bonne foi ». Le maçon fut laissé pour mort. Furieuse, la patrouille se fraya un chemin à travers la foule et porta ses pas plus loin. Avec une prudence infinie, maintenant des yeux anxieux et bons regardaient dans ma direction, passaient comme un jet de lampe sur ma fenêtre. Je me découvris à moitié et un sourire se détacha de ma pâleur. Je tenais à ces êtres par mille fils confiants dont pas un ne devait se rompre.

J'ai aimé farouchement mes semblables cette journée-là, bien au delà du sacrifice.*

129

Nous sommes pareils à ces crapauds qui dans l'austère nuit des marais s'appellent et ne se voient pas, ployant à leur cri d'amour toute la fatalité de l'univers.

130

J'ai confectionné avec des déchets de montagnes des hommes qui embaumeront quelque temps les glaciers.

131

A tous les repas pris en commun, nous invitons la liberté à s'asseoir. La place demeure vide mais le couvert reste mis.

132

Il semble que l'imagination qui hante à des degrés divers l'esprit de toute créature soit pressée de se séparer d'elle quand celle-ci ne lui propose que « l'impossible » et « l'inaccessible » pour extrême mission. Il faut admettre que la poésie n'est pas partout souveraine.

---

* N'était-ce pas le hasard qui m'avait choisi pour prince plutôt que le coeur mûri pour moi de ce village? (1945.)

Furor and Mystery

agreed-upon plan. They hurried without haste, literally streaming over the SS, paralyzing them, 'with the best of intentions.' The mason was left for dead. Furious, the patrol cut a path through the crowd and moved on. Now, with infinite prudence, eyes anxious and good looked in my direction, passed over my window like a stream of light. I half-showed myself and a smile stood out against my pallor. I was attached to these beings by a thousand trusting threads, not one of which had broken.

I loved my fellow men ferociously that day, far beyond the sacrifice.*

129

We are like those toads who in the austere night of the marshes call to each other and do not see each other, bending to their love cry all the fatality of the universe.

130

Out of the refuse of mountains I have constructed men who will briefly perfume the glaciers.

131

At all the meals we take in common, we invite freedom to sit down. The chair remains empty, but the place continues to be set.

132

It seems the imagination, which to some degree haunts every creature's mind, can't wait to separate from the latter when offered only "the impossible" and "the inaccessible" for ultimate mission. We must admit that poetry is not everywhere supreme.

*Wasn't it chance that had chosen me for prince, rather than the heart, ripened for me, of this village? (1945)

133

« Les oeuvres de bienfaisance devront être maintenues parce que l'homme n'est pas bienfaisant. » Sottise. Ah! pauvreté sanglante.

134

Nous sommes pareils à ces poissons retenus vifs dans la glace des lacs de montagne. La matière et la nature semblent les protéger cependant qu'elles limitent à peine la chance du pêcheur.

135

Il ne faudrait pas aimer les hommes pour leur être d'un réel secours. Seulement désirer rendre meilleure telle expression de leur regard lorsqu'il se pose sur plus appauvri qu'eux, prolonger d'une seconde telle minute agréable de leur vie. A partir de cette démarche et chaque racine traitée, leur respiration se ferait plus sereine. Surtout ne pas entièrement leur supprimer ces sentiers pénibles, à l'effort desquels succède l'évidence de la vérité à travers pleurs et fruits.

136

La jeunesse tient la bêche. Ah! qu'on ne l'en dessaisisse pas!

137

Les chèvres sont à la droite du troupeau. (Il est bien que la ruse côtoie l'innocence quand le berger est bon, le chien est sûr.)

138

Horrible journée! J'ai assisté, distant de quelque cent mètres, à l'exécution de B. Je n'avais qu'à presser la détente du fusil-mitrailleur et il pouvait être sauvé! Nous étions sur les hauteurs dominant Céreste, des armes à faire craquer les buissons et au moins égaux en nombre aux SS. Eux ignorant que nous étions là. Aux yeux qui imploraient partout autour de moi le signal d'ouvrir le feu, j'ai répondu non de la tête… Le soleil de juin glissait un froid polaire dans mes os.

133

"Charitable works will have to be maintained because man is not charitable." Stupidity. Ah! blood-stained poverty.

134

We are like those fish trapped alive in the ice of mountain lakes. Matter and nature seem to protect them but hardly limit the fisherman's luck.

135

You needn't love men to be of real help to them. You need only want to make the expression in their eyes better as they look on what is more impoverished than they, and to prolong by one second some pleasant moment in their lives. With this approach and each root treated, their breathing will grow more serene. Above all do not entirely deprive them of those painful paths on which exertion gives way to the clarity of truth, as tears and fruit.

136

The young hold the spade. Ah, may it not be taken from them!

137

The goats are on the right of the herd. (It is well that guile stay close to innocence when the shepherd is skilled, the dog reliable.)

138

Horrible day! I was present, some hundred meters away, at B's execution. I had only to pull the trigger on the machine gun and he was saved! We were on the heights overlooking Céreste, with weapons enough to break the bushes, and equal in number to the SS. They unaware of the fact that we were there. To the eyes everywhere around me that begged for the signal to open fire I responded no with a shake of the head... The June sun slid a polar cold into my bones.

Il est tombé comme s'il ne distinguait pas ses bourreaux et si léger, il m'a semblé, que le moindre souffle de vent eût dû le soulever de terre.

Je n'ai pas donné le signal parce que ce village devait être épargné *à tout prix.* Qu'est-ce qu'un village? Un village pareil à un autre? Peut-être l'a-t-il su, lui, à cet ultime instant?

139

C'est l'enthousiasme qui soulève le poids des années. C'est la supercherie qui relate la fatigue du siècle.

140

La vie commencerait par une explosion et finirait par un concordat? C'est absurde.

141

La contre-terreur c'est ce vallon que peu à peu le brouillard comble, c'est le fugace bruissement des feuilles comme un essaim de fusées engourdies, c'est cette pesanteur bien répartie, c'est cette circulation ouatée d'animaux et d'insectes tirant mille traits sur l'écorce tendre de la nuit, c'est cette graine de luzerne sur la fossette d'un visage caressé, c'est cet incendie de la lune qui ne sera jamais un incendie, c'est un lendemain minuscule dont les intentions nous sont inconnues, c'est un buste aux couleurs vives qui s'est plié en souriant, c'est l'ombre, à quelques pas, d'un bref compagnon ac-croupi qui pense que le cuir de sa ceinture va céder... Qu'importent alors l'heure et le lieu où le diable nous a fixé rendezvous!

142

Le temps des monts enragés et de l'amitié fantastique.

143

ÈVE-DES-MONTAGNES. Cette jeune femme dont la vie insécable avait l'exacte dimension du coeur de notre nuit.

He fell as though he didn't even see his executioners, and so light, it seemed to me, that the least puff of wind must have lifted him off the earth.

I did not give the signal because this village had to be spared *at any price.* What is a village? A village like any other? Did he perhaps know, in that last instant?

139

It is enthusiasm that lifts the weight of the years. It is the hoax that tells of the century's fatigue.

140

Life should start with an explosion and end with a peace agreement? Absurd.

141

The counter-terror is this valley little by little brimmed with mist, it is the fleeting buzz of the leaves like a swarm of torpid Roman candles, it is this heaviness dispersed, this muffled movement of animals and insects etching a thousand marks into the tender bark of the night, it is this grain of alfalfa in the dimple of a face caressed, this fire on the moon which will never catch fire, it is a miniscule day-after whose intentions are unknown to us, it is the brightly-colored bust that bowed smiling, it is the shadow a few feet away of a brief companion who bends over, worrying that the leather of his belt is going to give... Of what importance then the hour and the place the devil has fixed for our rendezvous!

142

Era of enraged mountains and fantastic friendship.

143

EVE-OF-THE-MOUNTAINS. This young woman whose indivisible life had the exact dimension of our night's heart.

144

Comme se sont piqués tes vieux os de papillon!

145

Du bonheur qui n'est que de l'anxiété différée. Du bonheur bleuté, d'une insubordination admirable, qui s'élance du plaisir, pulvérise le présent et toutes ses instances.

146

Roger était tout heureux d'être devenu dans l'estime de sa jeune femme le mari-qui-cachait-dieu.

Je suis passé aujourd'hui au bord du champ de tournesols dont la vue l'inspirait. La sécheresse courbait la tête des admirables, des insipides fleurs. C'est à quelques pas de là que son sang a coulé, au pied d'un vieux mûrier, sourd de toute l'épaisseur de son écorce.

147

Serons-nous plus tard sembables à ces cratères où les volcans ne viennent plus et où l'herbe jaunit sur sa tige?

148

« Le voilà! » Il est deux heures du matin. L'avion a vu nos sig- ´ naux et réduit son altitude. La brise ne gênera pas la descente en parachute du visiteur que nous attendons. La lune est d'étain vif et de sauge. « L'école des poètes du tympan », chuchote Léon qui a toujours le mot de la situation.

149

Mon bras plâtré me fait souffrir. Le cher docteur Grand Sec s'est débrouillé à merveille malgré l'enflure. Chance que mon sub-conscient ait dirigé ma chute avec tant d'à-propos. Sans cela la grenade que je tenais dans la main, dégoupillée, risquait fort d'éclater. Chance que les feldgendarmes n'aient rien entendu, grâce au moteur de leur camion qui tournait. Chance que je n'aie pas perdu connaissance avec ma tête en pot de géranium... Mes

144

How your old butterfly bones prickled!

145

Happiness which is no more than deferred anxiety. Blue-tinged happiness, admirably insubordinate, that springs from pleasure, pulverizes the present and all its pleading.

146

Roger was utterly happy he'd become the husband-who-hid-god in his young wife's opinion.

Yesterday I passed along the edge of the sunflower field whose sight used to exhilirate him. Dryness curved the heads of these admirable, these insipid flowers. It is a few feet away that his blood flowed, at the foot of an old mulberry, deaf with the full thickness of its bark.

147

Will we someday be like those craters where volcanoes no longer come and the grass yellows on its stem?

148

"There it is!" It's two o'clock in the morning. The plane has seen our signals and reduces its altitude. The breeze won't bother the descent, by parachute, of the visitor that we await. The moon is of bright tin and sage. "The eardrum poets' school," whispers Leon, who always coins the right phrase for any situation.

149

The arm inside my cast hurts. The dear Doctor Great Gaunt [Grand Sec] managed marvelously despite the swelling. Luck that my unconscious directed my fall so aptly. Otherwise the grenade I was holding in my hand, its pin pulled, might well have exploded. Luck that the feldgendarmes heard nothing, thanks to their truck motor, which was running. Luck that I didn't lose consciousness,

camarades me complimentent sur ma présence d'esprit. Je les persuade difficilement que mon mérite est nul. Tout s'est passé en dehors de moi. Au bout des huit mètres de chute j'avais l'impression d'être un panier d'os disloqués. Il n'en a presque rien été heureusement.

150

C'est un étrange sentiment que celui de fixer le destin de certains êtres. Sans votre intervention, la médiocre table tournante de la vie n'aurait pas autrement regimbé. Tandis que les voici livrés à la grande conjoncture pathétique...

151

Réponds « absent » toi-même, sinon tu risques de ne pas être compris.

152

Le silence du matin. L'appréhension des couleurs. La chance de l'épervier.

153

Je m'explique mieux aujourd'hui ce besoin de simplifier, de faire entrer tout dans un, à l'instant de décider si telle chose doit avoir lieu ou non. L'homme s'éloigne à regret de son labyrinthe. Les mythes millénaires le pressent de ne pas partir.

154

Le poète, susceptible d'exagération, évalue correctement dans le supplice.

155

J'aime ces êtres tellement épris de ce que leur cœur imagine la liberté qu'ils s'immolent pour éviter au peu de liberté de mourir. Merveilleux mérite du peuple. (Le libre arbitre n'existerait pas.

my head in a pot of geraniums… My comrades compliment me on my presence of mind. With difficulty I persuade them that I don't deserve the credit. Everything happened without my participation. After a fall of eight meters I felt like a basketful of broken bones. Happily, almost nothing happened.

150

It is a strange feeling, determining the fate of certain individuals. Without your intervention, life's mediocre séance table would not otherwise have jumped. Whereas here they are, delivered up to the great touching juncture…

151

Answer "Absent" for yourself, otherwise you risk not being understood.

152

The silence of the morning. The apprehension of colors. The luck of the hawk.

153

I understand better today this need to simplify, to make everything into one, at the instant of deciding if such and such must happen or not. Man withdraws from his labyrinth reluctantly. Millenary myths urge him not to leave.

154

Given to exaggeration, the poet reckons correctly under torture.

155

I love those so enamored of what their hearts imagine to be freedom that they immolate themselves to avoid the limited freedom of death. Marvelous merit of the people. (Perhaps free will

L'être se définirait par rapport à ses cellules, à son hérédité, la course brève ou prolongée de son destin… Cependant il existe entre *tout cela* et l'Homme une enclave d'inattendus et de métamorphoses dont il faut défendre l'accès et assurer le maintien.)

156

Accumule, puis distribue. Sois la partie du miroir de l'univers la plus dense, la plus utile et la moins apparente.

157

Nous sommes tordus de chagrin à l'annonce de la mort de Robert G. (Émile Cavagni), tué dans une embuscade à Forcalquier, dimanche. Les Allemands m'enlèvent mon meilleur frère d'action, celui dont le coup de pouce faisait dévier les catastrophes, dont la présence ponctuelle avait une portée déterminante sur les défaillances possibles de chacun. Homme sans culture théorique mais grandi dans les difficultés, d'une bonté au beau fixe, son diagnostic était sans défaut. Son comportement était instruit d'audace attisante et de sagesse. Ingénieux, il menait ses avantages jusqu'à leur extrême conséquence. Il portait ses quarante-cinq ans verticalement, tel un arbre de la liberté. Je l'aimais sans effusion, sans pesanteur inutile. Inébranlablement.

158

Nous découvrons, à l'évoquer, des ailes adaptables, des sourires sans rancune, au bagne vulgaire des voleurs et des assassins. L'Homme-au-poing-de-cancer, le grand Meurtrier interne a innové en notre faveur.

159

Une si étroite affinité existe entre le coucou et les êtres furtifs que nous sommes devenus, que cet oiseau si peu visible, ou qui revêt un grisâtre anonymat lorsqu'il traverse la vue, en écho à son chant écartelant, nous arrache un long frisson.

does not exist. Perhaps the individual is defined by his cells, his heredity, the brief or prolonged course of his destiny... Still, there exists between *all that* and Man an enclave of unanticipated beings and metamorphoses whose approach must be defended and whose continuity assured.)

156

Accumulate, then distribute. Be the most compact, most useful, and least apparent part of the universe's mirror.

157

We are racked with grief at news of the death of Robert G. (Emile Cavagni), killed in an ambush at Forcalquier, Sunday. The Germans deprive me of my best brother in action, whose helping hand averted catastrophes, whose punctilious presence bore directly on the possible failings of each of us. A man without theoretical training but brought up amid difficulties, of undeviating goodness, his judgment was impeccable. His behavior was shaped by stirring audacity and wisdom. Ingenious, he pushed his advantages to their farthest extreme. He carried his forty-five years vertically, like a tree of freedom. I loved him without effusiveness, without unnecessary weight. Unshakably.

158

We are discovering, by conjuring them, adaptible wings, smiles without rancor, in the vulgar prison of thieves and assassins. The Man-with-the-fist-of-cancer, the great internal Murderer has evolved in our favor.

159

Such a strong affinity exists between the cuckoo and the furtive creatures we've become that whenever this bird, hardly visible or clothed in grayish anonymity, crosses our sight, he tears from us, in echo to his wrenching cry, a lingering shudder.

160

Rosée des hommes qui trace et dissimule ses frontières entre le point du jour et l'émersion du soleil, entre les yeux qui s'ouvrent et le cœur qui se souvient.

161

Tiens vis-à-vis des autres ce que tu t'es promis toi seul. Là est ton contrat.

162

Voici l'époque où le poète sent se dresser en lui cette méridienne force *d'ascension*.

163

Chante ta soif irisée.

164

Fidèles et démesurément vulnérables, nous opposons la conscience de l'événement au gratuit (encore un mot de déféqué).

165

Le fruit est aveugle. C'est l'arbre qui voit.

166

Pour qu'un héritage soit réellement grand, il faut que la main du défunt ne se voie pas.

167

Ketty, la chienne, prend autant de plaisir que nous à réceptionner. Elle va de l'un à l'autre sans aboyer, en connaissance hardie de la chose. Le travail terminé, elle s'étale heureuse sur la dune des parachutes et s'endort.

160

Dew of men, tracing and dissembling its frontiers between daybreak and the emergence of the sun, between the eyes that open and the heart that remembers.

161

Maintain towards others what you promised to yourself alone. Therein lies your contract.

162

This is the era when the poet feels rising within him the meridian force of *ascension*.

163

Sing your iridescent thirst.

164

Faithful and immeasurably vulnerable, we oppose our consciousness of the event to the gratuitous (there's another saying purified).

165

The fruit is blind. It is the tree that sees.

166

For a legacy to be truly great, we must not see the hand of the deceased.

167

Ketty, the dog, enjoys taking delivery as much as we do. She goes from one to the other without barking, in fearless knowledge of the thing. The work done, she stretches out happily on the dune of parachutes and goes to sleep.

168

Résistance n'est qu'espérance. Telle la lune d'Hypnos, pleine cette nuit de tous ses quartiers, demain vision sur le passage des poèmes.

169

La lucidité est la blessure la plus rapprochée du soleil.

170

Les rares moments de liberté sont ceux durant lesquels l'inconscient se fait conscient et le conscient néant (ou verger fou).

171

Les cendres du froid sont dans le feu qui chante le refus.

172

Je plains celui qui fait payer à autrui ses propres dettes en les aggravant du prestige de la fausse vacuité.

173

Il en va de certaines femmes comme des vagues de la mer. En s'élançant de toute leur jeunesse elles franchissent un rocher trop élevé pour leur retour. Cette flaque désormais croupira là, prisonnière, belle par éclair, à cause des cristaux de sel qu'elle renferme et qui lentement se substituent à son vivant.

174

La perte de la vérité, l'oppression de cette ignominie dirigée qui s'intitule *bien* (le mal, non dépravé, inspiré, fantasque est utile) a ouvert une plaie au flanc de l'homme que seul l'espoir du grand lointain informulé (le vivant inespéré) atténue. Si l'absurde est maître ici-bas, je choisis l'absurde, l'antistatique, celui qui me rapproche le plus des chances pathétiques. Je suis homme de berges — creusement et inflammation — ne pouvant l'être toujours de torrent.

168

Resistance is only hope. Like the moon of Hypnos, full tonight in all its quarters, tomorrow vision over poems passing by.

169

Lucidity is the wound closest to the sun.

170

The rare moments of freedom are those during which the unconscious becomes conscious and the consciousness nothing (or a mad orchard).

171

Ashes of the cold are in the fire that sings refusal.

172

I pity the one who makes others pay his debts, adding to them the prestige of false vacuity.

173

It is the case with certain women as with ocean waves. Flinging themselves forward in their youth, they clear a rock too high for their return. From then on, a puddle stagnates there, imprisoned, beautiful in the lightning because of the salt crystals it contains, which slowly take the place of its living essence.

174

The loss of truth, the oppression of this managed ignominy which calls itself *good* (evil—fantastic, inspired, not depraved—is useful) has opened a wound in man's side which only the hope of the vast unformulated faraway (unhoped-for life) attenuates. If the absurd is master here below, I choose the absurd, the antistatic, whatever gets me closest to pathetic chance. I am a man of river-banks—excavation and inflammation—since it isn't always possible to be a man of torrents.

175

Le peuple des prés m'enchante. Sa beauté frêle et dépourvue de venin, je ne me lasse pas de me la réciter. Le campagnol, la taupe, sombres enfants perdus dans la chimère de l'herbe, l'orvet, fils du verre, le grillon, moutonnier comme pas un, la sauterelle qui claque et compte son linge, le papillon qui simule l'ivresse et agace les fleurs de ses hoquets silencieux, les fourmis assagies par la grande étendue verte, et immédiatement au-dessus les météores hirondelles...

Prairie, vous êtes le boîtier du jour.

176

Depuis le baiser dans la montagne, le temps se guide sur l'été doré de ses mains et le lierre oblique.

177

Les enfants réalisent ce miracle adorable de demeurer des enfants et de voir par nos yeux.

178

La reproduction en couleurs du *Prisonnier* de Georges de La Tour que j'ai piquée sur le mur de chaux de la pièce où je travaille, semble, avec le temps, réfléchir son sens dans notre condition. Elle serre le cœur mais combien désaltère! Depuis deux ans, pas un réfractaire qui n'ait, passant la porte, brûlé ses yeux aux preuves de cette chandelle. La femme explique, l'emmuré écoute. Les mots qui tombent de cette terrestre silhouette d'ange rouge sont des mots essentiels, des mots qui portent immédiatement secours. Au fond du cachot, les minutes de suif de la clarté tirent et diluent les traits de l'homme assis. Sa maigreur d'ortie sèche, je ne vois pas un souvenir pour la faire frissonner. L'écuelle est une ruine. Mais la robe gonflée emplit soudain tout le cachot. Le Verbe de la femme donne naissance à l'inespéré mieux que n'importe quelle aurore.

175

The population of the meadows enchants me. Its frail beauty, bereft of venom. I never tire of reciting it to myself. The field vole, the mole, somber children lost in the chimera of the grass, the blindworm, son of glass, the cricket, conformist as they come, the grasshopper who flaps and counts its linen, the butterfly who play-acts drunkenness and irritates the flowers with its silent hiccups, the ants made wiser by the vast verdant expanse, and just above it, the meteoric swallows...

Meadow, you are the day's container.

176

Since the kiss on the mountain, time is guided by the golden summer of her hands and the oblique ivy.

177

Children accomplish the charming miracle of remaining children and seeing through our eyes.

178

The color reproduction of Georges de la Tour's *Prisoner*, which I've stuck on the whitewashed wall of the room in which I work, seems over time to reflect its meaning into our circumstances. It wrings our hearts, but how deeply quenches our thirst! For two years now, not one resistance fighter who hasn't, coming through the door, burned his eyes on what that candle proves. The woman explains, the walled-in prisoner listens. The words that fall from this terrestrial silhouette of a red angel are essential words, words that immediately bring help. In the depths of the dark cell the minutes of the tallow's clarity lengthen and dilute the features of the seated man. His dry-nettle thinness—I see not one memory to make it shiver. His bowl is in ruins. But the swollen gown abruptly fills the dark cell. Better than any dawn, the Word of woman gives birth to the unhoped-for.

Reconnaissance à Georges de La Tour qui maîtrisa les ténèbres hitlériennes avec un dialogue d'êtres humains.

179

Venez à nous qui chancelons d'insolation, sœur sans mépris, ô nuit!

180

C'est l'heure où les fenêtres s'échappent des maisons pour s'allumer au bout du monde où va poindre notre monde.

181

J'envie cet enfant qui se penche sur l'écriture du soleil, puis s'enfuit vers l'école, balayant de son coquelicot pensums et récompenses.

182

Lyre pour des monts internés.

183

Nous nous battons sur le pont jeté entre l'être vulnérable et son ricochet aux sources du pouvoir formel.

184

Guérir le pain. Attabler le vin.

185

Quelquefois mon refuge est le mutisme de Saint-Just à la séance de la Convention du 9 Thermidor. Je comprends, oh combien, la *procédure* de ce silence, les volets de cristal à jamais tirés sur la *communication*.

186

Sommes-nous voués à n'être que des débuts de vérité?

My gratitude to Georges de la Tour who mastered the Hitlerian shadows with a dialogue between two human beings.

179

Come to us who stagger with sunstroke, unscornful sister, oh night!

180

It is the hour when the windows escape the houses to light up at the end of the world where our world is going to dawn.

181

I envy the child who bends over the sun's handwriting, then runs off toward school, sweeping away prizes and punishments with a red poppy.

182

Lyre for interned mountains.

183

We are fighting on the bridge thrown up between vulnerable being and its ricochet at the wellsprings of absolute power.

184

Heal the bread. Seat the wine at table.

185

Sometimes my refuge is the muteness of Saint-Just at the Convention of 9 Thermidor. I understand, oh how well, the *practice* of that silence, crystal shutters closed forever on *communication.*

186

Are we doomed to be only the beginnings of truth?

187

L'action qui a un sens pour les vivants n'a de valeur que pour les morts, d'achèvement que dans les consciences qui en héritent et la questionnent.

188

Entre le monde de la réalité et moi, il n'y a plus aujourd'hui d'épaisseur triste.

189

Combien confondent révolte et humeur, filiation et inflorescence du sentiment. Mais aussitôt que la vérité trouve un ennemi à sa taille, elle dépose l'armure de l'ubiquité et se bat avec les ressources mêmes de sa condition. Elle est indicible la sensation de cette profondeur qui se volatilise en se concrétisant.

190

Inexorable étrangeté! D'une vie mal défendue, rouler jusqu'aux dés vifs du bonheur.

191

L'heure la plus droite c'est lorsque l'amande jaillit de sa rétive dureté et transpose ta solitude.

192

Je vois l'espoir, veine d'un fluvial lendemain, décliner dans le geste des êtres qui m'entourent. Les visages que j'aime dépérissent dans les mailles d'une attente qui les ronge comme un acide. Ah, que nous sommes peu aidés et mal encouragés! La mer et son rivage, ce pas visible, sont un tout scellé par l'ennemi, gisant au fond de la même pensée, moule d'une matière où entrent, à part égale, la rumeur du désespoir et la certitude de résurrection.

187

The action that has a meaning for the living has value only for the dead, finds completion only in those consciousnesses that inherit and question it.

188

Between the world of reality and me, there is no more layer of sadness today.

189

How many confuse revolt and temper, filiation and the efflorescence of feeling. But as soon as truth finds an enemy made to its measure, it puts aside the armor of ubiquity and fights with the actual resources of its condition. Indescribable, the sensation of this depth which volatilizes in becoming concrete.

190

Inexorable strangeness! In the midst of a badly defended life, to roll the living dice of happiness.

191

The most upright hour is when the almond springs from its restive hardness and transposes your solitude.

192

I see hope, the vein of a fluvial day-after, declining in the gestures of those who surround me. The faces that I love are dwindling in the meshes of a waiting which corrodes like acid. Ah, how little we are helped and encouraged! The sea and its shore, this visible step, are a whole sealed by the enemy, lying at the bottom of our common thought, which is molded in material made equally from the murmur of despair and the certainty of resurrection.

193

L'insensibilité de notre sommeil est si complète que le galop du moindre rêve ne parvient pas à le traverser, à le rafraîchir. Les chances de la mort sont submergées par une inondation d'absolu telle qu'y penser suffit à faire perdre la tentation de la vie qu'on appelle, qu'on supplie. Il faut beaucoup nous aimer, cette fois encore, respirer plus fort que le poumon du bourreau.

194

Je me fais violence pour conserver, malgré mon humeur, ma voix d'encre. Aussi, est-ce d'une plume à bec de bélier, sans cesse éteinte, sans cesse rallumée, ramassée, tendue et d'une haleine, que j'écris ceci, que j'oublie cela. Automate de la vanité? Sincèrement non. Nécessité de contrôler l'évidence, de la faire créature.

195

Si j'en réchappe, je sais que je devrai rompre avec l'arôme de ces années essentielles, rejeter (non refouler) silencieusement loin de moi mon trésor, me reconduire jusqu'au principe du comportement le plus indigent comme au temps où je me cherchais sans jamais accéder à la prouesse, dans une insatisfaction nue, une connaissance à peine entrevue et une humilité questionneuse.

196

Cet homme autour duquel tourbillonnera un moment ma sympathie compte parce que son empressement à servir coïncide avec tout un halo favorable et mes projets à son égard. Dépêchons-nous d'œuvrer ensemble avant que ce qui nous fait converger l'un vers l'autre ne tourne inexplicablement à l'hostile.

197

Être du bond. N'être pas du festin, son épilogue.

198

Si la vie pouvait n'être que du sommeil désappointé…

193

The numbness of our sleep is so total that not the gallop of the least dream manages to cross it, to refresh it. The chances of death are submerged in a flood so absolute that thinking of it is enough to stop our being tempted by the life we summon, we entreat. It is necessary to love us a great deal, this time too, to breathe more deeply than the executioner's lung.

194

I do myself violence to preserve my voice in ink, despite my mood. Thus, it is with a pen whose nib is a battering ram—ceaselessly extinguished, ceaselessly relit, collected, tensed—and with one breath that I write this, and leave out that. Automaton of vanity? Sincerely not. The necessity is to examine the evidence, to turn it into a created entity.

195

If I make it through, I know I'll have to break with the aroma of these essential years, silently push faraway from me (not repress) my treasure, guide myself back to the principle of the most indigent behavior, as in that time when I was looking for myself without achieving prowess, in naked dissatisfaction, scarcely-glimpsed knowledge, and inquisitive humility.

196

The man around whom my affinity will swirl momentarily counts since his eagerness to serve coincides with a wholly favorable halo and my plans for him. Let's be quick to work together before what joins us to each other inexplicably turns hostile.

197

Be part of the leap. Do not be part of the banquet, its epilogue.

198

If life could be but disappointed sleep...

199

Il y a deux âges pour le poète : l'âge durant lequel la poésie, à tous égards, le maltraite, et celui où elle se laisse follement embrasser. Mais aucun n'est entièrement défini. Et le second n'est pas souverain.

200

C'est quand tu es ivre de chagrin que tu n'as plus du chagrin que le cristal.

201

Le chemin du secret danse à la chaleur.

202

La présence du désir comme celle du dieu ignore le philosophe. En revanche le philosophe châtie.

203

J'ai vécu aujourd'hui la minute du pouvoir et de l'invulnérabilité absolus. J'étais une ruche qui s'envolait aux sources de l'altitude avec tout son miel et toutes ses abeilles.

204

Ó vérité, infante mécanique, reste terre et murmure au milieu des astres impersonnels!

205

Le doute se trouve à l'origine de toute grandeur. L'injustice historique s'évertue à ne pas le mentionner. Ce doute-là est génie. Ne pas le rapprocher de l'incertain qui, lui, est provoqué par l'émiettement des pouvoirs de la sensation.

199

There are two ages for the poet: the age when poetry mistreats him in every respect, and the other, when she allows herself to be madly embraced. But neither is clearly defined. And the second is not supreme.

200

It is when you are drunk with pain that you feel no more pain than the crystal.

201

The road to the secret dances in the heat.

202

The presence of desire like that of a god knows nothing about the philosopher. In return the philosopher castigates.

203

Today I lived a moment of absolute power and invulnerability. I was a hive that took flight at the fountainhead of altitude, with all its honey and all its bees.

204

Oh truth, mechanical infanta, remain earth and murmur in the midst of the impersonal stars!

205

Doubt is at the origin of all greatness. Historical injustice does its utmost not to mention it. This doubt is genius. Don't confuse it with uncertainty, which is caused by the crumbling of the power to feel.

206

Toutes les feintes auxquelles les circonstances me contraignent allongent mon innocence. Une main gigantesque me porte sur sa paume. Chacune de ses lignes qualifie ma conduite. Et je demeure là comme une plante dans son sol bien que ma saison soit de nulle part.

207

Certains de mes actes se frayent une voie dans ma nature comme le train parcourt la campagne, suivant la même involonté, avec le même art qui fuit.

208

L'homme qui ne voit qu'une source ne connaît qu'un orage. Les chances en lui sont contrariées.

209

Mon inaptitude à *arranger* ma vie provient de ce que je suis fidèle non à un seul mais à tous les êtres avec lesquels je me découvre en parenté sérieuse. Cette constance persiste au sein des contradictions et des différends. L'humour veut que je conçoive, au cours d'une de ces interruptions de sentiment et de sens littéral, ces êtres ligués dans l'exercice de ma suppression.

210

Ton audace, une verrue. Ton action, une image spécieuse, par faveur coloriée.

(J'ai toujours présent en mémoire le propos niais de ce charbonnier de Saumanes qui affirmait que la Révolution française avait purgé la contrée d'un seigneur parfaitement criminel : un certain Sade. Un de ses exploits avait consisté à égorger les trois filles de son fermier. La culotte du Marquis était tendue avant que la première beauté n'eût expiré...

L'idiot n'en put démordre, l'avarice montagnarde ne voulant évidemment rien céder.)

Furor and Mystery

206

All the pretense to which the circumstances force me extends my innocence. A gigantic hand is carrying me in its palm. Each of its lines qualifies my conduct. And I remain there like a plant in its earth although my season comes from nowhere.

207

Certain acts of mine clear a path through my nature, as a train runs through the countryside, following the same unintentionality with the same fleeing art.

208

The man who sees only one wellspring knows only one storm. The chances within him are thwarted.

209

My inability to *fix* my life comes from the fact that I am faithful not to one but to all of those beings with whom I find myself in serious kinship. This constancy persists at the very heart of contradictions and differences. In a moment when emotion and literal meaning are interrupted, humor leads me to conceive of these beings as allies in the exercise of my elimination.

210

Your audacity, a wart. Your action, a specious image, preferably in color.

(Always present in my memory is the inane remark of the coal-merchant in Saumanes who asserted that the French Revolution had purged the region of a thoroughly criminal nobleman: a certain Sade. One of his exploits had consisted of murdering his farmer's three daughters. The Marquis's underwear was taut before the first beauty had expired...

This idiot couldn't let it go, the mountain-dweller's greed obviously unwilling to make any concessions.)

211

Les justiciers s'estompent. Voici les cupides tournant le dos aux bruyères aérées.

212

Enfonce-toi dans l'inconnu qui creuse. Oblige-toi à tournoyer.

213

J'ai, ce matin, suivi des yeux Florence qui retournait au Moulin du Calavon. Le sentier volait autour d'elle : un parterre de souris se chamaillant! Le dos chaste et les longues jambes n'arrivaient pas à se rapetisser dans mon regard. La gorge de jujube s'attardait au bord de mes dents. Jusqu'à ce que la verdure, à un tournant, me le dérobât, je repassai, m'émouvant à chaque note, son admirable corps musicien, inconnu du mien.

214

Je n'ai pas vu d'étoile s'allumer au front de ceux qui allaient mourir mais le dessin d'une persienne qui, soulevée, permettait d'entrevoir un ordre d'objets déchirants ou résignés, dans un vaste local où des servantes heureuses circulaient.

215

Têtes aux sèves poisseuses survenues, on ne sait trop pourquoi, dans notre hiver et figées là, depuis. Un futur souillé s'inscrit dans leurs lignes. Tel ce Dubois que sa graisse spartiate de mouchard entérine et perpétue. Justes du ciel et balle perdue, accordez-lui les palmes de votre humour…

216

Il n'est plus question que le berger soit guide. Ainsi en décide le politique, ce nouveau fermier général.

211

The just are growing blurred. Here are the greedy, turning their backs on the vaporous heather.

212

Plunge into the unknown that cuts furrows. Make a point of spiraling.

213

I followed Florence with my eyes this morning as she returned to the Calavon Mill. The path flew around her: an orchestra pit of mice was squabbling! The chaste back and long legs never quite grew smaller in my eyes. The throat of jujube lingered at the edge of my teeth. Until the greenery at a turning hid her from me, I scanned, aroused by every note, her admirable musician body, unknown to my own.

214

I haven't seen a star light up in the forehead of those who were going to die, but rather the pattern of a blind which, raised, allowed a glimpse of orderly objects, wrenching and resigned, in a vast room where happy servants circulated.

215

Heads of sticky sap have unexpectedly arisen in our winter, no one really knows why, and congealed there ever since. A soiled future is inscribed in their lines. Like this Dubois whose Spartan police-spy fat confirms and perpetuates him. Just men of heaven and stray bullet, bestow on him the palms of your humor...

216

It is no longer possible that the shepherd be guide. This, decided by politics, the new farmer-general.

217

Olivier le Noir m'a demandé une bassine d'eau pour nettoyer son revolver. Je suggérai la graisse d'arme. Mais c'est bien l'eau qui convenait. Le sang sur les parois de la cuvette demeurait hors de portée de mon imagination. A quoi eût servi de se représenter la silhouette honteuse, effondrée, le canon dans l'oreille, dans son enroulement gluant? Un justicier rentrait, son labeur accompli, comme un qui, ayant bien rompu sa terre, décrotterait sa bêche avant de sourire à la flambée de sarments.

218

Dans ton corps conscient, la réalité est en avance de quelques minutes d'imagination. Ce temps jamais rattrapé est un gouffre étranger aux actes de ce monde. Il n'est jamais une ombre simple malgré son odeur de clémence nocturne, de survie religieuse, d'enfance incorruptible.

219

Brusquement tu te souviens que tu as un visage. Les traits qui en formaient le modelé n'étaient pas tous des traits chagrins, jadis. Vers ce multiple paysage se levaient des êtres doués de bonté. La fatigue n'y charmait pas que des naufrages. La solitude des amants y respirait. Regarde. Ton miroir s'est changé en feu. Insensiblement tu reprends conscience de ton âge (qui avait sauté du calendrier), de ce surcroît d'existence dont tes efforts vont faire un pont. Recule à l'intérieur du miroir. Si tu n'en consumes pas l'austérité du moins la fertilité n'en est pas tarie.

220

Je redoute l'échauffement tout autant que la chlorose des années qui suivront la guerre. Je pressens que l'unanimité confortable, la boulimie de justice n'auront qu'une durée éphémère, aussitôt retiré le lien qui nouait notre combat. Ici, on se prépare à revendiquer l'abstrait, là on refoule en aveugle tout ce qui est susceptible d'atténuer la cruauté de la condition humaine de ce siècle et lui

217

Olivier le Noir [Oliver the Black] asked me for a basin of water to clean his revolver. I suggested gun oil. But water was exactly what was called-for. The blood on the sides of the washbowl exceeded my imagination. What good would it have done to dwell on the shameful silhouette, the gun in his ear, slumped in his viscid coil? A just man was back, his work done, like one who having scrupulously broken up his earth would scrape his spade clean, before smiling into the blaze of the vineshoots.

218

In your conscious body, reality is ahead of the imagination by several minutes. A period of time never-recaptured, this chasm is foreign to the acts of this world. It is never a simple shadow, despite its odor of nocturnal clemency, religious remnant, incorruptible childhood.

219

Abruptly you remember that you have a face. The features it was modeled on were not all sad, once. Toward this multiple landscape rose beings endowed with goodness. Their fatigue charmed more than shipwrecks. The solitude of lovers breathed in them. Look. Your mirror has changed into fire. Imperceptibly you grow aware of your age again (it had leapt off the calendar), of this superfluity of existence which your efforts will make into a bridge. Withdraw into the mirror's interior. If you don't consume its austerity, at least its fertility has not run dry.

220

I dread the overexcitement as much as the chlorosis of the years following the war. I have a presentiment that comfortable unanimity, the bulimia of justice, will be short-lived, as soon as the ties are cut that bound our combat. Here, people prepare to demand the abstract; there, they blindly repress all that might attenuate the cruelty of the human condition in this century, permitting

permettre d'accéder à l'avenir, d'un pas confiant. Le mal partout déjà est en lutte avec son remède. Les fantômes multiplient les conseils, les visites, des fantômes dont l'âme empirique est un amas de glaires et de névroses. Cette pluie qui pénètre l'homme jusqu'à l'os c'est l'espérance d'agression, l'écoute du mépris. On se précipitera dans l'oubli. On renoncera à mettre au rebut, à retrancher et à guérir. On supposera que les morts inhumés ont des noix dans leurs poches et que l'arbre un jour fortuitement surgira.

O vie, donne, s'il est temps encore, aux vivants un peu de ton bon sens subtil sans la vanité qui abuse, et par-dessus tout, peut-être, donne-leur la certitude que tu n'es pas aussi accidentelle et privée de remords qu'on le dit. Ce n'est pas la flèche qui est hideuse, c'est le croc.

221

La carte du soir

Une fois de plus l'an nouveau mélange nos yeux
De hautes herbes veillent qui n'ont d'amour qu'avec le feu
    et la prison mordue
Après seront les cendres du vainqueur
Et le conte du mal
Seront les cendres de l'amour
L'églantier au glas survivant
Seront tes cendres
Celles imaginaires de ta vie immobile sur son cône d'ombre.

222

Ma renarde, pose ta tête sur mes genoux. je ne suis pas heureux et pourtant tu suffis. Bougeoir ou météore, il n'est plus de coeur gros ni d'avenir sur terre. Les marches du crépuscule révèlent ton murmure, gîte de menthe et de romarin, confidence échangée entre les rousseurs de l'automne et ta robe légère. Tu es l'âme de la montagne aux flancs profonds, aux roches tues derrière des lèvres d'argile. Que les ailes de ton nez frémissent. Que ta

it to reach the future with a confident step. Already evil everywhere is struggling against its remedy. Ghosts issue repeated advice, repeatedly visit, ghosts whose empirical soul is a mass of mucus and neuroses. This rain penetrating man to the bone is but hope for aggression, attentive listening to contempt. They will rush into amnesia. They will forgo discarding, excising, and healing. They will suppose that the buried dead have nuts in their pockets and that the tree will someday, fortuitously, sprout.

Oh life, give the living, if there is still time, a little of your good subtle sense, without deceptive vanity, and perhaps above all give them the certitude that you are not as accidental and remorseless as they say. It is not the arrow that is hideous, it is the hook.

221

Map of the evening

Once more the new year mingles our eyes.
High grasses keep watch, who love only gunfire and addictive
    prison.
Afterwards will be the conquerer's ashes
And the tale of evil;
Will be love's ashes;
The wild rose lasting longer than the death knell;
Will be your ashes,
The imaginary ones of your immobile life on its cone
    of shadow.

222

My vixen, rest your head on my knees. I am not happy, and yet you are enough. Candlestick or meteor, there is no full heart or future left on earth. The steps of dusk reveal your murmur, lair of mint and rosemary, whispered secret between autumn's russets and your ethereal dress. You are the soul of the mountain with its deep flanks, its rocks hushed behind lips of clay. How the wings of your nose tremble. How your hand secures the path and draws

main ferme le sentier et rapproche le rideau des arbres. Ma renarde, en présence des deux astres, le gel et le vent, je place en toi toutes les espérances éboulées, pour un chardon victorieux de la rapace solitude.

223

Vie qui ne peut ni ne veut plier sa voile, vie que les vents ramènent fourbue à la glu du rivage, toujours prête cependant à s'élancer par-dessus l'hébétude, vie de moins en moins *garnie,* de moins en moins patiente, désigne-moi ma part si tant est qu'elle existe, ma part justifiée dans le destin commun au centre duquel ma singularité fait tache mais retient l'amalgame.

224

Autrefois au moment de me mettre au lit, l'idée d'une mort temporaire au sein du sommeil me rassérénait, aujourd'hui je m'endors pour vivre quelques heures.

225

L'enfant ne voit pas l'homme sous un jour sûr mais sous un jour simplifié. Là est le secret de leur inséparabilité.

226

Un jugement qui engage ne fortifie pas toujours.

227

L'homme est capable de faire ce qu'il est incapable d'imaginer. Sa tête sillonne la galaxie de l'absurde.

228

Pour qui oeuvrent les martyrs? La grandeur réside dans le départ qui oblige. Les êtres exemplaires sont de vapeur et de vent.

Furor and Mystery

the curtain of the trees closer. My vixen, in the presence of the two stars, frost and wind, I place in you every broken hope, for a victorious thistle of rapacious solitude.

223

Life that cannot and does not wish to lower its sail, life that the winds return to the birdlime of the shore, foundered but always ready to leap beyond its stupor, life less and less *adorned,* less and less patient, assign me my role, if it exists, my legitimate role in the common destiny at whose center my singularity stands out as a stain but binds the amalgam.

224

Formerly, at the moment when I went to bed, the idea of a temporary death in the bosom of sleep restored me; today I sleep to be alive for a few hours.

225

The child does not see the man in an unflinching light, but in a simplified one. Therein lies the secret of their inseparability.

226

A judgment that engages does not always strengthen.

227

Man is capable of doing what he is incapable of imagining. His head tills the galaxy of the absurd.

228

For whom do martyrs do their work? Greatness resides in the departure that compels us. Exemplary beings are of vapor and wind.

229

La couleur noire renferme *l'impossible* vivant. Son champ mental est le siège de tous les inattendus, de tous les paroxysmes. Son prestige escorte les poètes et prépare les hommes d'action.

230

Toute la vertu du ciel d'août, de notre angoisse confidente, dans la voix d'or du météore.

231

Peu de jours avant son supplice, Roger Chaudon me disait : « Sur cette terre, on est un peu dessus, beaucoup dessous. L'ordre des époques ne peut être inversé. C'est, au fond, ce qui me tranquillise, malgré la joie de vivre qui me secoue comme un tonnerre... »

232

L'exceptionnel ne grise ni n'apitoie son meurtrier. Celui-là, hélas! a les yeux qu'il faut pour tuer.

233

Considère sans en être affecté que ce que le mal pique le plus volontiers ce sont les cibles non averties dont il a pu s'approcher à loisir. Ce que tu as appris des hommes — leurs revirements incohérents, leurs humeurs inguérissables, leur goût du fracas, leur subjectivité d'arlequin — doit t'inciter, une fois l'action consommée, à ne pas t'attarder trop sur les lieux de vos rapports.

234

Paupières aux portes d'un bonheur fluide comme la chair d'un coquillage, paupières que l'œil en furie ne peut faire chavirer, paupières, combien suffisantes!

229

The color black contains the living *impossible.* Its mental domain is the seat of all surprises, all paroxysms. Its prestige escorts poets and trains men of action.

230

All the virtue of the August sky, of our confiding anguish, in the golden voice of the meteor.

231

Shortly before his torture, Roger Chaudon said to me, "On this earth you sometimes get the upper hand, mostly you get the worst of it. The order of the times can't be reversed. That's basically what keeps me calm, despite the joy of being alive which shakes me like a thunderbolt…"

232

The exceptional neither fascinates its murderer nor moves him to compassion. Alas! he has the eyes required for killing.

233

Take into account, without being affected by it, that what evil most willingly strikes are those ill-informed targets it has managed to approach at leisure. What you've learned about men—their incoherent reversals, their incurable moods, their taste for uproar, their buffoonish subjectivity—must prompt you, once an action is finished, not to linger too long on the scene.

234

Eyelids at the doors of a happiness as fluid as the flesh of a shellfish, eyelids the enraged eye cannot overwhelm, eyelids, what an honorable job you do!

235

L'angoisse, squelette et cœur, cité et forêt, ordure et magie, intègre désert, illusoirement vaincue, victorieuse, muette, maîtresse de la parole, femme de tout homme, ensemble, et Homme.

236

« Mon corps était plus immense que la terre et je n'en connaissais qu'une toute petite parcelle. J'accueille des promesses de félicité si innombrables, du fond de mon âme, que je te supplie de garder pour nous seuls ton nom. »

237

Dans nos ténèbres, il n'y a pas une place pour la Beauté. Toute la place est pour la Beauté.

LA ROSE DE CHÊNE

Chacune des lettres qui composent ton nom, ô Beauté, au tableau d'honneur des supplices, épouse la plane simplicité du soleil, s'inscrit dans la phrase géante qui barre le ciel, et s'associe à l'homme acharné à tromper son destin avec son contraire indomptable: l'espérance.

235

Anguish, skeleton and heart, town and forest, filth and magic, upright desert, seemingly vanquished, victorious, mute, mistress of the word, woman for all men together, and Man.

236

"My body was more immense than the earth and I knew only a tiny part of it. From the bottom of my soul, I welcome such innumerable promises of bliss that I beg you to keep your name our secret."

237

In our shadows, there is not one space alone for Beauty. The whole space is for Beauty.

—NK

THE OAKEN ROSE

Each of the letters that compose your name, oh Beauty, on the honor roll of tortures, espouses the even simplicity of the sun, inscribes itself in the giant phrase that crosses the sky, and joins with man determined to elude his destiny by means of its indomitable contrary: hope.

—NK

HYPNOS MOON

(from *Search for the Base and the Summit*)

In mid-July of 1944, the order from Algiers reached me in the Maquis at Céreste to be ready to take off during the next clandestine landing operation. The plane would alight after dark on one of our fields on Mont Ventoux and bring me out. Instead of delighting me, the prospect of leaving vexed me. I suspected that if Allied Headquarters in North Africa was sending for one of us, it was because the invasion of the southern zone was imminent. I foresaw that in this eventuality the need for information could justify my presence over there, since the department for which I was responsible, air operations, figured prominently in the concerns of the High Command. In fact the latter believed that the Germans, in retreating from the Mediterranean coast, might be able to hold the foothills of the Lower Alps and compromise the Allies' rapid advance along the length of the Rhone. My comrades and I were skeptical as to the extent and possible success of such a venture. The enemy army, already reeling, could only have set up not very dangerous pockets of resistance. The Maquis, given the right arms, was well-suited—if supported by air—to stop the most aggressive units from meeting up and becoming entrenched. We were in a position to know this. But we also knew that opinion on the opposite side of the Mediterranean differed. The reports of agents parachuted into occupied France, then smuggled out again, always tended to exaggerate things, first and foremost the dangers. This is common, since remarkable merit is preferred to anything less. But why did those in Algiers appear to be, by turns, so naïve and so malevolent? With an indifference each day more pronounced to the fate and future of the young people in the Resistance. These last were endowed with humane devotion and good will. Outlaws operating within the most sovereign of laws, and docile humus beneath hope's spade. Yes, why this duplicity, whose symptoms so disconcerted us? Because a good

Furor and Mystery

many politicians and members of the military are perverts of the imagination, dotards of differential calculus. Beyond a doubt they are too fond of permanent posts and comfort, of every kind of driving ambition and of comfort. And the practical counterpart of that was spread out, here, in the form of memorial plaques, the grass revivified! In Algiers, they turned a blind eye to the barometer...

One evening the message announcing the plane's arrival came over the airwaves. The hours that preceded it I had spent in talking with my companions, consulting them, taking note of their suggestions, in order to transmit these to the other side of the sea. It was to their great credit that their morale was not in tatters. Spring and the beginning of summer had been murderous. Our encounters with the SS and the militia ended most often, depending on the condition of the forces present, in implacable extermination or retreat. Most of my comrades from the beginning of the action had been killed or executed. Several had disappeared, others had resigned. Those of our leaders who were newcomers lacked tenacity, pure courage, moral focus. At least, so I imagined. Divisions arising from our differences were gouging their way between us. I had grown gloomier. I no longer exchanged anything with others except a glance. My attitude was certainly blameworthy. Ever since the death of Emile Cavagni, I had felt very alone. With the disappearance of this man, a massive piece of sun had shattered and emptied of happiness. The false optimism that I had to maintain around me asphyxiated me. The obligation to keep our partisan band going, at any price, stuck to my skin like an ecclesiastical charge, even though I realized that in it alone lay salvation or, at the very least, the solution that was the least constricting. At different critical points in the Lower Alps, Zyngerman, Noel, Chaudon, Aubert, Besson, Grillet, Rostagne held their own, as best they could; that is to say, with all their experience as seasoned fighters they stood firm, in the most extreme difficulties. Yet admirable young people, captive only yesterday to the terror of the occupier but quickly delivered from it by the legend of our existence, were now multiplying, rushing to the final blood transfusion. That something which had lain dying, among the partisans as among their enemies, abruptly revived, grew brutally destupefied. Combat resumed its speed at the same time as its suffering.

The last companion with whom I spoke was Roger Chaudon. He, for one, advised me strongly not to leave. Grimly, he insisted on painting a bleak portrait of *the milieu* which was going to be mine in North Africa, the intrigues I would witness with disgust. Chaudon, of whose martyrdom I was to learn with impotent shame several days later in Algiers, is one of those I will long revisit in my memory, for it was he in particular who had the gift of purifying every question by the *just* tenor of his response. He loved life as one does at forty, with an eagle's gaze and the effusiveness of a tit-mouse. His generosity increased his scope, rather than hobbling him. He believed, without a trace of foolishness, that the virtue of our ten fingers added to the tenacity of our hearts, as well as to the guile we must assume in the face of evil—then discard like cast-off clothing afterwards, or be contaminated—possessed resources against tyranny that we must not lose. He understood the din made by the devil's advocates: "Their progeny is assured for years to come. They've looked after themselves so well that they have sons even among us. We will know another fearful era. I've staked my life against the enterprise." Such was his thought.

It is two o'clock in the morning on the immense field of laven-der. The air is crisp, the breeze has risen. The crest of Mount Ventoux retains on its slopes a whole pelt of frozen woolly clouds, clouds that have ceased to live. The landing signals have been set up in a triangle on the improvised runway. Holding his lamp ready to throw out its beam of light, the director of the operation listens for the sound of the engine that will be curving down to us. The mi-nuscule machine suddenly looms from the shadows, hesitates an instant, skims over us, then lands. A few embraces, a wave goodbye, I slip into the cramped cabin. I have just enough time to smile at Arthur who has scarcely left my side until now, Arthur who hunches his coyote head into his shoulders. The plane has taken off. An American pilot, an escaped prisoner, and an eccentric who specializes in summary executions are my traveling companions. In my new independence I feel a fine and happy anguish, mixed with a twinge of remorse whose origin is perfectly clear to me. Not without self-mockery, I see myself as one of those colored images in childhood magazines: hunting the great beasts, taking the citadel. The others converse with shouted words, and gesticulate. The Lysander heads south, at a low altitude. The plane is not armed. Its course is followed by the moon which juts out over it, a sly colossus. The moon's moist gaze has always nauseated me. Tonight more than ever. My attention turns, rather, to the gorges of dark earth below the undulating line of mountains. Why have I tensed, then suddenly come undone? I am bending over, beneath a rush of streaming gratitude. Fires, torches light up everywhere, mount from the earth, puffs of luminous words addressed to me, the one who is leaving. From inside hell, as I pass over, they extend this link to me, this friendship as piercing as a cry, this incorruptible flower: fire. How the stars of Corsica, at crossing's end, looked dim and simpering to me!

It ought not to depend, alas, on my resources that a fervor of first dawn find voices worthy of it, nor that its ferocious beauty be understood and safeguarded. Beaten but invincible, periodically prostrate and trampled by the pack, will man remain forever the reed from *before* Pascal?

1945

—NK

A NOTE ON THE MAQUIS

(from *Search for the Base and the Summit*)

Show the risky side of the enterprise, but with designedly retrospective art, torn from our hearts in its newness, in its truth or its sincere approximation of truth. It is the enemy's "faults," his orders to humiliate before exterminating, that are above all in our favor. Without forced labor in Germany, persecution, contamination and crimes, only a small number of young men would have joined the maquis and taken up arms. *France in 1940 did not believe, personally, in cruelty or servitude*—not the France delivered up to Hitler's fantastic rake by the mental poverty of some, the well-prepared treason of others, finally the all-powerful noxiousness of enemy interests. And, too, the enigma of the years 1939–1940 weighed on the insouciance of the previous day like a lead cape.

In the rapid sequence of hopes and disappointments, of sudden advances followed by depressing deceptions, which have stood out as landmarks of these last forty years, one can distinguish, quite rightly, the mark of a malign fate, the very same whose intervention one glimpses periodically during extreme periods of History, as though its mission were to prohibit any change, other than superficial, in the underlying condition of men. But I must banish this perception. The year fast approaching has a free hand…

Contrary to advanced thinking, the courage born of despair attracts few initiates. As late as 1942, only a handful of solitary men attempted to engage in close combat. The marvel is that this disparate cohort, composed of coddled children badly trained, consummate individualists, workers by tradition in revolt, generous believers, boys abhorring exile from their native soil, peasants of a singularly obscure patriotism, unstable imaginative spirits, precocious adventurers, side by side with old steeds back from the Foreign Legion, and men attracted to the Spanish War—this conglomeration, in the hands of intelligent and clear-sighted men, was

Furor and Mystery

on the point of becoming an extraordinary orchard, such as France had known only four or five times in the course of its existence and on its soil. But something that was hostile or simply foreign to this aspiration then arose and flung it back into nothingness. For fear of an evil whose powers were to grow precisely out of that dead time left in the wake of this abandonment!

To enlarge, until it becomes light—which will always be fleeting—the glimmer during which we're shaken, we begin to act, we suffer, and persist, we must approach it without prejudice, relieved of the archetypes who suddenly, without forewarning, no longer work. To obtain a valid result from any action whatsoever, we must strip it of disquieting appearances, of the spells and legends the imagination grants it, even before bringing it, with the help of the mind and circumstances, to a happy conclusion; we must distinguish the true from the false opening through which we're going to proceed into the future. To observe it naked, its prow facing the times. Frequently the evidence, which is not a feeling but a glance exchanged in passing, offers itself to us half-hidden. We will point out beauty everywhere it stands a chance of outliving that temporary status it seems to secure amid our sufferings. And cause to dream at length those who do not ordinarily have dreams, and plunge into reality those whose minds are given to the wasted games of sleep.

1944

—NK

LE CARNET D'HYPNOS

(from *Le Bâton de rosier*)

Le carnet d'Hypnos fut enfoui en juillet 1944, lors de mon départ pour Alger, dans le mur intérieur d'une maison à demi démolie de Céreste. Je le retrouvai à mon retour, et en détruisis, pour des raisons personnelles, la plupart des pages. Un feuillet fut conservé comme témoin.

L'ouvrage parut en 1946 dans la collection Espoir, *dirigé chez Gallimard par Albert Camus. A notre amitié est attaché le poème "De moment en moment," choisi par Camus alors que, parcourant le Vaucluse tous deux, il me demanda d'ouvrir avec ce poème* La Postérité du soleil, *livre illustré de photographies de Henriette Grindat, mais qui ne devait paraître qu'après la mort de Camus.*

THE HYPNOS NOTEBOOK

(from *The Rose-Tree Staff*)

In July 1944, when I left for Algiers, the Hypnos notebook was hidden in the interior wall of a half-demolished house in Céreste. I reclaimed it on my return and destroyed, for personal reasons, most of its pages. One leaf was preserved, in witness.

The work appeared in 1946 in the Espoir *[Hope] collection, which was edited at Gallimard by Albert Camus. Connected with our friendship is the poem "From Moment to Moment," chosen by Camus when, as the two of us were wandering through the Vaucluse, he asked if he could use it to open* The Sun's Posterity, *a book illustrated with photographs by Henriette Grindat, but which was not to appear until after Camus' death.*

—NK

LES LOYAUX ADVERSAIRES

LOYAL ADVERSARIES

SUR LA NAPPE D'UN ÉTANG GLACÉ

Je t'aime,
Hiver aux graines belliqueuses.
Maintenant ton image luit
Là où son cœur s'est penché.

CRAYON DU PRISONNIER

Un amour dont la bouche est un bouquet de brumes,
Éclot et disparaît.
Un chasseur va le suivre, un guetteur l'apprendra,
Et ils se haïront tous deux, puis ils se maudiront tous trois.
Il gèle au dehors, la feuille passe à travers l'arbre.

ON THE SHEET OF A FROZEN POND

I love you,
Winter with warlike seeds.
Now your image gleams
Where his heart inclined.

—MAC

PRISONER'S PENCIL

A lover whose mouth is a bouquet of mists
Blossoms and fades away.
A hunter sets off in pursuit, a sentinel will learn of it,
And they will hate each other, these two; then all three
    of them will put a curse on one another.
It is icing up outside, the leaf passes through the tree.

—NK

UN OISEAU...

Un oiseau chante sur un fil
Cette vie simple, à fleur de terre.
Notre enfer s'en réjouit.

Puis le vent commence à souffrir
Et les étoiles s'en avisent.

Ô folles, de parcourir
Tant de fatalité profonde!

L'ORDRE LÉGITIME
EST QUELQUEFOIS INHUMAIN

Ceux qui partagent leurs souvenirs,
La solitude les reprend, aussitôt fait silence.
L'herbe qui les frôle éclôt de leur fidélité.

Que disais-tu? Tu me parlais d'un amour si lointain
Qu'il rejoignait ton enfance.
Tant de stratagèmes s'emploient dans la mémoire!

Furor and Mystery

A BIRD…

A bird perched on a wire is singing
This simple life, at the earth's surface.
Our inferno glories in it.

Then the wind begins to suffer
And the stars take note.

Oh madwomen, to wander
Over so much deep fatality!

—NK

THE LEGITIMATE ORDER

Those who share their memories,
Solitude reclaims them, silence soon.
From their faithfulness blooms the grass grazing them.

What were you saying? You spoke to me of a love so distant
That it rejoined your childhood.
So many stratagems serve memory!

—MAC

René Char

SUR LE VOLET D'UNE FENÊTRE

Visage, chaleur blanche,
Soeur passante, soeur disant,
Suave persévérance,
Visage, chaleur blanche.

CHAUME DES VOSGES

1939

Beauté, ma toute-droite, par des routes si ladres,
A l'étape des lampes et du courage clos,
Que je me glace et que tu sois ma femme de décembre.
Ma vie future, c'est ton visage quand tu dors.

ON A WINDOW SHUTTER

Face, white warmth,
Passing sister, speaking sister,
Silken perseverance
Face, white warmth.

—NK

STRAW OF THE VOSGES

1939

Beauty, my upright one, over such mean roads,
At the stage of lamps and concluded courage,
Let me ice over, be my December wife.
My future life is your face when you sleep.

—MAC

LE THOR

Dans le sentier aux herbes engourdies où nous nous étonnions, enfants, que la nuit se risquât à passer, les guêpes n'allaient plus aux ronces et les oiseaux aux branches. L'air ouvrait aux hôtes de la matinée sa turbulente immensité. Ce n'étaient que filaments d'ailes, tentation de crier, voltige entre lumière et transparence. Le Thor s'exaltait sur la lyre de ses pierres. Le mont Ventoux, miroir des aigles, était en vue.

Dans le sentier aux herbes engourdies, la chimère d'un age perdu souriait à nos jeunes larmes.

PÉNOMBRE

J'étais dans une de ces forêts où le soleil n'a pas accès mais où, la nuit, les étoiles pénètrent. Ce lieu n'avait le permis d'exister, que parce que l'inquisition des États l'avait négligé. Les servitudes abandonnées me marquaient leur mépris. La hantise de punir m'était retirée. Par endroit, le souvenir d'une force caressait la fugue paysanne de l'herbe. Je me gouvernais sans doctrine, avec une véhémence sereine. J'étais l'égal de choses dont le secret tenait sous le rayon d'une aile. Pour la plupart, l'essentiel n'est jamais né, et ceux qui le possèdent ne peuvent l'échanger sans se nuire. Nul ne consent à perdre ce qu'il a conquis à la pointe de sa peine! Autrement ce serait la jeunesse et la grâce, source et delta auraient la même pureté.

J'étais dans une de ces forêts où le soleil n'a pas accès mais où, la nuit, les étoiles pénètrent pour d'implacables hostilités.

Furor and Mystery

LE THOR

In the path of numbed grasses where we were astonished as children that night risked going past, wasps no longer went to brambles nor birds to branches. The air opened to the morning's guests its turbulent immensity. There were only filaments of wings, the temptation to shout, a vaulting between light and transparency. Le Thor exalted on the lyre of its stones. Mont Ventoux, mirror to eagles, was in sight.

In the path of numbed grasses, the chimera of a lost age smiled at our young tears.

—NK

PENUMBRA

I was in one of those forests where the sun has no access, but where stars penetrate by night. This place could exist only because the inquisition of the State had overlooked it. Forsaken easements showed me their scorn. The obsession to chastise was taken from me. Here and there, the memory of a strength caressed the peasant flights of the grass. I ruled myself without doctrine, in serene vehemence. I was the equal of things whose secret fitted under the beam of a wing. For most, the essential is never born, and its possessors cannot exchange it without harm to themselves. None consents to lose what was conquered by dint of pain! Otherwise, it would be youth and grace, spring and delta would be equally pure;

I was in one of those forests where the sun has no access, but where stars penetrate by night for a relentless warring.

—MAC

CUR SECESSISTI ?

Neige, caprice d'enfant, soleil qui n'as que l'hiver pour devenir un astre, au seuil de mors cachot de pierre, venez vous abriter. Sur les pentes d'Aulan, mes fils qui sont incendiaires, mes fils qu'on tue sans leur fermer les yeux, s'augmentent de votre puissance.

CETTE FUMÉE QUI NOUS PORTAIT

Cette fumée qui nous portait était sœur du bâton qui dérange la pierre et du nuage qui ouvre le ciel. Elle n'avait pas mépris de nous, nous prenait tels que nous étions, minces ruisseaux nourris de désarroi et d'espérance, avec un verrou aux mâchoires et une montagne dans le regard.

CUR SECESSISTI?

Snow, child's caprice, sun with only the winter to become a star, at the threshold of my stone dungeon, come take shelter. On the slopes of Aulan, my incendiary sons, my sons who are killed without closing their eyes, are made greater by your power.

—MAC

THIS SMOKE WHICH CARRIED US

This smoke which bore us was sister to the rod disturbing the rock and to the cloud opening the sky. It did not scorn us, took us as we were, narrow rivulets nourished on confusion and hope, with a bolt to our jaws and a mountain in our gaze.

—MAC

LA PATIENCE

Le Moulin

Un bruit long qui sort par le toit;
Des hirondelles toujours blanches;
Le grain qui saute, l'eau qui broie;
Et l'enclos où l'amour se risque,
Étincelle et marque le pas.

Vagabonds

Vagabonds, sous vos doux haillons,
Deux étoiles rébarbatives
Croisent leurs jambes narratives,
Trinquent à la santé des prisons.

Le Nombre

Ils disent des mots qui leur restent au coin des yeux;
Il suivent une route où les maisons leur sont fermées;
Ils allument parfois une lampe dont la clarté les met en pleurs;
Ils ne sont jamais comptés, ils sont trop!
Ils sont l'équivalent des livres dont la clé fut perdue.

Auxiliaires

Ceux qu'il faut attacher sur terre
Pour satisfaire la beauté,
Familiers autant qu'inconnus,
À l'image de la tempête,

PATIENCE

The Mill

From under the roof a long din;
Swallows always white;
Grain that leaps, water that grinds.
And the enclosure where love takes its chances,
Sparkles, and marks time.

Vagabonds

Vagabonds, beneath your gentle rags,
Two prickly stars
Cross their narrative legs,
Drink to the health of jails.

The Numerous

They speak the words that linger at the corners of their eyes;
They take a road where houses are closed to them;
Sometimes they light a lamp whose brightness makes them cry;
They are never counted, they're far too many!
Just like books whose key no one can find.

Auxiliaries

Those we have to tie to the earth
In order to satisfy beauty,
As familiar as they are unknown,
In the likeness of a storm,

René Char

Qu'attendent-ils les uns des autres?
Un nuage soudain les chasse.
Il suffit qu'ils aient existé
Au même instant qu'une mouette.

What do they hope from each other?
A sudden cloud and they're gone.
But just the same, they've existed
While a seagull spread its wings.

—NK & PT

René Char

REDONNEZ-LEUR

Redonnez-leur ce qui n'est plus présent en eux,
Ils reverront le grain de la moisson s'enfermer dans l'épi et s'agiter
  sur l'herbe.
Apprenez-leur, de la chute à l'essor, les douze mois de leur visage.
Ils chériront le vide de leur coeur jusqu'au désir suivant;
Car rien ne fait naufrage ou ne se plaît aux cendres;
Et qui sait voir la terre aboutir à des fruits,
Point ne l'émeut l'échec quoiqu'il ait tout perdu.

DIS…

Dis ce que le feu hésite à dire
Soleil de l'air, clarté qui ose,
Et meurs de l'avoir dit pour tous.

RESTORE TO THEM

Restore to them what is no longer present in them;
They will once again see the grain of the harvest slip into the stalk
    and sway over the grass.
Teach them, from falling to soaring, the twelve months of their
    face.
They will cherish the emptiness of their hearts until the next
    desire;
For nothing is altogether destroyed, nor takes deep pleasure in
    ashes;
And he who can see that the earth ends in fruit
Is unmoved by failure, though he has lost all.

—MAC & NK

SAY...

Say what the fire hesitates to say
Sun of the air, daring clarity,
And die of having said it for all.

—NK

LE POÈME PULVERISÉ
(1945–1947)

THE PULVERIZED POEM
(1945–1947)

ARGUMENT

Comment vivre sans inconnu devant soi ?

Les hommes d'aujourd'hui veulent que le poème soit à l'image de leur vie, faite de si peu d'égards, de si peu d'espace et brûlée d'intolérance.

Parce qu'il ne leur est plus loisible d'agir suprêmement, dans cette préoccupation fatale de se détruire par son semblable, parce que leur inerte richesse les freine et les enchaîne, les hommes d'aujourd'hui, l'instinct affaibli, perdent, tout en se gardant vivants, jusqu'à la poussière de leur nom.

Né de l'appel du devenir et de l'angoisse de la rétention, le poème, s'élevant de son puits de boue et d'étoiles, témoignera presque silencieusement, qu'il n'était rien en lui qui n'existât vraiment ailleurs, dans ce rebelle et solitaire monde des contradictions.

ARGUMENT

How can we live without the unknown in front of us?

Men of today want the poem to be in the image of their lives, composed of such little consideration, of such little space, and burned with intolerance.

Because it is no longer given to them to act supremely, in this fatal preoccupation of self-destruction at the hands of their fellow-men, because their inert wealth holds them back and enslaves them, men of today, their instinct weakened, lose—still keeping alive— even the dust of their names.

Born from the summons of becoming and from the anguish of retention, the poem, rising from its well of mud and of stars, will bear witness, almost silently, that it contained nothing which did not truly exist elsewhere, in this rebellious and solitary world of contradictions.

—MAC

René Char   245

LES TROIS SOEURS

Mon amour à la robe de phare bleu,
je baise la fièvre de ton visage
où couche la lumière qui jouit en secret.

J'aime et je sanglote. Je suis vivant
et c'est ton coeur cette Étoile du Matin
à la durée viclorieuse qui rougit avant
de rompre le combat des Constellations.

Hors de toi, que ma chair devienne la voile
qui répugne au vent.

I

Dans l'urne des temps secondaires
L' enfant à naître était de craie.
La marche fourchue des saisons
Abritait d'herbe l'inconnu.

La connaissance divisible
Pressait d'averses le printemps.
Un aromate de pays
Prolongeait la fleur apparue.

Communication qu' on outrage,
Ecorce ou givre déposés;
L'air investit, le sang attise
L'oeil fait mystère du baiser.

Donnant vie à la route ouverte,
Le tourbillon vint aux genoux;
Et cet élan, le lit des larmes
S'en emplit d'un seul battement.

THE THREE SISTERS

My love with your blue lighthouse dress,
I kiss the fever of your face
where the light sleeps secretly in its pleasure.

I love and am weeping. I am alive
and your heart is this Morning Star
enduring victorious blushing before
breaking off the combat of Constellations.

Apart from you, let my flesh become the sail
Revolting at the wind.

I

In the urn of secondary times
The babe to be born was of chalk.
The forked march of the seasons
Sheltered the unknown with grass.

Knowledge divisible
Pressured spring with showers.
A country aromatic
Prolonged the apparent flower.

Communication offended,
Bark or frost laid down;
The air invests, the blood stirs up;
The eye makes a mystery of the kiss.

Enlivening the open road,
The tornado came kneeling;
From this impulse, the bed of tears
Filled up in a single beat.

René Char

II

La seconde crie et s'évade
De l'abeille ambiante et du tilleul vermeil.
Elle est un jour de vent perpétuel,
Le dé bleu du combat, le guetteur qui sourit
Quand sa lyre profère : "Ce que je veux, sera."

C' est l'heure de se taire
De devenir la tour
Que l'avenir convoite.

Le chasseur de soi fuit sa maison fragile;
Son gibier le suit n'ayant plus peur.

Leur clarté est si haute, leur santé si nouvelle,
Que ces deux qui s'en vont sans rien signifier
Ne sentent pas les soeurs les ramener à elles
D'un long baillon de cendre aux forêts blanches.

III

Cet enfant sur ton épaule
Est ta chance et ton fardeau.
Terre en quoi l'orchidée brûle,
Ne le fatiguez pas de vous.

Restez fleur et frontière,
Restez manne et serpent;
Ce que la chimère accumule
Bientût délaisse le refuge.

Meurent les yeux singuliers
Et la parole qui découvre.

The second cries out and escapes
Ambient bee and crimson limetree.
She's a day of constant wind,
Blue dice of combat, the watcher smiling
When his lyre plays: "What I want, will be."

It's the time for silence
Becoming the tower
The future envies.

The self-hunter flees his fragile house:
His prey follows him no longer fearful.

Their brightness is so high, their health so new,
That these two going off meaning nothing
Don't feel the sisters bring them back
With a long ashen gag to the white forests.

III

This child on your shoulder
Is your luck and your burden.
Earth where the orchid burns,
Don't tire him with yourself.

Remain frontier and flower,
Remain snake and manna;
What the chimera accumulates
Soon leaves the refuge behind

May the strange eyes die
And the word discovering.

René Char

La plaie qui rampe au miroir
Est maîtresse des deux bouges.

Violente l'épaule s'entrouvre;
Muet apparait le volcan.
Terre sur quoi l'olivier brille,
Tout s'évanouit en passage.

The wound cringing in the mirror
Is mistress of two dens.

Violent the shoulder opens;
Mute the volcano appears.
Land on which the olive burns,
All vanishes in passing.

—MAC

Char's note to "Three Sisters"

...."Three Fates are breathing on the fingers of the man they have desired to be a child. In vain:

Land on which the olive burns

Everything vanishes in passing...

The key remains quicksilver."

René Char   251

BIENS ÉGAUX

Je suis épris de ce morceau tendre de campagne, de son accoudoir de solitude au bord duquel les orages viennent se dénouer avec docilité, au mât duquel un visage perdu, par instant s'éclaire et me regagne. De si loin que je me souvienne, je me distingue penché sur les végétaux du jardin désordonné de mon père, attentif aux sèves, baisant des yeux formes et couleurs que le vent semi-nocturne irriguait mieux que la main infirme des hommes. Prestige d'un retour qu'aucune fortune n'offusque. Tribunaux de midi, je veille. Moi qui jouis du privilège de sentir tout ensemble accablement et confiance, défection et courage, je n'ai retenu personne sinon l'angle fusant d'une Rencontre.

Sur une route de lavande et de vin, nous avons marché côte à côte dans un cadre enfantin de poussière à gosier de ronces, l'un se sachant aimé de l'autre. Ce n'est pas un homme à tête de fable que plus tard tu baisait derrière les brumes de ton lit constant. Te voici nue et entre toutes la meilleure seulement aujourd'hui où tu franchis la sortie d'un hymne raboteux. L'espace pour toujours est-il cet absolu et scintillant congé, chétive volte-face? Mais prédisant cela j'affirme que tu vis; le sillon s'éclaire entre ton bien et mon mal. La chaleur reviendra avec le silence comme je te soulèverai, Inanimée.

EQUAL SHARES

I am in love with this tender patch of countryside, with its armrest of solitude, at whose edge storms come gently undone, on whose mast a lost face for an instant lights up and reaches me again. As far back as I can remember, I see myself bent over the plants in my father's disorderly garden, attentive to sap, my eyes embracing forms and colors that the faint nocturnal wind watered better than the feeble hand of man. Marvel of a return that no fortune offends. Noon tribunals, I keep watch. I who have the privilege of feeling at once uncertainty and confidence, defection and courage. I have held on to no one except the fusing angle of an Encounter.

On a road of lavender and wine, we walked side by side in a childhood setting of bramble-throated dust, knowing we were loved by one another. It is not a man with a head of fable that you kissed later behind the mists of your constant bed. Here you are, naked and of all the others the best, only today as you find your way out of a rough-hewn hymn. Is space forever this absolute and sparkling leave-taking, this frail about-face? But predicting that, I affirm that you live; the furrow lights up between your blessing and my pain. Heat will come back with silence as I lift you, Inanimate.

—MAC & NK

DONNERBACH MÜHLE

Hiver 1939

Novembre de brumes, entends sous le bois la cloche du dernier sentier franchir le soir et disparaître,

le voeu lointain du vent séparer le retour dans les fers de l'absence qui passe.

Saison d'animaux pacifiques, de filles sans méchanceté, vous détenez des pouvoirs que mon pouvoir contredit; vous avez les yeux de mon nom, ce nom qu'on me demande d'oublier.

Glas d'un monde trop aimé, j'entends les monstres qui piétinent sur une terre sans sourire. Ma soeur vermeille est en sueur. Ma soeur furieuse appelle aux armes.

La lune du lac prend pied sur la plage où le doux feu végétal de l'été descend à la vague qui l'entraîne vers un lit de profondes cendres.

> Tracée par le canon,
> — vivre, limite immense —
> la maison dans la forêt s'est allumée:
> Tonnerre, ruisseau, moulin.

Char's note to "Donnerbach Mühle"

During the winter of 1939, as an artilleryman on the Lower Rhine, boring myself to death behind the badly used guns, each of my leaves, preferably at night, led me and a comrade to the lake at Donnerbach Mühle, three kilometers from Struth, to

DONNERBACH MÜHLE

Winter 1939

November of mists, beneath the woods hear the bell of the final path as it leaps the evening and disappears,

the distant promise of the wind that separates our return to shackles from the absence passing by.

Seasons of peaceable animals, of girls without malice, you possess powers that my power contradicts; you have the eyes of my name, this name I am told to forget.

Funeral knell for a world too well-loved, I hear the monsters trampling the earth, unsmiling. My vermilion sister is bathed in sweat. My furious sister calls to arms.

The lake moon gets a footing on the beach where summer's soft vegetal fire falls on the waves that sweep it toward a bed of deepest ash.

> In the sights of the gun
> — to live, an immense limit —,
> the house in the forest has lit up:
> thunder, millstream, mill.

—NK

the forest ranger's house, where we partook of a frugal but delicious meal, served by the ranger couple. The return through the freezing air, voluptuous snow on the ground, amid fleeing herds of deer and wild boar, was a starry celebration.

René Char

255

HYMNE À VOIX BASSE

L'Hellade, c'est le rivage déployé d'une mer géniale d'où s'élancèrent à l'aurore le souffle de la connaissance et le magnétisme de l'intelligence, gonflant d'égale fertilité des pouvoirs qui semblèrent perpétuels; c'est plus loin, une mappemonde d'étranges montagnes : une chaîne de volcans sourit à la magie des héros, à la tendresse serpentine des déesses, guide le vol nuptial de l'homme, libre enfin de se savoir et de périr oiseau; c'est la réponse à tout, même à l'usure de la naissance, même aux détours du labyrinthe. Mais ce sol massif fait du diamant de la lumière et de la neige, cette terre imputrescible sous les pieds de son peuple victorieux de la mort mais mortel par évidence de pureté, une raison étrangère tente de châtier sa perfection, croit couvrir le balbutiement de ses épis.

O Grèce, miroir et corps trois fois martyrs, t'imaginer c'est te rétablir. Tes guérisseurs sont dans ton peuple et ta santé est dans ton droit. Ton sang incalculable, je l'appelle, le seul vivant pour qui la liberté a cessé d'être maladive, qui me brise la bouche, lui du silence et moi du cri.

HYMN IN A QUIET VOICE

The Hellades, the extended shore of an inspired sea, whence at dawn were launched the breath of knowledge and the magnetism of intelligence, swelling with an equal fertility from the powers which seemed perpetual; further off, a globe of strange mountains: a chain of volcanoes smiles at the magic of heroes, at the serpentine tenderness of goddesses, guides the nuptial flight of man, finally free to know himself and perish as a bird; it's the answer to everything, even to the wear and tear of birth, even to the detours of the labyrinth. But this massive ground made of the diamond of light and snow, this incorruptible earth under the feet of its people vanquishers of death but mortal by evidence of purity, a foreign reason tries to chastise its perfection, believes it covers over the stammering of its stalks.

Oh Greece, mirror and body thrice martyrs, to imagine you is to reestablish you. Your healers are in your people and your health in your right. Your incalculable blood, I call on it, the only living thing for which freedom has ceased to be morbid, which breaks my mouth apart, it of silence and myself of the cry.

—MAC

René Char

J'HABITE UNE DOULEUR

Ne laisse pas le soin de gouverner ton coeur à ces tendresses parentes de l'automne auquel elles empruntent sa placide allure et son affable agonie. L'oeil est précoce à se plisser. La souffrance connaît peu de mots. Préfère te coucher sans fardeau : tu rêveras du lendemain et ton lit te sera léger. Tu rêveras que ta maison n'a plus de vitres. Tu es impatient de t'unir au vent, au vent qui parcourt une année en une nuit. D'autres chanteront l'incorporation mélodieuse, les chairs qui ne personnifient plus que la sorcellerie du sablier. Tu condamneras la gratitude qui se répète. Plus tard, on t'identifiera à quelque géant désagrégé, seigneur de l'impossible.

Pourtant.

Tu n'as fait qu'augmenter le poids de ta nu Tu es retourné à la pêche aux murailles, à la canicule sans été. Tu es furieux contre ton amour au centre d'une entente qui s'affole. Songe à la maison parfaite que tu ne verras jamais monter. A quand la récolte de l'abîme? Mais tu as crevé les yeux du lion. Tu crois voir passer la beauté au-dessus de lavandes noires...

Qu'est-ce qui t'a hissé, une fois encore, un peu plus haut, sans te convaincre?

Il n'y a pas de siège pur.

THE PAIN I DWELL IN

Do not leave the task of governing your heart to those affections akin to autumn whose placid demeanor and whose affable death-pangs they borrow. Eyes are early in their narrowing. Suffering knows few words. Prefer to sleep unburdened: you will dream of the morrow and your bed will be light for you. You will dream that your house has window panes no longer. You are impatient to join with the wind, the wind rushing through a year in one night. Others will sing of the melodious embodying of substances, flesh personifying no longer other than an hourglass witchery. You will condemn gratitude repeating itself. Later they will identify you with some disaggregated giant, lord of the impossible.

However.

You have only increased the weight of your night. You have returned to high wall fishing, to the dog-days with no summer. You are raging against your love at the center of a frenzied understanding. Think of the perfect house you will never see built. When shall it be, the harvest of the abyss? But you have put out the eyes of the lion. You think you see beauty passing above the black lavender…

What has lifted you once again, slightly higher still, without convincing you?

There is no untainted seat.

—MAC

LE MUGUET

J'ai sauvegardé la fortune du couple. Je l'ai suivi dans son obscure loyauté. La vieillesse du torrent m'avait lu sa page de gratitude. Un jeune orage s'annonçait. La lumière de la terre me frôlait. Et pendant que se retraçait sur la vitre l'enfance du justicier (la clémence était morte), à bout de patience je sanglotais.

SEUIL

Quand s'ébranla le barrage de l'homme, aspiré par la faille géante de l'abandon du divin, des mots dans le lointain, des mots qui ne voulaient pas se perdre, tentèrent de résister à l'exorbitante poussée. Là se décida la dynastie de leur sens.

J'ai couru jusqu'à l'issue de cette nuit diluvienne. Planté dans le flageolant petit jour, ma ceinture pleine de saisons, je vous attends, ô mes amis qui allez venir. Déjà je vous devine derrière la noirceur de l'horizon. Mon âtre ne tarit pas de voeux pour vos maisons. Et mon bâton de cyprès rit de tout son coeur pour vous.

LILY OF THE VALLEY

I have preserved the fortune of the couple. I have followed it in its obscure faithfulness. The old age of the torrent had read me its page of gratitude. A young storm was brewing. The light of the earth was grazing me. And while the childhood of the justice-lover was retracing itself on the glass (clemency was dead), I was at the end of my patience, sobbing.

—MAC

THRESHOLD

When man's dam crumbled, sucked into the giant gap left by the abandonment of the divine, words in the distance, words that were determined not to drown, tried to resist the mighty push. There, the dynasty of meanings was decided.

I have run to the end of that diluvian night. Planted in the trembling early morning, my belt full of seasons, I await you, oh my friends who are going to come. I can already guess at you behind the dark of the horizon. My hearth is overflowing with good wishes for your houses. And my cypress staff laughs for you from the bottom of its heart.

—NK

L'EXTRAVAGANT

Il ne déplaçait pas d'ombre en avançant, traduisant une audace tôt consumée, bien que son pas fût assez vulgaire. Ceux qui, aux premières heures de la nuit, ratent, leur lit et le perdent ensuite de vue jusqu'au lendemain, peuvent être tentés par les similitudes. Ils cherchent à s'extraire de quelques pierres trop sages, trop chaudes, veulent se délivrer de l'emprise des cristaux à prétention fabuleuse, que la morne démarche du quotidien sécrète, aux lieux de son choix, avec des attouchements de suaire, Tel n'était ce marcheur que le voile du paysage lunaire, très bas, semblait ne pas gêner dans son mouvement. Le gel furieux effleurait la surface de son front sans paraître *personnel.* Une route qui s'allonge, un sentier qui dévie sont conformes à l'élan de la pensée qui fredonne. Par la nuit d'hiver fantatiquement propre parce qu'elle était commune à la généralité des habitants de l'univers qui ne la pénétraient pas, le dernier comédien n'allait plus exister. Il avait perdu tout lien avec le volume ancien des sources propices aux interrogations, avec les corps heureux qu'il s'était plu à animer auprès du sien lorsqu'il pouvait encore assigner une cime à son paisir, une neige à son talent. Aujourd'hui il rompait avec la tristesse devenue un objet aguerri, avec la frayeur du convenu. La terre avait faussé sa persuasion, la terre, de sa vitesse un peu courte, avec son imagination safranée, son usure crevassée par les actes des monstres. Personne n'aurait à l'oublier car l'utile ne l'avait pas assisté, ne l'avait pas dessiné en entier au regard des autres. Sur le plafond de chaux blanche de sa chambre, quelques oiseaux étaient passés mais leur éclair avait fondu dans son sommeil.

Le voile du paysage lunaire maintenant très haut déploie ses couleurs aromatiques au-dessus du personnage que je dis. Il sort éclairé du froid et tourne à jamais le dos au printemps qui n'existe pas.

THE EXTRAVAGANT ONE

He displaced no shadow in his advance, betraying an audacity soon burned out, although his step was rather commonplace. Those who miss their beds in the night's early hours and then lose sight of them until the morrow may be tempted by resemblances. They try to break away from stones too wise, too warm, wishing to escape from the hold of crystals of fabulous claim which daily usage secretes, in places of its choosing, with a shroud's light touch. Such was not this man who appeared to be unhindered by the low-hanging veil of the lunar landscape. The raging frost brushed his forehead lightly without seeming personal. A road extending, a path diverging are consistent with the forward thrust of thought humming. In the winter night miraculously clean, because it was common to those dwelling in the universe who did not penetrate into it, the last player would no longer exist. He had lost every tie with the ancient swell of springs favorable to questioning, with the joyous bodies he had pleased to quicken near his own when he could still assign a summit to his pleasure, a snowfall to his talent. Today he broke with sadness, now a thing inured, with the dread of the accepted. Earth had warped his belief, earth, with its somewhat limited pace, with its saffron-hued imagining, its attrition rifted with the acts of monsters. No one would have to forget him, for self-interest had never aided him, had never sketched him whole for another's gaze. Across the whitewashed ceiling of his room, birds had passed, but their flash had melted into his sleep.

The veil of the lunar landscape, now lifted high, unfolds its aromatic colors above this personage of whom I speak. He comes forth lit by the cold and forever turns his back on the springtime never there.

—MAC

René Char

PULVÉRIN

La nouvelle sincérité se débat dans la pourpre de la naissance. Diane est transfigurée. Partout où l'arche du soleil développe sa course, partout essaime le nouveau mal tolérant. Le bonheur est modifié. En aval sont les sources. Tout au-dessus chante la bouche des amants.

AFFRES, DÉTONATION, SILENCE

Le Moulin du Calavon. Deux années durant, une ferme de cigales, un château de martinets. Ici tout parlait torrent, tantôt par le rire, tantôt par les poings de la jeunesse. Aujourd'hui, le vieux réfractaire faiblit au milieu de ses pierres, la plupart mortes de gel, de solitude et de chaleur. À leur tour les présages se sont assoupis dans le silence des fleurs.

Roger Bernard: l'horizon des monstres était trop proche de sa terre.

Ne cherchez pas dans la montagne; mais si, à quelques kilomètres de là, dans les gorges d'Oppedette, vous rencontrez la foudre au visage d'écolier, allez à elle, oh, allez à elle et souriez-lui car elle doit avoir faim, faim d'amitié.

COAL DUST

Sincerity made new. Struggles in the crimson of birth. Diane is transfigured. Everywhere the arc of the sun unfolds its trajectory, there swarms the new and tolerant evil. Happiness is changed. Upstream are the springs. Even higher up sings the mouth of the lovers.

—MAC & PT

TORMENT, DETONATION, SILENCE

The Calavon Mill. Two years running, a farm for cicadas, a castle for swifts. Here everything spoke mountain stream, some-times with laughter, sometimes with the fists of youth. Today, the old rebel grows weak in the middle of its stones, most dead of frost, solitude and heat. In their turn the omens have dozed off in the silence of the flowers.

Roger Bernard: the monsters' horizon was too close to your earth.

Don't look on the mountain; but if, a few kilometers from there, in the Oppedette gorges, you meet the lightning with a schoolboy face, go to it, oh, go to it and smile, for it must be hungry, hungry for friendship.

—NK

JACQUEMARD ET JULIA

Jadis l'herbe, à l'heure où les routes de la terre s'accordaient dans leur déclin, élevait tendrement ses tiges et allumait ses clartés. Les cavaliers du jou au regard de leur amour et les châteaux de leurs bien-aimées comptaient autant de fenêtrés
que l'abîme porte d'orages légers.

Jadis l'herbe connaissait mille devises qui ne se contrariaient pas. Elle était la providence des visages baignés de larmes. Elle incantait les animaux, donnait asile à l'erreur. Son étendue était comparable au ciel qui a vaincu la peur du temps et allégi la douleur.

Jadis l'herbe était bonne aux fous et hostile ai bourreau. Elle convolait avec le seuil de toujours. Les jeux qu'elle inventait avaient des ailes à leursourire (jeux absous et également fugitifs). Elle n'était dure pour aucun de ceux qui perdant leur chemin souhaitent le perdre à jamais.

Jadis l'herbe avait établi que la nuit vaut moins que son pouvoir, que les sources ne compliquen pas à plaisir leur parcours, que la graine qui s'age nouille est déjà à demi dans le bec de l'oiseau. Jadis,terre et ciel se haïssaient mais terre et ciel vivaient.

L'inextinguible sécheresse s'écoule. L'homme est un étranger pour l'aurore. Cependant à la poursuite de la vie qui ne peut être encore imaginée, il y a des volontés qui frémissent, des murmures qui vont s'affronter et des enfants sains et saufs qui *découvrent*.

JACQUEMARD AND JULIA

Once the grass, at the hour when the roads of earth were harmonious in their decline, lifted its blades tenderly and turned on its lights. The horsemen of the day were born in the look of their love and the castles of their lovers contained as many windows as the abyss holds slight storms.

Once the grass knew a thousand devices not in contradiction. It was the providence of those faces bathed in tears. It enchanted the animals, lent shelter to error. Its expanse was comparable to the sky which has vanquished the fear of time and softened the suffering.

Once the grass was good to madmen and hostile to executioners. It wedded the threshold of always. The games it invented had wings to their smile (games absolved and just as fleeting). It was hard for none of those who, losing their way, hope to lose it forever.

Once the grass prescribed that night's worth is less than its power, that springs don't complicate their course lightly, that seed kneeling down is already half in the bird's beak. Once, earth and sky hated each other, but earth and sky were living.

The inexhaustible drought runs off. Man is a stranger to dawn. However, in pursuit of the life that can't yet be imagined, there are wishes trembling, murmurs about to join together, and children safe and sound, *discovering.*

—MAC

LE BULLETIN DES BAUX

Ta dictée n'a ni avènement ni fin. Souchetée seulement d'absences, de volets arrachés, de pures inactions.

Juxtapose à la fatalité la résistance à la fatalité. Tu connaîtras d'étranges hauteurs.

La beauté naît du dialogue, de la rupture du silence et du regain de ce silence. Cette pierre qui t'appelle dans son passé est libre. Cela se lit aux lignes de sa bouche.

La durée que ton coeur réclame existe ici en dehors de toi.

Oui et non, heure après heure, se réconcilient dans la superstition de l'histoire. La nuit et la chaleur, le ciel et la verdure se rendent invisibles pour être mieux sentis.

Les ruines douées d'avenir, les ruines incohérentes avant que tu n'arrives, homme comblé, vont de leurs parcelles à ton amour. Ainsi se voit promise et retirée à ton irritable maladresse la rose qui ferme le royaume.

La graduelle présence du soleil désaltère la tragédie. Ah! n'appréhende pas de renverser ta jeunesse.

BULLETIN FROM LES BAUX

Your dictation has neither advent nor end. Only marked with absences, torn-off shutters, pure inactions.

Juxtapose to fate the resistance to fate. You will know strange heights.

Beauty is born of dialogue, of the breaking of silence and the renewal of that silence. The stone that calls you into its past is free. That can be read in the lines of its mouth.

The duration that your heart demands exists here, outside of you.

Yes and no, hour after hour, are reconciled in the superstition of history. Night and heat, sky and vegetation become invisible in order to be better felt.

Ruins gifted with future, ruins incoherent before you arrived, stream from their smallest fragments toward your love, abundantly replenished man. Just so, the rose that closes the kingdom is promised and withdrawn from your irritable clumsiness.

The gradual presence of sun quenches the tragedy. Ah! do not be afraid to overturn your youth.

—NK

René Char

LE REQUIN ET LA MOUETTE

Je vois enfin la mer dans sa triple harmonie, la mer qui tranche de son croissant la dynastie des douleurs absurdes, la grande volière sauvage, la mer crédule comme un liseron.

Quand je dis : *j'ai levé la loi, j'ai franchi la morale, j'ai maillé le cœur,* ce n'est pas pour me donner raison devant ce pèse-néant dont la rumeur étend sa palme au delà de ma persuasion. Mais rien de ce qui m'a vu vivre et agir jusqu'ici n'est témoin alentour. Mon épaule peut bien sommeiller, ma jeunesse accourir. C'est de cela seul qu'il faut tirer richesse immédiate et opérante. Ainsi, il y a un jour de pur dans l'année, un jour qui creuse sa galerie merveilleuse dans l'écume de la mer, un jour qui monte aux yeux pour couronner midi. Hier la noblesse était déserte, le rameau était distant de ses bourgeons. Le requin et la mouette ne communiquaient pas.

O Vous, arc-en-ciel de ce rivage polisseur, approchez le navire de son espérance. Faites que toute fin supposée soit une neuve innocence, un fiévreux en-avant pour ceux qui trébuchent dans la matinale lourdeur.

THE SHARK AND THE SEAGULL

Finally I catch sight of the sea in its triple harmony, the sea whose crescent slices into the dynasty of absurd griefs, the great preserver of wild birds, the sea believing like a bindweed.

When I say: *I have liberated the law, I have gone past morality, I have buckled my heart,* it isn't to claim I am right before this scale of emptiness whose sound extends its palm beyond my conviction. But nothing of what has seen me live and act until now is around to bear witness. My shoulder may slumber, my youth may rush forth. From that alone wealth immediate and workable should be drawn. So there's one pure day in the year, one day that furrows its marvelous moulding in the foam of the sea, one day rising as high as the eyes to crown noontime. Yesterday nobility was wasteland, the branch was far from its buds. The shark and the seagull did not converse.

Oh rainbow of this shining shore, bring the ship close to its hope. Make every supposed goal find some new innocence, a feverish forwardness for those who are stumbling in the heaviness of morning.

—MAC

MARTHE

Marthe que ces vieux murs ne peuvent pas s'approprier, fontaine où se mire ma monarchie solitaire, comment pourrais-je jamais vous oublier puisque je n'ai pas à me souvenir de vous: vous êtes le présent qui s'accumule. Nous nous unirons sans avoir à nous aborder, à nous prevoir comme deux pavots font en amour une anémone géante.

Je n'entrerai pas dans votre coeur pour limiter sa mémoire. Je ne retiendrai pas votre bouche pour l'empêcher de s'entrouvrir sur le bleu de l'air et la soif de partir. Je veux être pour vous la liberté et le vent de la vie qui passe le seuil de toujours avant que la nuit ne devienne introuvable.

MARTHA

Martha whom these old walls cannot make their own, fountain mirroring my solitary monarchy, how could I forget you since I needn't remember you: you are the present accumulating. We will come together without having to approach each other or forewarn each other, as two poppies make in love one huge anemone.

I will not enter your heart to limit its memory. I will not possess your mouth to hinder it from opening to the blue of air, the thirst for leaving. I want to be freedom for you, and the wind of life that crosses the threshold of always before night turns unfindable.

—NK

René Char

SUZERAIN

Nous commençons toujours notre vie sur un crépuscule admirable. Tout ce qui nous aidera, plus tard, à nous dégager de nos déconvenues s'assemble autour de nos premiers pas.

La conduite des hommes de mon enfance avait l'apparence d'un sourire du ciel adressé à la charité terrestre. On y saluait le mal comme une incartade du soir. Le passage d'un météore attendrissait. Je me rends compte que l'enfant que je fus, prompt à s'éprendre comme à se blesser, a eu beaucoup de chance. J'ai marché sur le miroir d'une rivière pleine d'anneaux de couleuvre et de danses de papillons. J'ai joué dans des vergers dont la robuste vieillesse donnait des fruits. Je me suis tapi dans des roseaux, sous la garde d'êtres forts comme des chênes et sensibles comme des oiseaux.

Ce monde net est mort sans laisser de charnier. Il n'est plus resté que souches calcinées, surfaces errantes, informe pugilat et l'eau bleue d'un puits minuscule veillée par cet Ami silencieux.

La connaissance eut tôt fait de grandir entre nous. *Ceci n'est plus,* avais-je coutume de dire. *Ceci n'est pas,* corrigeait-il. *Pas* et *plus* étaient disjoints. Il m'offrait, à la gueule d'un serpent qui souriait, mon impossible que je pénétrais sans souffrir. D'où venait cet Ami? Sans doute, du moins sombre, du moins ouvrier des soleils. Son énergie que je jugeais grande éclatait en fougères patientes, humidité pour mon espoir. Ce dernier, en vérité, n'était qu'une neige de l'existence, l'affinité du renouveau. Un butin s'amoncelait, dessinant le littoral cruel que j'aurais un jour à parcourir. Le coeur de mon Ami m'entrait dans le coeur comme un trident, coeur souverain égaillé dans des conquêtes bientôt réduites en cendres, pour marquer combien la tentation se déprime chez qui s'établit, se rend. Nos confidences ne construiraient pas d'église; le mutisme reconduisait tous nos pouvoirs.

Il m'apprit à voler au-dessus de la nuit des mots, loin de l'hébétude des navires a l'ancre. Ce n'est pas le glacier qui nous importe

LIEGE LORD

We always begin our lives in an admirable twilight. Everything that will help us later to survive our dashed hopes gathers around our first steps.

The conduct of the men of my childhood looked like a celestial smile addressed to earthly charity. Evil was greeted as a sudden outburst of evening. The passage of a meteor kindled tenderness. I realize that the child I was, as quick to fall in love as to be hurt, had great luck. I trod the mirror of a river brimming with the coils of snakes and the dances of butterflies. I played in orchards whose robust old age yielded fruits. I took cover in reeds, under the protection of beings as strong as oaks and sensitive as birds.

This clear-cut world died without leaving behind it a charnel house. Nothing remained but calcinated stumps, wandering surfaces, disorganized fist fights, and the blue water of a tiny well, watched over by a silent Friend.

We quickly came to know each other. *This no longer exists,* I had a habit of saying. *This does not exist,* he would correct me. *Not* and *no longer* were distinct. With the jaws of a smiling snake, he offered me what I had found impossible, which I entered without suffering. Where did this Friend come from? No doubt from the least somber, least toiling of suns. His energy, which I thought huge, unfurled in patient ferns, moistening my hope. The latter was nothing more, in truth, than the snow of existence, an affinity with renewal. Spoils grew, outlining the cruel shores I would one day have to wander. My Friend's heart entered mine like a trident, a sovereign heart dispersed among conquests soon reduced to ashes, showing how temptation fades in those who settle, who give up. Our confidences would not establish any church; muteness escorted all our powers.

He taught me to soar above the night of words, far from the stupor of boats at anchor. It is not the glacier that matters to us,

René Char   275

mais ce qui le fait possible indéfiniment, sa solitaire vraisemblance. Je nouai avec des haines enthousiastes que j'aidai à vaincre puis quittai. (Il suffit de fermer les yeux pour ne plus être reconnu.) Je retirai aux choses l'illusion qu'elles produisent pour se préserver de nous et leur laissai la part qu'elles nous concèdent. Je vis qu'il n'y aurait jamais de femme pour moi dans MA ville. La frénésie des cascades, symboliquement, acquitterait mon bon vouloir.

J'ai remonté ainsi l'âge de la solitude jusqu'à la demeure suivante de L'HOMME VIOLET. Mais il ne disposait là que du morose état civil de ses prisons, de son expérience muette de persécuté, et nous n'avions, nous, que son signalement d'évadé.

but what renders it indefinitely possible, its reclusive credibility. I wrestled with passionate hatreds that I helped to vanquish, then left behind. (You can go unrecognized simply by closing your eyes.) I stripped from things the illusion they produce to preserve themselves from us, and left them the part they concede to us. I saw there would be no woman for me in MY city. The frenzy of waterfalls would demonstrate, symbolically, my good will.

In this way I climbed again the age of solitude, up to the next dwelling of the VIOLET MAN. But there he had at his disposal only the morose civil servants in his prisons, his mute and persecuted experience, and we ourselves had only his official description as a fugitive.

—NK

Char's note to "Liege Lord"

The stiffened silhouette of Jean-Pancrace Nouguier, the Gunsmith, who welcomed me on the threshold of his house, which one might have taken for a dream of Da Vinci's, when in fact it had been built by his own active hands. The strange nobility of this man, a former tree-pruner, whom a fall had left half-crippled, without, however, immobilizing or embittering him.

Still farther along: D. A. F. de Sade, the violet man, whose plaintive letters I was reading, letters written shortly before he died, at Charenton, to the notary Roze, the grandfather of my godmother Louise.

René Char

À LA SANTÉ DU SERPENT

I

Je chante la chaleur à visage de nouveau-né, la chaleur désespérée.

II

Au tour du pain de rompre l'homme, d'être la beauté du point du jour.

III

Celui qui se fie au tournesol ne méditera pas dans la maison. Toutes les pensées de l'amour deviendront ses pensées.

IV

Dans la boucle de l'hirondelle un orage s'informe, un jardin se construit.

V

Il y aura toujours une goutte d'eau pour durer plus que le soleil sans que l'ascendant du soleil soit ébranlé.

VI

Produis ce que la connaissance veut garder secret, la conaissance aux cent passages.

VII

Ce qui vient au monde pour ne rien troubler ne mérite ni égards ni patience.

VIII

Combien durera ce manque de l'homme mourant au centre de la création parce que la création l'a congédié?

HERE'S TO THE SNAKE!

I

I sing of heat with the face of a newborn, desperate heat.

II

It's bread's turn to break man, to be the beauty of dawn.

III

The one who relies on the sunflower will not be musing in the house. All the thoughts of love will become his thoughts.

IV

In the swoop of the swallow, a storm builds, a garden forms.

V

There'll always be a drop of water lasting longer than the sun without shaking the sun's ascendancy.

VI

Produce what knowledge wants to keep secret, knowledge with a hundred passages.

VII

What comes into being without troubling anything deserves neither attention nor patience.

VIII

How long will there be this lack of man dying in the center of creation, because creation has sent him away?

René Char

IX

Chaque maison était une saison. La ville ainsi se répétait. Tous les habitants ensemble ne connaissaient que l'hiver, malgré leur chair réchauffée, malgré le jour qui ne s'en allait pas.

X

Tu es dans ton essence constamment poète, constamment au zénith de ton amour, constamment avide de vérité et de justice. C'est sans doute un mal nécessaire que tu ne puisses l'être assidument dans ta conscience.

XI

Tu feras de l'âme qui n'existe pas un homme meilleur qu'elle.

XII

Regarde l'image téméraire où se baigne ton pays, ce plaisir qui t'a longtemps fui.

XIII

Nombreux sont ceux qui attendent que l'écueil les soulève, que le but les franchisse, pour se définir.

XIV

Remercie celui qui ne prend pas souci de ton remords. Tu es son égal.

XV

Les larmes méprisent leur confident.

XVI

Il reste une profondeur mesurable là où le sable subjugue la destinée.

IX

Every house was a season. So the town repeated itself. All the inhabitants together knew nothing but winter, despite their bodies warmed over, despite the day that did not leave.

X

You are in your essence constantly a poet, constantly at the height of your love, constantly avid of truth and justice. No doubt it's a necessary evil that you can't be such steadily in your consciousness.

XI

You'll make of the nonexistent soul someone who's its better.

XII

Look at the foolhardy image your country bathes in, this pleasure which has escaped you for ages.

XIII

Numerous are they who wait for the shoal to lift them up, for the goal to certify them, so as to define themselves.

XIV

Be grateful to the person who doesn't care about your remorse. You are his equal.

XV

Tears despise the one they confide in.

XVI

There remains a calculable depth where sand subjugates fate.

René Char

XVII

Mon amour, peu importe que je sois né : tu deviens visible à la place où je disparais.

XVIII

Pouvoir marcher sans tromper l'oiseau, du coeur de l'arbre à l'extase du fruit.

XIX

Ce qui t'accueille à travers le plaisir n'est que la gratitude mercénaire du souvenir. La présence que tu as choisie ne délivre pas d'adieu.

XX

Ne te courbe que pour aimer. Si tu meurs, tu aimes encore.

XXI

Les ténèbres que tu t'infuses sont régies par la luxure de ton ascendant solaire.

XXII

Néglige ceux aux yeux de qui l'homme passe pour n'être qu'une étape de la couleur sur le dos tourmenté de la terre. Qu'ils dévident leur longue remontrance. L'encre du tisonnier et la rougeur du nuage ne font qu'un.

XXIII

Il n'est pas digne du poète de mystifier l'agneau, d'investir sa laine.

XXIV

Si nous habitons un éclair, i1 est le coeur de l'éternel.

XXV

Yeux qui, croyant inventer le jour, avez éveillé le vent, que puis-je pour vous? Je suis l'oubli.

XVII

My beloved, it matters little that I've been born: you become visible just where I disappear.

XVIII

To be able to walk, without deceiving the bird, from the tree's heart to the fruit's ecstasy.

XIX

What welcomes you through pleasure is only the mercenary gratitude of memory. The presence you've chosen delivers no farewell.

XX

Don't bend over except to love. If you die, you keep on loving.

XXI

The shadows you steep in are ruled by the lewdness of your solar climb.

XXII

Ignore those in whose eyes a person is just a stage of color on the tormented back of the earth. Let them reel off their long remonstrance. The poker's ink and the cloud's crimson are of a piece.

XXIII

It's unworthy of the poet to mystify the lamb, to take on his wool.

XXIV

If we inhabit a lightning flash, it's the heart of the eternal.

XXV

Thinking you invented daytime, you eyes who awoke the wind, what can I do for you? I am forgetfulness.

René Char

XXVI

La poésie est de toutes les eaux claires celle qui s'attarde le moins
   aux reflets de ses ponts.

Poésie, la vie future à l'intérieur de l'homme requalifié.

XXVII

Une rose pour qu'il pleuve. Au terme d'innombrables années, c'est
ton souhait.

XXVI

Poetry is of all the clear waters the one which lingers least in the
reflections of its bridges.

Poetry, future life inside man newly qualified.

XXVII

A rose for it to rain. At the end of innumerable years, it's your
wish.

—MAC

L'ÂGE DE ROSEAU

Monde las de mes mystères, dans la chambre d'un visage, ma nuit est-elle prévue?

Cette terre pour navire, dominée par le cancer, démembrée par la torture, cette offense va céder.

Monde enfant des genoux d'homme, chapelet de cicatrices, aigrelette buissonnée, avec tant d'êtres probables, je n'ai pas été capable de faire ce monde impossible. Que puis-je réclamer!

CHANSON DU VELOURS À CÔTES

Le jour disait: "Tout ce qui peine m'accompagne, s'attache à moi, se veut heureux. Témoins de ma comédie, retenez mon pied joyeux. J'appréhende midi et sa flèche méritée. Il n'est de grâce a quérir pour prévaloir à ses yeux. Si ma disparition sonne votre élargissement, les eaux froides de l'été ne me recevront que mieux."

La nuit disait: "Ceux qui m'offensent meurent jeunes. Comment ne pas les aimer? Prairie de tous mes instants, ils ne peuvent me fouler. Leur voyage est mon voyage et je reste obscurité."

Il était entre les deux un mal qui les déchirait. Le vent allait de l'un à l'autre; le vent ou rien, les pans de la rude étoffe et l'avalanche des montagnes, ou rien.

THE AGE OF THE REED

World tired of my mysteries, in the room of a face, has my night been foreseen?

This earth as a ship, dominated by cancer, dismembered by torture, this offense is going to cease.

World child of human knees, rosary of scars, sourish in its bushes, with so many probable beings, I haven't been capable to make this world impossible. What can I complain of?

—MAC

CORDUROY SONG

Day said: "Everything that labors accompanies me, is attached to me, wishes to be happy. Witnesses of my comedy, retain my joyous foot. I fear high noon and its deserved arrow. No grace can be sought that might prevail in its eyes. If my disappearance tolls your release, the cold waters of summer will only receive me better."

Night said: "Those who offend me die young. How could I not love them? Meadow of all my instants, they cannot trample me. Their journey is my journey and I remain darkness."

There was between the two an affliction that tore them apart. The wind went from one to the other; the wind or nothing, the flaps of the rough cloth and the mountains' avalanche, or nothing.

—NK

René Char

LE MÉTÉORE DU 13 AOÛT

[Le Météore du 13 août]

À la seconde où tu m'apparus, mon coeur eut tout le ciel pour l'éclairer. Il fut midi à mon poème. Je sus que l'angoisse dormait.

[Novae]

Premier rayon qui hésite entre l'imprécation du supplice et le magnifique amour.

L'optimisme des philosophies ne nous est plus suffisant.

La lumière du rocher abrite un arbre majeur. Nous nous avançons vers sa visibilité.

Toujours plus large fiançailles des regards. La tragédie qui s'élabore jouira même de nos limites.

Le danger nous ôtait toute mélancholie. Nous parlions sans nous regarder. Le temps nous tenait unis. La mort nous évitait.

Alouettes de la nuit, étoiles, qui tournoyez aux sources de l'abandon, soyez progrès aux fronts qui dorment.

J'ai sauté de mon lit bordé d'aubépines. Pieds nus, je parle aux enfants.

[La lune change de jardin]

Où vais-je égarer cette fortune d'excréments qui m'escorte comme une lampe?

THE METEOR OF AUGUST 13th

[The Meteor of August 13th]

At the second you appeared to me, my heart had all the sky to light its way. It was my poem's noon. I knew that anguish was asleep.

[Novae]

First ray which hesitates between the curse of agony and magnificent love.

The optimism of philosophies is no longer enough for us.

The rock's light shelters a major tree. We go forward toward its visibility.

Ever deeper wedding of the eyes. The tragedy now unfolding will delight even in our limits.

Danger took from us all melancholy. We talked without looking at each other. Time held us, as one. Death avoided us.

Larks of the night, stars, who whirl at the wellsprings of abandon, be progress for sleeping foreheads.

I have leapt from my hawthorn-bordered bed. Barefoot, I talk to children.

[The Moon Changes Gardens]

Where am I going to scatter this fortune of excrement that escorts me like a lamp?

René Char

289

Hymnes provisoires! Hymnes contredits!

Folles, et, à la nuit, lumières obéissantes.

Orageuse liberté dans les langes de la foudre, sur la souveraineté du vide, aux petites mains de l'homme.

Ne t'étourdis pas de lendemains. Tu regardes l'hiver qui enjambe les plaies et ronge les fenêtres, et, sur la porche de la mort, l'inscrutable torture.

Ceux qui dorment dans la laine, ceux qui courent dans le froid, ceux qui offrent leur médiation, ceux qui ne sont pas ravisseurs faute de mieux, s'accordent avec le météore, ennemi du coq.

Illusoirement, je suis à la fois dans mon âme et hors d'elle, loin devant la vitre et contre la vitre, saxifrage éclaté. Ma convoitise est infinie. Rien ne m'obsède que le vie.

Étincelle nomade qui meurt dans son incendie.

Aime riveraine. Dépense ta vérité. L'herbe qui cache l'or de ton amour ne connaîtra jamais le gel.

Sur cette terre des périls, je m'émerveille de l'idolatrie de la vie.

Que ma présence qui vous cause énigmatique malaise, haine sans rémission, soit météore dans votre âme.

Un chant d'oiseau surprend la branche du matin.

Provisional hymns! Hymns contradicted!

Demented and—to the night—obedient lights.

Stormy freedom swaddled in lightning, above the sovereignty of the void, in man's small hands.

Don't anesthetize yourself with tomorrows. You watch winter, which strides over wounds and gnaws at the windows, and on death's porch, inscrutable torture.

Those who sleep in wool, those who run in the cold, those who offer their mediation, those who are not plunderers, for want of better, agree with the meteor, enemy of the cock.

My illusion is to be at once inside my soul and outside it, far in front of the windowpane and up against the windowpane, a split saxifrage. My desire is infinite. Nothing obsesses me but life.

Nomadic spark dying in its fire.

Love a river girl. Spend your truth. The grass that hides your love's gold will never know frost.

On this perilous earth, I marvel at life's idolatry.

May my presence, which causes you enigmatic uneasiness, unremitting hatred, be a meteor in your soul.

A birdsong surprises the morning's branch.

—NK

René Char

LYRE

Lyre sans bornes des poussières,
Surcroît de notre coeur.

LYRE

Boundless lyre of dust,
Superabundance of our heart.

—NK

LA FONTAINE NARRATIVE
(1947)

THE NARRATIVE FOUNTAIN
(1947)

FASTES

L'été chantait sur son roc préféré quand tu m'es apparue, l'été chantait à l'écart de nous qui étions silence, sympathie, liberté triste, mer plus encore que la mer dont la longue pelle bleue s'amusait à nos pieds.

L'été chantait et ton cœur nageait loin de lui. Je baisais ton courage, entendais ton désarroi. Route par l'absolu des vagues vers ces hauts pics d'écume où croisent des vertus meurtrières pour les mains qui portent nos maisons. Nous n'étions pas crédules. Nous étions entourés.

Les ans passèrent. Les orages moururent. Le monde s'en alla. J'avais mal de sentir que ton cœur justement ne m'apercevait plus. Je t'aimais. En mon absence de visage et mon vide de bonheur. Je t'aimais, changeant en tout, fidèle à toi.

Furor and Mystery

ANNALS

Summer was singing on its favorite rock when you appeared to me, summer was singing apart as we who were silence, sympathy, sorrowful freedom, were sea still more than the sea whose long blue spade was playing at our feet.

Summer was singing and your heart swam far from it.
I embraced your courage, heard your confusion. Road along the absolute of waves toward those high peaks of foam where virtues sail, murderous to hands bearing our houses. We were not credulous. We were surrounded.

The years passed by. The storms died down. The world went its way. I suffered to think it was your heart which no longer perceived me. I loved you. In my absence of visage and my emptiness of joy. I loved you, changing in every way, faithful to you.

—MAC

René Char

LA SORGUE

Chanson pour Yvonne

Rivière trop tôt partie, d'une traite, sans compagnon,
Donne aux enfants de mon pays le visage de ta passion.

Rivière où l'éclair finit et où commence ma maison,
Qui roule aux marches d'oubli la rocaille de ma raison.

Rivière, en toi terre est frisson, soleil anxiété.
Que chaque pauvre dans sa nuit fasse son pain de ta moisson.

Rivière souvent punie, rivière à l'abandon.

Rivière des apprentis à la calleuse condition,
Il n'est vent qui ne fléchisse à la crête de tes sillons.

Rivière de l'âme vide, de la guenille et du soupçon,
Du vieux malheur qui se dévide, de l'ormeau, de la compassion.

Rivière des farfelus, des fiévreux, des équarisseurs,
Du soleil lâchant sa charrue pour s'acoquiner au menteur.

Rivière des meilleurs que soi, rivière des brouillards éclos,
De la lampe qui désaltère l'angoisse autour de son chapeau.

Rivière des égards au songe, rivière qui rouille le fer,
Où les étoiles ont cette ombre qu'elles refusent à la mer.

Furor and Mystery

THE SORGUE

Song for Yvonne

River too soon gone, unswerving, unaccompanied,
Give to the children of my country the face of your passion.

River where the lightning ends and where my house begins,
That rolls the rubble of my reason around the steps of forgetting.

River, in you earth is trembling, sun disquietude.
May every pauper in his night bake his bread of your harvest.

River often punished, river neglected.

River of apprentices in calloused condition,
There is no wind that does not bend before your wave crests.

River of the empty soul, of tatters and suspicion,
Of the old sorrow told, of young elm, of compassion.

River of the feverish, the crackpot, of those who quarter carcasses,
Of sun abandoning its plough to cosy up to liars.

River of its betters, river of mists in bloom,
Of the lamp that quenches anguish around its shade.

River of respect for dreams, river that rusts iron,
In which stars cast the shadows they deny the sea.

René Char

Rivière des pouvoirs transmis et du cri embouquant les eaux,
De l'ouragon qui mord la vigne et annonce le vin nouveau.

Rivière au coeur jamais détruit dans ce monde fou de prison,
Garde-nous violent et ami des abeilles de l'horizon.

River of transmitted powers and cries coming into the channel,
Of the hurricane that nips the grapevine and announces the new
  wine.

River whose heart is never destroyed in this world mad for prison,
Keep us violent, a friend to the bees on the horizon.

—NK

René Char

TU AS BIEN FAIT DE PARTIR, ARTHUR RIMBAUD!

Tu as bien fait de partir, Arthur Rimbaud! Tes dix-huit ans réfractaires à l'amitié, à la malveillance, à la sottise des poètes de Paris ainsi qu'au ronronnement d'abeille stérile de ta famille ardennaise un peu folle, tu as bien fait de les éparpiller aux vents du large, de les jeter sous le couteau de leur précoce guillotine. Tu as eu raison d'abandonner le boulevard des paresseux, les estaminets des pisse-lyres, pour l'enfer des bêtes, pour le commerce des rusés et le bonjour des simples.

Cet élan absurde du corps et de l'âme, ce boulot de canon qui atteint sa cible en la faisant éclater, oui, c'est bien là la vie d'un homme! On ne peut pas, au sortir de l'enfance, indéfiniment étrangler son prochain. Si les volcans changent peu de place, leur lave parcourt le grand vide du monde et lui apporte des vertus qui chantent dans ses plaies.

Tu as bien fait de partir, Arthur Rimbaud! Nous sommes quelques-uns à croire sans preuve le bonheur possible avec toi.

LES PREMIERS INSTANTS

Nous regardions couler devant nous l'eau grandissante. Elle effaçait d'un coup la montagne, se chassant de ses flancs maternels. Ce n'était pas un torrent qui s'offrait à son destin mais une bête ineffable dont nous devenions la parole et la substance. Elle nous tenait amoureux sur l'arc tout-puissant de son imagination. Quelle intervention eût pu nous contraindre? La modicité quotidienne avait fui, le sang jeté était rendu à sa chaleur. Adoptés par l'ouvert, poncés jusqu'à l'invisible, nous étions une victoire qui ne prendrait jamais fin.

YOU WERE RIGHT TO LEAVE, ARTHUR RIMBAUD!

You were right to leave, Arthur Rimbaud! Your eighteen years resisting friendship, malice, the stupidity of Paris poets, and the buzzing of that sterile bee, your cracked Ardennes family—you were right to scatter all these to the four winds, flinging them beneath the blade of their precocious guillotine. You did well to walk away from the boulevard of the lazy, the bars of piss-poor lyres, for the inferno of the beasts, the commerce of the cunning, and the greeting of the simple.

That absurd burst of body and soul, that cannonball shattering its target on impact, yes, that's the life of a man! On leaving childhood, one cannot endlessly continue strangling his neighbor. If volcanos change place only slightly, their lava flows over the great void of the world and carries to it virtues that sing in its wounds.

You were right to leave, Arthur Rimbaud! We are a few who, without proof, believe happiness possible with you.

—NK

THE FIRST MOMENTS

We were watching the water as it flowed, increasing before us. It effaced the mountain suddenly, expelling itself from her maternal side. Not a torrent submitting to its fate but an ineffable beast whose word and substance we became. It held us amorous on the all-powerful arch of its imagination. What intervention could have constrained us? Daily tameness had fled, blood cast aside was rendered to its heat. Adopted by the open, abraded to invisibility, we were a victory that would never end.

—MAC

René Char

LE MARTINET

Martinet aux ailes trop larges qui vire et crie sa joie autour de la maison. Tel est le coeur.

Il dessèche le tonnerre. Il sème dans le ciel serein. S'il touche au sol il se déchire.

Sa repartie est l'hirondelle. Il déteste la familière. Que vaut dentelle de la tour?

Sa pause est au creux le plus sombre. Nul n'est plus à l'étroit que lui.

L'été de la longue clarté il filera dans les ténèbres par les persiennes de minuit.

Il n'est pas d'yeux pour le tenir. Il crie, c'est toute sa présence. Un mince fusil va l'abattre. Tel est le coeur.

THE SWIFT

Swift, whose wings are too wide, who spirals and cries out his joy around the house. Such is the heart.

He dries up the thunder. He sows in the quiet sky. If he touches the ground, he breaks.

The swallow is his counterpart. He detests her domesticity. What good is the tower's lace?

He will pause in the darkest crevice. None is more stringently lodged than he.

In the long brilliance of summer, he slips through the shutters of midnight into shadow.

No eyes can hold him. His presence is all in his cry. A slender gun is going to strike him down. Such is the heart.

—PT

René Char

MADELEINE À LA VEILLEUSE

par Georges de La Tour

Je voudrais aujourd'hui que l'herbe fût blanche pour fouler l'évidence de vous voir souffrir: je ne regarderais pas sous votre main si jeune la forme dure, sans crépi de la mort. Un jour discrétionnaire, d'autres pourtant moins avides que moi, retireront votre chemise de toile, occuperont votre alcôve. Mais ils oublieront en partant de noyer la veilleuse et un peu d'huile se répandra par le poignard de la flamme sur l'impossible solution.

MADELEINE WITH THE VIGIL-LAMP
by Georges de La Tour

I would wish today that the grass were white to trample the visible signs of your suffering: I'd not look under your hand, so young, at death's hard form without rough-cast. One discretionary day, others, though less avid than I, will remove your rough linen blouse, will occupy your alcove. But they will forget to extinguish the lamp in their departing and a little oil will spill out by the dagger of the flame onto the impossible solution.

—MAC

René Char

À UNE FERVEUR BELLIQUEUSE

Notre-Dame de Lumières qui restez seule sur votre rocher, brouillée avec votre église, favorable à ses insurgés, nous ne vous devons rien qu'un regard d'ici-bas.

Je vous ai quelquefois détestée. Vous n'étiez jamais nue. Votre bouche était sale. Mais je sais aujourd'hui que j'ai exagéré car ceux qui vous baisaient avaient souillé leur table.

Les passants que nous sommes n'ont jamais exigé que repos leur vint avant l'épuisement. Gardienne des efforts, vous n'êtes pas marquée, sinon du peu d'amour dont vous fûtes couverte.

Vous êtes le moment d'un mensonge éclairé, le gourdin encrassée, la lampe punissable. J'ai la tête assez chaude pour vous mettre en débris ou prendre votre main. Vous êtes sans défense.

Trop de coquins vous guettent et guettent votre effroi. Vous n'avez d'autre choix que la complicité. Le sévère dégoût que de bâtir pour eux, de devoir en retour leur servir d'affidée!

J'ai rompu le silence puisque tous sont partis et que vous n'avez rien qu'un bois de pins pour vous. Ah! courez à la route, faites-vous des amis, coeur enfant devenez sous le nuage noir.

Le monde a tant marché depuis votre venue qu'il n'est plus qu'un pot d'os, qu'un voeu de cruauté. Ô Dame évanouie, servante de hasard, les lumières se rendent où l'affamé les voit.

1943

Furor and Mystery

TO A WARLIKE ARDOR

Notre-Dame de Lumières remaining alone on your rock, at odds with your church, favoring its insurgents, we owe you nothing but a glance from here below.

I have sometimes detested you. You were never naked. Your mouth was dirty. But I know today that I exaggerated because those who kissed you had soiled their table.

The passersby we are have never required rest to come before exhaustion. Guardian of the efforts, you were not marked, except with the bit of love which covered you.

You are the moment of an inspired lie, filthy bludgeon, punishable lamp. I have a head hot enough to shatter you or to take your hand. You are without defense.

Too many rascals spy on you and spy on your fright. You have no other choice than complicity. What severe disgust to build for them, to have in turn to act as their confederate!

I have broken the silence because they've all left and you have nothing but a pine woods for you. Ah! Run to the road, make friends, become a heart child under the black cloud.

The world has advanced so much since your coming that it is only a pot of bones, a vow of cruelty. Oh Lady fainted away, servant of chance, the lights go where the famished person sees them.

1943

—MAC

René Char

ASSEZ CREUSÉ

Assez creusé, assez miné sa part prochaine. Le pire est dans chacun, en chasseur, dans son flanc. Vous qui n'êtes ici qu'une pelle que le temps soulève, retournez-vous sur ce que j'aime, qui sanglote à côté de moi, et fracassez-nous, je vous prie, que je meure une bonne fois.

ENOUGH

You've dug enough, undermined enough the part that comes next. The worst exists in each, a hunter, deep within. You who are only a shovel here, hefted by time, turn around and look at what I love, which lies beside me sobbing, and smash us to pieces, I beg you, let me die once and for all.

—NK

René Char

ALLÉGEANCE

Dans les rues de la ville il y a mon amour. Peu importe où il va dans le temps divisé. Il n'est plus mon amour, chacun peut lui parler. I1 ne se souvient plus; qui au juste l'aima?

Il cherche son pareil dans le vœu des regards. L'espace qu'il parcourt est ma fidélité. Il dessine l'espoir et léger l'éconduit. Il est prépondérant sans qu'il y prenne part.

Je vis au fond de lui comme une épave heureuse. A son insu, ma solitude est son trésor. Dans le grand méridien où s'inscrit son essor, ma liberté le creuse.

Dans les rues de la ville il y a mon amour. Peu importe où il va dans le temps divisé. Il n'est plus mon amour, chacun peut lui parler. Il ne se souvient plus; qui au juste l'aima et l'éclaire de loin pour qu'il ne tombe pas?

FIDELITY

In the streets of the town goes my love. Small matter where she moves in divided time. She is no longer my love, anyone may speak with her. She remembers no longer: who exactly loved her?

She seeks her equal in glances, pledging. The space she traverses is my faithfulness. She traces a hope and lightly dismisses it. She is dominant without taking part.

I live in her depth, a joyous shipwreck. Without her knowing, my solitude is her treasure. In the great meridian where her soaring is inscribed, my freedom delves deep in her.

In the streets of the town goes my love. Small matter where she moves in divided time. She is no longer my love, anyone may speak with her. She remembers no longer: who exactly loved her, and lights her from afar, lest she should fall?

—MAC

ALLEGIANCE

My dear one has gone into the streets of the city. It doesn't matter where, since time has been torn apart. Anyone can speak to my love, no longer mine, and shorn of memory; whose love was left behind?

Seeking to be mirrored in the vows of unknown eyes, moving through that space which is my loyalty, my love gives shape to the hope it casts away with scorn, always in the foreground, absent everywhere.

Happy to be shipwrecked within the depths of my love, who doesn't know its treasure is my solitude, my freedom hollows out the orbit of its flight, inscribing on the sky a curve of longitude.

My dear one has gone into the streets of the city. It doesn't matter where, since time has been torn apart. Anyone can speak to my love, no longer mine, and shorn of memory; whose love was left behind to light my dear one's steps lest they come to harm?

—PT

OTHER WRITINGS

LE MARTEAU SANS MAÎTRE

THE HAMMER WITH NO MASTER

ARTINE

Au silence de celle qui laisse rêveur.

Dans le lit qu'on m'avait préparé il y avait: un animal sanguinolent et meurtri, de la taille d'une brioche, un tuyau de plomb, une rafale de vent, un coquillage glacé, une cartouche tirée, deux doigts d'un gant, une tache d'huile; il n'y avait pas de porte de prison, il y avait le goût de l'amertume, un diamant de vitrier, un cheveu, un jour, une chaise cassée, un ver à soie, l'objet volé, une chaîne de pardessus, une mouche verte apprivoisée, une branche de corail, un clou de cordonnier, une roue d'omnibus.

Offrir au passage un verre d'eau à un cavalier lancé à bride abattue sur un hippodrome envahi par la foule suppose, de part et d'autre, un manque absolu d'adresse; Artine apportait aux esprits qu'elle visitait cette sécheresse monumentale.

L'impatient se rendait parfaitement compte de l'ordre des rêves qui hanteraient dorénavant son cerveau, surtout dans le domaine de l'amour où l'activité dévorante se manifestait couramment en dehors du temps sexuel; l'assimilation se développant, la nuit noire, dans les serres bien closes.

Artine traverse sans difficulté le nom d'une ville. C'est le silence qui détache le sommeil.

Les objets désignés et rassemblés sous le nom de nature-précise font partie du décor dans lequel se déroulent les actes d'érotisme des *suites fatales,* épopée quotidienne et nocturne. Les mondes imaginaires chauds qui circulent sans arrêt dans la campagne à l'époque des moissons rendent l'œil agressif et la solitude in-tolérable à celui qui dispose du pouvoir de destruction. Pour les

ARTINE (1930)

To the silence of one who leaves us dreaming.

In the bed prepared for me were: an animal bruised and slightly bleeding, no larger than a bun, a lead pipe, a gust of wind, an icy seashell, a spent cartridge, two fingers of a glove, a spot of oil; there was no prison door, rather the taste of bitterness, a glazier's diamond, one hair, one day, a broken chair, a silkworm, the stolen object, an overcoat chain, a tame green fly, a branch of coral, a cobbler's nail, a bus wheel.

To offer a glass of water to a horseman as he passes hurtling headlong on a racetrack invaded by the mob takes an absolute awkwardness on both sides; Artine brought to the minds she visited this monumental drought.

Impatient, he was perfectly aware of the order of dreams which would henceforth haunt his brain, especially in the realm of love whose devouring activities usually appeared in other than sexual moments; assimilation developing, through the dead of darkness, in hothouses closed tight.

Artine traverses effortlessly the name of a town. Silence unleashes sleep.

The objects described by and gathered under the name of *nature-précise*[1] form part of the setting for erotic acts bound to *fatal consequences,* an epic daily and nocturnal. Hot imaginary worlds circulating ceaselessly in the countryside at harvest-time render the eye aggressive and solitude intolerable to the wielder of

[1] Here the term plays on "nature morte" or still-life.

extraordinaires bouleversements il est tout de même préférable de s'en remettre entièrement à eux.

L'état de léthargie qui précédait Artine apportait les éléments indispensables à la projection d'impressions saisissantes sur l'écran de ruines flottantes: édredon en flammes précipité dans l'insondable gouffre de ténèbres en perpétuel mouvement.

Artine gardait en dépit des animaux et des cyclones une intarissable fraîcheur. A la promenade, c'était la transparence absolue.

A beau surgir au milieu de la plus active dépression l'appareil de la beauté d'Artine, les esprits curieux demeurent des esprits furieux, les esprits indifférents des esprits extrêmement curieux.

Les apparitions d'Artine dépassaient le cadre de ces contrées du sommeil, où le *pour* et le *pour* sont animés d'une égale et meurtrière violence. Elles évoluaient dans les plis d'une soie brûlante peuplée d'arbres aux feuilles de cendre.

La voiture à chevaux lavée et remise à neuf l'emportait presque toujours sur l'appartement tapissé de salpêtre lorsqu'il s'agissait d'accueillir durant une soirée interminable la multitude des ennemis mortels d'Artine. Le visage de bois mort était particulièrement odieux. La course haletante de deux amants au hasard des grands chemins devenait tout à coup une distraction suffisante pour permettre au drame de se dérouler, derechef, à ciel ouvert.

Quelquefois une manœuvre maladroite faisait tomber sur la gorge d'Artine une tête qui n'était pas la mienne. L'énorme bloc de soufre se consumait alors lentement, sans fumée, présence en soi et immobilité vibrante.

destructive power. For extraordinary upheavals, however, it is preferable to rely altogether upon them.

The lethargic state preceding Artine added what was indispensable to the projection of striking impressions onto the screen of floating ruins: eiderdown in flames cast into the unfathomable abyss of perpetually moving shadows.

In spite of animals and cyclones, Artine retained an inexhaustible freshness. On outings, this was the most absolute transparency.

From the most active depression, the array of Artine's beauty may arise, but the curious minds remain nevertheless furious, the indifferent minds extremely curious.

Artine's appearances went past the border of those countries of sleep where the *for* and the *for* are endowed with an equal and murderous violence. They occurred in the folds of a burning silk peopled with ashen-leaved trees.

Washed and renovated, the horse-drawn chariot nearly always won out over the saltpeter-papered apartment playing host for an interminable evening to the multitude of Artine's mortal enemies. The dead-wood face was particularly odious. The breathless race of two lovers at random along the highways suddenly became a diversion sufficient for a dramatic unfolding thereupon, out in the open air.

Sometimes, a careless movement caused a head other than mine to sink on Artine's breast. The enormous sulphur block consumed its substance slowly and smoke-lessly, presence in itself vibrating motionless.

Le livre ouvert sur les genoux d'Artine était seulement lisible les jours sombres. A intervalles irréguliers les héros venaient apprendre les malheurs qui allaient à nouveau fondre sur eux, les voies multiples et terrifiantes dans lesquelles leur irréprochable destinée allait à nouveau s'engager. Uniquement soucieux de la Fatalité, ils étaient pour la plupart d'un physique agréable. Ils se déplaçaient avec lenteur, se montraient peu loquaces. Ils exprimaient leurs désirs à l'aide de larges mouvements de tête imprévisibles. Ils paraissaient en outre s'ignorer totalement entre eux.

The book open on Artine's knees could be read only on overcast days. At irregular intervals heroes would come to learn the calamities once more to befall them, and in what numerous and fearful directions their irreproachable fate would start out afresh. Concerned only with Fatality, they presented for the most part an agreeable appearance. They moved about slowly and were not loquacious. They expressed their desires in broad unforeseeable motions of their heads. Moreover, they seemed to be utterly unconscious of each other.

The poet has slain his model.

—MAC

Char's footnote to Artine:

The accompanying text for Artine was written by André Breton and Paul Eluard, in December of 1930, in Breton's apartment at 42, rue Fontaine in Paris, as an ad in a Parisian newspaper:

> *Unseen women, watch out!*
> *POET SEEKS model for poems. Sittings exclus, during sleep René Char, 8 ter, rue des Saules, Paris. (Usel. Come before compl. Night. Light is fatal to me.)*

....

WHO HAS SEEN, André Breton and Paul Eluard are asking, who has seen OUR FRIEND René Char since he found a mod. woman for a poem, a woman he dreamed of, a beautiful woman forbid. him to wake up? The woman was as dang. for the poet as the poet for the woman. We left them at the edge of a precip. No one. Who can tell us where this vanished perfume is leading us?

This is where ARTINE by René Char is placed. (Editions surréalistes.)

COURBET: LES CASSEURS DE CAILLOUX

Sable paille ont la vie douce le vin ne s'y brise pas
Du colombier ils récoltent les plumes
De la goulotte ils ont la langue avide
Ils retardent l'orteil des filles
Dont ils percent les chrysalides
Le sang bien souffert tombe dans l'anecdote de leur légèreté

Nous dévorons la peste du feu gris dans la rocaille Quand on
    intrigue à la commune
C'est encore sur les chemins ruinés qu'on est le mieux Là les
    tomates des vergers l'air nous les porte au
      crépuscule
Avec l'oubli de la méchanceté prochaine de nos femmes
Et l'aigreur de la soif tassée aux genoux

Fils cette nuit nos travaux de poussière
Seront visibles dans le ciel
Déjà l'huile du plomb ressuscite.

COURBET: THE STONE-BREAKERS

Sand, straw, have an easy life, wine doesn't shatter in them
They gather feathers from the dovecote
Their tongue is eager for the gullet
They slow the girl's toes going
Whose chrysalids they pierce
Blood fitly suffered falls in talkative lightness

In the rock we devour the gray fire's plague
When gossip spreads in the commune
We fare even better on ruined paths
There, a breeze brings us orchard tomatoes at twilight
A disregard for our wives' next nastiness
And thirst's sharp taste amassed in our knees

Son, tonight, our works of dust
Will be visible in the sky
Already oil returns to life from lead.

—MAC

René Char

LES MATINAUX

THE MORNING ONES

BANDEAU DES MATINAUX

Premiers levés qui ferez glisser de votre bouche le bâillon d'une inquisition insensée — qualifiée de connaissance — et d'une sensibilité exténuée, illustration de notre temps, qui occuperez tout le terrain au profit de la seule vérité poétique constamment aux prises, elle, avec l'imposture, et indéfiniment révolutionnaire, à vous.

1950

ABOUT THE MORNING ONES

You, the first to rise, who will slip from your mouth the gag of a mad inquisition—said to be knowledge—and of an exhausted sensitivity, an illustration of our moment, who will occupy all the terrain to profit the only poetic truth, constantly in a struggle with imposture, and indefinitely revolutionary, here's to you.

1950

—MAC

René Char

COMPLAINTE DU LÉZARD AMOUREUX

N'égraine pas le tournesol,
Tes cyprès auraient de la peine,
Chardonneret, reprends ton vol
Et reviens à ton nid de laine.

Tu n'es pas un caillou du ciel
Pour que le vent te tienne quitte,
Oiseau rural; l'arc-en-ciel
S'unifie dans la marguerite.

L'homme fusille, cache-toi;
Le tournesol est son complice.
Seules les herbes sont pour toi,
Les herbes des champs qui se plissent.

Le serpent ne te connaît pas,
Et la sauterelle est bougonne;
La taupe, elle, n'y voit pas;
Le papillon ne hait personne.

Il est midi, chardonneret.
Le seneçon est là qui brille.
Attarde-toi, va, sans danger:
L'homme est rentré dans sa famille!

L'écho de ce pays est sûr.
J'observe, je suis bon prophète;

COMPLAINT OF THE LIZARD IN LOVE

Let the sunflower keep its seeds—
Your cypress trees would be distressed,
Goldfinch, spread your wings again,
Go back to your woolly nest.

Were you a pebble from the sky,
The wind would acquit you for your flight,
Country bird; the rainbow's hues
Will, in the daisy, all unite.

Man would shoot you down—watch out!
The sunflower is on his side;
Only the grass belongs to you,
The folding grass where you can hide.

The snake will not know who you are,
From grasshoppers talk is hard won;
As for moles, they cannot see;
Butterflies don't hate anyone.

Little goldfinch, now it's noon.
The ragwort's yellow flame shines clear.
It's safe for you to linger here—
The man's gone home to his dining-room.

Trust the echo of this land.
From my low wall I spy on fate;

René Char

Je vois tout de mon petit mur,
Même tituber la chouette.

Qui, mieux qu'un lézard amoureux,
Peut dire les secrets terrestres?
O léger gentil roi des cieux,
Que n'as-tu ton nid dans ma pierre!

Orgon, aout 1947

Nothing will escape my eye:
Sometimes the owl can't fly straight!

To tell the secrets of the land
A lizard who's in love is best.
Oh! weightless, worthy king of the skies,
Couldn't you use my stone for your nest?

Orgon, August 1947

—PT

QU'IL VIVE!

Ce pays n'est qu'un vœu de l'esprit, un contre-sépulcre.

Dans mon pays, les tendres preuves du printemps et les oiseaux mal habillés sont préférés aux buts lointains.

La vérité attend l'aurore à côté d'une bougie. Le verre de fenêtre est négligé. Qu'importé à l'attentif.

Dans mon pays, on ne questionne pas un homme ému.

Il n'y a pas d'ombre maligne sur la barque chavirée.

Bonjour à peine, est inconnu dans mon pays.

On n'emprunte que ce qui peut se rendre augmenté.

Il y a des feuilles, beaucoup de feuilles sur les arbres de mon pays. Les branches sont libres de n'avoir pas de fruits.

On ne croit pas à la bonne foi du vainqueur.

Dans mon pays, on remercie.

LONG LIVE!

This country is only a wish of the spirit, a counter-sepulchre.

In my country, tender proofs of spring and badly-dressed birds are preferred to far-off goals.

Truth waits for dawn beside a candle. Window-glass is neglected. To the watchful, what does it matter?

In my country, we don't question a person deeply moved.

There is no malignant shadow on the capsized boat.

A cool greeting is unknown in my country.

We borrow only what can be returned increased.

There are leaves, many leaves, on the trees of my country. The branches are free to bear no fruit.

We don't believe in the good faith of the victor.

In my country, we say thank you.

—MAC

René Char

335

MONTAGNE DÉCHIRÉE

Oh! la toujours plus rase solitude
Des larmes qui montent aux cimes.

Quand se déclare la débâcle
Et qu'un vieil aigle sans pouvoir
Voit revenir son assurance,
Le bonheur s'élance à son tour,
A flanc d'abîme les rattrape.

Chasseur rival, tu n'as rien appris,
Toi qui sans hâte me dépasses
Dans la mort que je contredis.

Le Rébanqué, Lagnes, 29 aout 1949

TORN MOUNTAIN

Oh! the ever starker solitude
Of tears that mount the peaks.

When the ice first cracks
And an old eagle without power
Feels his confidence come back,
Happiness in its turn soars up
To catch them at the edge of the abyss.

Rival hunter, you've learned nothing,
You who without haste outdistance me
In the death I contradict.

Le Rébanqué, Lagnes, August 29, 1949

—NK

René Char

LE CARREAU

Pures pluies, femmes attendues,
La face que vous essuyez,
De verre voué aux tourments,
Est la face du révolté;
L'autre, la vitre de l'heureux,
Frissonne devant le feu de bois.

Je vous aime mystères jumeaux,
Je touche à chacun de vous;
J'ai mal et je suis léger.

L'AMOUREUSE EN SECRET

Elle a mis le couvert et mené à la perfection ce à quoi son amour assis en face d'elle parlera bas tout à l'heure, en la dévisageant. Cette nourriture semblable à l'anche d'un hautbois.

Sous la table, ses chevilles nues caressent à présent la chaleur du bien-aimé, tandis que des voix qu'elle n'entend pas la complimentent. Le rayon de la lampe emmêle, tisse sa distraction sensuelle.

Un lit, très loin, sait-elle, patiente et tremble dans l'exil des draps odorants, comme un lac de montagne qui ne sera jamais abandonné.

WINDOWPANE

Pure rains, awaited women,
The face you graze,
Of glass doomed to torment,
Is the rebel's face;
The other, the happy windowpane,
Shivers before the wood fire.

I love you, twin mysteries,
I touch on each of you;
I hurt and I am weightless.

—NK

THE WOMAN SECRETLY IN LOVE

She has set the table and brought to perfection all that her love, seated across from her, will soon respond to quietly, watching her face. This food like the reed of an oboe.

Under the table, her naked ankles now caress the warmth of the beloved, while voices she does not hear compliment her. The ray of lamplight tangles, weaves her sensual distraction.

A bed faraway, she knows, waits and trembles in the exile of its fragrant sheets, like a country lake that will never be abandoned.

—NK

L'ADOLESCENT SOUFFLETÉ

Les mêmes coups qui l'envoyaient au sol le lançaient en même temps loin devant sa vie, vers les futures années où, quand il saignerait, ce ne serait plus à cause de l'iniquité d'un seul. Tel l'arbuste que réconfortent ses racines et qui presse ses rameaux meurtris contre son fût résistant, il descendait ensuite à reculons dans le mutisme de ce savoir et dans son innocence. Enfin il s'échappait, s'enfuyait et devenait souverainement heureux. Il atteignait la prairie et la barrière des roseaux dont il cajolait la vase et percevait le sec frémissement. Il semblait que ce que la terre avait produit de plus noble et de plus persévérant, l'avait, en compensation, adopté.

Il recommencerait ainsi jusqu'au moment où, la nécessité de rompre disparue, il se tiendrait droit et attentif parmi les hommes, à la fois plus vulnérable et plus fort.

THE ADOLESCENT CHASTISED

The same blows that cast him to the ground projected him at once far ahead into his life, toward the future years when, wounded, he would no longer bleed from the iniquity of one being. Like the bush solaced by its roots, pressing its bruised boughs against its resistant bole, he would then descend backward into the silence of this knowledge and into its innocence. At last he escaped fleeing, and attained a sovereign happiness. He reached the meadow and the barrier of reeds whose slime he coaxed and whose dry quivering he watched. It seemed that the noblest and most enduring things that the earth had brought forth had, in compensation, adopted him.

Thus he would start again until, no longer needing to break off the battle, he could hold himself upright and attentive among men, more vulnerable and yet stronger.

—MAC

René Char

ANOUKIS ET PLUS TARD JEANNE

Je te découvrirai à ceux que j'aime, comme un long éclair de chaleur, aussi inexplicablement que tu t'es montrée à moi, Jeanne, quand, un matin s'astreignant à ton dessein, tu nous menas de roc en roc jusqu'à cette fin de soi qu'on appelle un sommet. Le visage à demi masqué par ton bras replié, les doigts de ta main sollicitant ton épaule, tu nous offris, au terme de notre ascension, une ville, les souffrances et la qualification d'un génie, la surface égarée d'un désert, et le tournant circonspect d'un fleuve sur la rive duquel des bâtisseurs s'interrogeaient. Mais je te suis vite revenu, Faucille, car tu consumais ton offrande. Et ni le temps, ni la beauté, ni le hasard qui débride le coeur ne pouvaient se mesurer avec toi.

J'ai ressuscité alors mon antique richesse, notre richesse à tous, et dominant ce que demain détruira, je me suis souvenu que tu étais Anoukis l'Etreigneuse, aussi fantastiquement que tu étais Jeanne, la soeur de mon meilleur ami, et aussi inexplicablement que tu étais l'Etrangère dans l'esprit de ce misérable carillonneur dont le père répétait autrefois que Van Gogh était fou.

Saint-Rémy-des-Alpilles, 18 septembre 1949

ANOUKIS AND LATER JEANNE

I will unveil you to those I love, like a long stroke of summer lightning, as inexplicably as you showed yourself to me, Jeanne, on a morning made to your design when you led us from rock to rock up to that end of self we call a summit. Your face half-masked by the arm you bent, the fingers of your hand seeking your shoulder, you offered us at the end of our ascent a city, the sufferings and qualifications of a genius, the scattered surface of a desert, and the circumspect turning of a river, on whose bank some builders stood questioning. But quickly I came back to you, my Reaper, for you were consuming your offering. And neither time, nor beauty, nor the luck that unbridles the heart could compare with you.

It was then I revived my ancient wealth, the wealth of all of us, and dominating what tomorrow will destroy, I remembered you were Anoukis the Clasper, just as incredibly as you were Jeanne, my best friend's sister, and as inexplicably as you were the Foreigner to that miserable bell-ringer whose father always used to say Van Gogh was crazy.

Saint-Rémy-des-Alpilles, September 18, 1949

—NK

RECOURS AU RUISSEAU

Sur l'aire du courant, dans les joncs agités, j'ai retracé ta ville. Les maçons au large feutre sont venus; ils se sont appliqués à suivre mon mouvement. Ils ne concevaient pas ma construction. Leur compétence s'alarmait.

Je leur ai dit que, confiante, tu attendais proche de là que j'eusse atteint la demie de ma journée pour connaître mon travail. A ce moment, notre satisfaction commune l'effacerait, nous le recommencerions plus haut, identiquement, dans la certitude de notre amour. Railleurs, ils se sont écartés. Je voyais, tandis qu'ils remettaient leur veste de toile, le gravier qui brillait dans le ciel du ruisseau et dont je n'avais, moi, nul besoin.

LES LICHENS

Je marchais parmi les bosses d'une terre écurée, les haleines secrètes, les plantes sans mémoire. La montagne se levait, flacon empli d'ombre qu'étreignait par instant le geste de la soif. Ma trace, mon existence se perdaient. Ton visage glissait à reculons devant moi. Ce n'était qu'une tache à la recherche de l'abeille qui la ferait fleur et la dirait vivante. Nous allions nous séparer. Tu demeurerais sur le plateau des arômes et je pénétrerais dans le jardin du vide. Là, sous la sauvegarde des rochers, dans la plénitude du vent, je demanderais à la nuit véritable de disposer de mon sommeil pour accroître ton bonheur. Et tous les fruits t'appartiendraient.

RECOURSE TO THE STREAM

On the surface of the current, among the quivering rushes,
I retraced your town. The masons came with their broad felt hats;
they endeavored to follow my movement. They could make no
sense of my plan. Their competence took fright.

I told them that, confident, you were awaiting nearby for me
to finish half my day so as to know of my work. At that moment,
our common satisfaction effacing it, we would begin it again un-
changed, higher up, in the certainty of our love. Scoffing, they
withdrew. I saw, as they donned once more their jackets of heavy
cloth, the gravel sparkling in the sky of the stream, of which I, for
my part, had no need.

—MAC

THE LICHENS

I walked among the hummocks of a land scoured bare, the
secret breaths, the plants without memory. The mountain rose
up, a shadow-filled flask embraced now and again by the gesture
of thirst. My track, my existence were slowly fading. Your face
slipped away retreating in front of me. It was only a spot in search
of the bee that would make of it a flower and call it alive. We were
going to separate. You would remain on the high plain of scents
and I would enter the garden of the void. There, in the safekeeping
of rocks, in the wind's fullness, I would place my sleep at the
disposition of the true night for it to deepen your happiness.
And all the fruits would be yours by right.

—MAC

René Char

LA PAROLE EN ARCHIPEL
(1952–1960)

THE WORD AS ARCHIPELAGO
(1952–1960)

LETTERA AMOROSA

DEDICATION

Non è già part'in voi che con forz' invin-
cibile d'amore tutt' a se non mi tragga.
MONTEVERDI, *Lettera amorosa.*

Time shored-up, years of affliction… Natural law! Once again they will grant existence, despite themselves, to the Work universally admired.

I cherish you. Soon bereft is he who would presume not to believe in woman, like the hornet at grips with his less and less spacious skill. I cherish you while the heavy pinnace of death changes course.

"It was, blessèd world, in a month of thirsting Eros that she lit up the structure of my being, the conch of her belly: I intermingled them forever. And it was in an instant of my understanding that she changed the blurred and straying path of my destiny into a luminous, sun-haloed road, for the furtive bliss of this earth of lovers."

*

The heart suddenly deprived, the desert's
host becomes almost legibly the fortunate heart,
the heart amplified, the diadem.

I don't have any more fever this morning. My head is clear and vacant again, resting like a rock on an orchard in its own image. The wind that came out of the north yesterday makes the bruised flanks of the trees quiver here and there.

René Char

I sense that this place owes to you a less distrustful sensibility and different eyes from those through which it looked at all things formerly. You've left, but you remain under these changed circumstances since it and I are hurting. To reassure you, in my mind, I've called off possible visitors, along with the attendant tasks and exchange of ideas. I am resting, as you say I must. I often go into the mountains to sleep. It is then that aided by nature, benevolent just now, I escape the splinters stuck into my flesh, old accidents, violent assaults.

Will you be able to tolerate so breathless a man close against you?

Moons and night, you are a wolf of black velvet, a village, watching over my love.

"Look hard at your eyelids," my mother used to say, bent over me as I was drifting into schoolboy sleep. I would see a little floating pebble, sometimes indolent, sometimes shrill, a worn stone to grow green in the grass. I used to cry. I would have wished it in my soul, and only there.

Song of Insomnia:

At love's summons she will come, the Lover,
Gloria of summer, oh fruits!
The arrow of the sun will move across her lips,
The naked clover curling on her flesh
Like miniature iris, orchid,
Oldest gift of pleasure's meadows
That the waterfall distills, the mouth releases.

I'd like to slip into a forest where the plants would clasp and close behind us, a forest many hundreds of years old, but it hasn't yet been sown. Painful in one's short life to have passed beside the fire with the hands of a sponge fisherman. "Two sparks, your grandmothers," mocks time's alto, pitilessly.

My song of praise spirals around the curls on your forehead, like a straight-beaked hawk.

Autumn! The park counts out its very different trees. This one russet, as always; that other, at road's end, a bubbling-up of thorns. The robin has arrived, the country's gentle lute. The drops of his song fall on the windowpane. The lawn's deep grass is shuddering with the magic murders of insects. Listen, but don't understand.

Sometimes I think it would be good to drown at the surface of a pond where no boat would risk sailing. Then come back to life amidst the current of a cataract where your colors bubbled.

What encloses the city where you're kept must crack. Wind, wind, wind around the trunks and on the thatch.

I raised my eyes to the window of your room. Did you take everything away? It is only a snowflake that melts on my eyelid. Ugly season, when we think we feel regret, or we make plans, while really we grow apathetic.

The air that I can always feel about to fail most beings, if it flows through you has a profusion and a sparkling ease.

I laugh marvelously with you. There's our extraordinary luck.

Absent wherever someone absent is celebrated.

I can only be and only want to live in the spaciousness and freedom of my love. Together, we are not the product of a signed surrender nor cause for an even more depressing servitude. That's why the guerrilla warfare we engage in, mischievously, one against the other, is above reproach.

You are pleasure, each wave separated from the one that follows. Finally, all charge at once. It is the sea creating itself, inventing itself. You are pleasure, coral of spasms.

Who hasn't dreamed, while strolling city boulevards, of a world that would begin not with the word, but with intentions?

Our words are slow to come to us, as though—separated—they contained enough sap to remain closed all one winter; or better, as if at each end of the silent distance, taking aim at one another, they were not permitted to spring forth and join. Our voices flow between us; but every avenue, every arbor, every patch of undergrowth attracts them, holds them, questions them. Everything serves as a pretext for their lingering.
Often I speak only for you, so the earth will forget me.

After the wind it was always more beautiful, even though nature's sorrow continued.

I've just come home. I walked for a long time. You are the Continual. I make a fire. I sit down in the curative armchair. Within the folds of the barbarous flames, my weariness climbs in its turn. Kindly transformation alternating with funereal.

Outside, the painless day drags by, which the willow switches give up thrashing. Above them are the woods' moderation, torn by dogs barking and the hunter's cry.

The ark belonging to us all, most perfect, a shipwreck in the very moment it is decked with flags. In its debris and dust, man with a newborn's head quickens again. Already half-liquid, half-flower.

The earth roars like a tiger, nights when the birds are coupling. A conspiracy of dead branches couldn't withstand it.

If there were only us on earth, my love, we would be without accomplices, without allies. Ingenuous forerunners or stupefied survivors.

My apprenticeship in life—several fights whose endings settled nothing, though their aims were valid—has taught me to look at the human person beneath that angle of the sky whose stormy blue becomes him most.

Mouth wide-open, a hunger for something better than light (more deeply notched, more gripping) breaks loose from its chains.

He who watches over pleasure's summit is the equal of the sun, as of the night. He who keeps watch has no wings, he does not pursue.

I open the door to your room. Our games sleep here. Placed by your own hand. Hardened blazons, this morning, like the honey of the cherry tree.

My exile is enclosed in hail. My exile climbs its tower of patience. Why does the sky curve like a vault?

There are certain places where the rare soul suddenly exults. Surrounded only by indifferent space. There, it rises from the frozen earth, unfolds its fur like song, to shelter that which overwhelms it, shielding it against the gaze of the cold.

Why does the field sown with wounds thrive more than all the rest? Men with old gazes, who have received the order of the trans-pierced sky, receive this news unastonished.

René Char

Sharpener of my own pain, I suffer to hear the fountains on your route dividing up the apple of storms.

A tiny bell rings on the slope of mosses where you dozed, my angel of detours. The soil spread with dwarf gravel was the humid opposite of the long sky, the trees intrepid dancers.

Respite, on the fence, for your foam-sated muzzle, nightmare colt, your race has long been run.

This hibernation of thought occupied with just one person, whom absence strives to place halfway between the artificial and the supernatural.

It isn't simple to stay buoyed by the wave of courage when your eyes are following a bird who flies toward the decline of day.

I do not confuse solitude with the desert's lyre. The cloud tonight encircling your ear is not of soporific snow, but of spindrift seized from spring.

There are two yellow iris in the green water of the Sorgue. If the current carried them away, it would mean they were decapitated.

My comic greed, my icy wish: to seize your head like a bird of prey over the abyss. I held you many times beneath the rain of the cliffs, like a hooded falcon.

Here, again, are the steps of the concrete world, the dark perspective where silhouettes of men gesticulate amid pillaging and discord. A few compensatory women oversee the fire of the harvest, blend with the clouds.

Thank you for existing, never breaking, iris, my flower of gravity. At the water's edge, you inspire miraculous affection, you do not weigh on the dying whose vigil you keep, you extinguish wounds that time has no effect on, you do not lead to a dismaying house, you let all the reflected windows form one single face of passion, you accompany the return of day along all the free green avenues.

ALONG THE RIVER'S EDGE

I. IRIS.

1) Name of a divinity in Greek mythology who was the female messenger of the gods. Unfurling her scarf, she produced the rainbow.

2) A woman's proper name, which poets use to designate the beloved or even a lady whose name they wish to keep secret.

3) Small planet.

II. IRIS. Specific name of a butterfly, the gray nymph butterfly, called the large iridescent March butterfly. Warns of the funereal visitor.

III. IRIS. Blue eyes, black eyes, green eyes are those whose iris is blue, black, green.

IV. IRIS. Plant. Yellow iris of rivers.
... Plural iris, iris of Eros, iris of *Lettera amorosa*.

—NK

René Char

LASCAUX

I

HOMME-OISEAU MORT ET BISON MOURANT

Long corps qui eut l'enthousiasme exigeant,
A présent perpendiculaire à la Brute blessée.

O tué sans entrailles!
Tué par celle qui fut tout et, réconciliée, se meurt;
Lui, danseur d'abîme, esprit, toujours à naître,
Oiseau et fruit pervers des magies cruellement sauvé.

II

LES CERFS NOIRS

Les eaux parlaient à l'oreille du ciel.
Cerfs, vous avez franchi l'espace millénaire,
Des ténèbres du roc aux caresses de l'air.

Le chasseur qui vous pousse, le génie qui vous voit,
Que j'aime leur passion, de mon large rivage!
Et si j'avais leurs yeux, dans l'instant où j'espère?

Other Writings

LASCAUX

I

DEAD BIRD-MAN AND DYING BISON

Long body that knew urgent exaltation,
Perpendicular now to the wounded Beast.

Oh, killed without entrails!
Killed by her who was all things and, reconciled, is dying;
He, dancer of chasms, spirit, not yet born,
Bird and perverse fruit of magic cruelly saved.

II

BLACK STAGS

The waters were murmuring into the ear of the sky.
Stags, you have leapt clear of millenary space,
From the shadows of the rock to the caresses of the air.

The hunter who pursues, the genius who sees you,
How I love their passion, from my wide riverbank!
And what if I had their eyes in my moments of hope?

René Char

III

LA BÊTE INNOMMABLE

La Bête innommable ferme la marche du gracieux troupeau,
    comme un cyclope bouffe.
Huit quolibets font sa parure, divisent sa folie.
La Bête rote dévotement dans l'air rustique.
Ses flancs bourrés et tombants sont douloureux, vont se vider
    de leur grossesse.
De son sabot à ses vaines défenses, elle est enveloppée de fétidité.

Ainsi m'apparaît dans la frise de Lascaux, mère fantastiquement
    déguisée,
La Sagesse aux yeux pleins de larmes.

IV.

JEUNE CHEVAL À LA CRINIÈRE VAPOREUSE

Que tu es beau, printemps, cheval,
Criblant le ciel de ta crinière,
Couvrant d'écume les roseaux!
Tout l'amour tient dans ton poitrail:
De la Dame Blanche d'Afrique
A la Madeleine au miroir,
L'idole qui combat, la grâce qui médite.

III

THE UNSPEAKABLE BEAST

The beast, unspeakable, brings up the rear of the graceful herd,
    a cyclopean buffoon.
Eight jibes make up her jewels, divide her madness.
The Beast devoutly belches into the rustic air.
Her full and falling flanks are painful, are about to empty out
    their pregnancy.
From her hooves to her useless horns, she is sheathed in stench.

Thus Wisdom appears to me in the Lascaux frieze, mother
    fantastically disguised,
Her eyes brimming with tears.

IV

YOUNG HORSE WITH VAPOROUS MANE

How beautiful you are, springtime, mare,
Sifting the sky with your mane,
Covering the reeds with foam!
All of love fits into your breast:
From the White Lady of Africa
To Madeleine before her mirror,
Warrior idol, meditative grace.

René Char   359

Cette part jamais fixée, en nous sommeillante, d'où jaillira DEMAIN LE MULTIPLE.

L'âge du renne, c'est-à-dire l'âge du souffle. Ô vitre, ô givre, nature conquise, dedans fleurie, dehors détruite!

Insouciants, nous exaltons et contrecarrons justement la nature et les hommes. Cependant, terreur, au-dessus de notre tête, le soleil entre dans le signe de ses ennemis.

La lutte contre la cruauté profane, hélas, voeu de fourmi ailée. Sera-t-elle notre novation?

Au soleil d'hiver quelques fagots noués et ma flamme au mur.

Terre où je m'endors, espace où je m'éveille, qui viendra quand vous ne serez plus là? (*que deviendrai-je* m'est d'une chaleur presque infinie).

That never-defined part of us, lying dormant within, from which THE MULTIPLE TOMORROW will spring.

The reindeer age, that is, the age of the breath, oh window-pane, oh frost, nature conquered, flowering inside, outside destroyed!

Careless, we exalt and thwart precisely nature and men. Meanwhile above our heads terror, the sun enters the sign of its enemies.

The struggle against desecrating cruelty, alas, the wish of a winged ant. Will that be our new obligation?

Under the winter sun, a few bundles of sticks and my flame by the wall.

Earth where I fall asleep, space where I awaken, who will appear when you are no longer there? (*what will I become* is of nearly infinite heat to me).

—NK

René Char

QUATRE FASCINANTS

I.

LE TAUREAU

Il ne fait jamais nuit quand tu meurs,
Cerné de ténèbres qui crient,
Soleil aux deux pointes semblables.

Fauve d'amour, vérité dans l'épée,
Couple qui se poignarde unique parmi tous.

II.

LA TRUITE

Rives qui croulez en parure
Afin d'emplir tout le miroir,
Gravier où balbutie la barque
que le courant presse et retrousse,
Herbe, herbe toujours étirée,
Herbe, herbe jamais en répit,
Que devient votre créature
Dans les orages transparents
Où son coeur la précipita?

FOUR WHO FASCINATE

I.

THE BULL

It is never night when you die,
Rimmed with shouting shadows,
Twin-pointed sun.

Beast of love, the truth in a sword,
Crossed plunging blades: a unique couple.

II.

THE TROUT

Crumbling rivershores, necklace
To fill the whole mirror,
Pebbles below the babbling boat
Currents pull back and propel.
Grasses, grasses endlessly stretched out,
Grasses, grasses never left to rest,
What has become of your quick one
Among the transparent storms
Into which her heart swept her?

René Char

III.

LE SERPENT

Prince des contresens, exerce mon amour
À tourner son Seigneur qui je hais de n'avoir
Que trouble répression ou fastueux espoir.

Revanche à tes couleurs, débonnaire serpent,
Sous le couvert du bois, et en toute maison.
Par le lien qui unit la lumière à la peur,
Tu fais semblant de fuir, ô serpent marginal!

IV.

L'ALOUETTE

Extrême braise du ciel et première ardeur du jour,
Elle reste sertie dans l'aurore et chante la terre agitée,
Carillon maître de son haleine et libre de sa route.

Fascinante, on la tue en l'émerveillant.

III.

THE SNAKE

Prince of twisted meanings, teach my love
To get around her Lord I hate whose scope
Is turbid repression, opulence of hope.

Now may your colors triumph, courtly snake,
Sheltered by the woods and in each house.
Along the line uniting light and fear,
O marginal snake! you pretend you've gone away.

IV.

THE LARK

The sky's ultimate ember, and first warmth of day,
Set into dawn she sings the unquiet earth,
Carillon, master of breathing and free to go where she will.

She fascinates, to be killed she must be dazzled.

—PT

René Char   365

LA MINUTIEUSE

L'inondation s'agrandissait. La campagne rase, les talus,
les menus arbres désunis s'enfermaient dans des flaques dont
quelques-unes en se joignant devenaient lac. Une alouette au ciel
trop gris chantait. Des bulles çà et là brisaient la surface des eaux,
à moins que ce ne fût quelque minuscule rongeur ou serpent
s'échappant à la nage. La route encore restait intacte. Les abords
d'un village se montraient. Résolus et heureux nous avancions.
Dans notre errance il faisait beau. Je marchais entre Toi et cette
Autre qui était Toi. Dans chacune de mes mains je tenais serré
votre sein nu. Des villageois sur le pas de leur porte ou occupés à
quelque besogne de planche nour saluaient avec faveur. Mes doigts
leur cachaient votre merveille. En eussent-ils été choqués? L'une
de vous s'arrêta pour causer et pour sourire. Nous continuâmes.
J'avais désormais la nature à ma droite et devant moi la route. Un
boeuf au loin, en son milieu, nous précédait. La lyre de ses cornes,
il me parut, tremblait. Je t'aimais. Mais je reprochais à celle qui
était demeurée en chemin, parmi les habitants des maisons, de se
montrer trop familière. Certes, elle ne pouvait figurer parmi nous
que ton enfance attardée. Je me rendis à l'évidence. Au village la
retiendraient l'école et cette façon qu'ont les communautés aguer-
ries de temporiser avec le danger. Même celui d'inondation. Main-
tenant nous avions atteint l'orée de très vieux arbres et la solitude
des souvenirs. Je voulus m'enquérir de ton nom éternel et chéri
que mon âme avait oublié: "Je suis la Minutieuse." La beauté des
eaux profondes nous endormit.

THE METICULOUS ONE

The flood was rising. The razed countryside, the embankments, the slender disconnected trees were surrounded by puddles, of which several flowed together to become a lake. In the too-gray sky a lark was singing. Bubbles here and there broke the surface of the waters, unless it were some minuscule rodent or snake swimming to safety. The road was still intact. The outskirts of a village could be seen. Resolute and happy we strode forward. The weather in our wandering was beautiful. I walked between You and that Other who was You. In each of my hands I held one of your naked breasts. Villagers on their thresholds or busy with some gardening task greeted us with approval. My fingers hid your wonders from them. Would they have been shocked? One of you stopped to talk and smile. We continued on. Henceforth I had nature to my right and the road ahead of me. In his element, a distant ox preceded us. The lyre of his horns, it seemed to me, was trembling. I loved you. But I reproached the one who'd stayed behind, among the house-dwellers, for acting too familiar. Certainly, she could only play the part, among us, of your belated childhood. I bowed to the facts. In the village, school would keep her, and the way war-hardened communities have of temporizing with danger. Even that of a flood. Now we had reached the verge of very old trees and the solitude of memories. I wanted to ask your eternal and cherished name, which my soul had forgotten: "I am the Meticulous One." The beauty of the deep waters lulled us to sleep.

—NK

L'INOFFENSIF

Je pleure quand le soleil se couche parce qu'il te dérobe à ma vue et parce que je ne sais pas m'accorder avec ses rivaux nocturnes. Bien qu'il soit au bas et maintenant sans fièvre, impossible d'aller contre son déclin, de suspendre son effeuillaison, d'arracher quelque envie encore à sa lueur moribonde. Son départ te fond dans son obscurité comme le limon du lit se délaye dans l'eau du torrent par-delà l'éboulis des berges détruites. Dureté et mollesse au ressort différent ont alors des effets semblables. Je cesse de recevoir l'hymne de ta parole; soudain tu n'apparais plus entière à mon côté; ce n'est pas le fuseau nerveux de ton poignet que tient ma main mais la branche creuse d'un quelconque arbre mort et déjà débité. On ne met plus un nom à rien, qu'au frisson. Il fait nuit. Les artifices qui s'allument me trouvent aveugle.

Je n'ai pleuré en vérité qu'une seule fois. Le soleil en disparaissant avait coupé ton visage. Ta tête avait roulé dans la fosse du ciel et je ne croyais plus au lendemain.

Lequel est l'homme du matin et lequel celui des ténèbres?

Other Writings

THE HARMLESS MAN

I weep when the sun goes down because it takes you from my sight and I am not congenial with its nocturnal rivals. Although it is now low, and has no fever, I cannot keep it from declining, suspend its shedding of leaves, or glean more longing from its moribund glimmer. Going, it melts you in darkness, as the alluvium of the bed liquifies in the water of the current, out beyond the falling earth of the wasting banks. Hardness and softness differ in their origins, but here have similar effects. I am no longer granted the hymn of your words; suddenly you appear no longer whole at my side; this is not the nervous spindle of your wrist I hold in my hand but the hollow branch of some tree or other, dead and already sawed up. Nothing any longer has a name, except the shudder. It is night. The fireworks flaring show that I am blind.

In truth I wept only once. The sun when it disappeared cut off your face. Your head rolled into the grave of the sky and I no longer believed in tomorrow.

Which is the man for morning, and which for the dark?

—MAC

René Char

LE MORTEL PARTENAIRE

Il la défiait, s'avançait vers son coeur, comme un boxeur ourlé, ailé et puissant, bien au centre de la géométrie attaquante et défensive de ses jambes. Il pesait du regard les qualités de l'adversaire qui se contentait de rompre, cantonné entre une virginité agréable et son expérience. Sur la blanche surface où se tenait le combat, tous deux oubliaient les spectateurs inexorables. Dans l'air de juin voltigeaient le prénom des fleurs du premier jour de l'été. Enfin une légère grimace courut sur la joue du second et une raie rose s'y dessina. La riposte jaillit sèche et conséquente. Les jarrets soudain comme du linge étendu, l'homme flotta et tituba. Mais les poings en face ne poursuivirent pas leur avantage, renoncèrent à conclure. A présent les têtes meurtries des deux battants dodelinaient l'une contre l'autre. À cet instant le premier dut à dessein prononcer à l'oreille du second des paroles si parfaitement offensantes, ou appropriées, ou énigmatiques, que celui-ci fila, prompte, totale, précise, une foudre qui coucha net l'incompréhensible combattant.

Certains êtres ont une signification qui nous manque. Qui sont-ils? Leur secret tient au plus profond du secret même de la vie. Ils s'en approchent. Elle les tue. Mais l'avenir qu'ils ont ainsi éveillé d'un murmure, les devinant, les crée. O dédale de l'extrême amour!

THE MORTAL PARTNER

He challenged her, went straight for her heart, like a boxer—trim, winged, powerful—centered in the offensive and defensive geometry of his legs. His glance weighed the fine points of his adversary who was content to break off fighting, suspended between a pleasant virginity and knowledge of him. On the white surface where the combat was being held, both forgot the inexorable spectators. The given names of the flowers of summer's first day fluttered in the June air. Finally a slight grimace crossed the adversary's cheek and a streak of pink appeared. The riposte flashed back, brusque and to the point. His legs suddenly like linen on the line, the man floated, staggered. But the opposing fists did not pursue their advantage, refusing to conclude the match. Now the two fighters' battered heads nodded against each other. At that instant the first must have purposely pronounced into the other's ear words so perfectly offensive, or appropriate, or enigmatic, that the latter let fly a lightning bolt, abrupt, complete, precise, which knocked the incomprehensible fighter out cold.

Certain beings have a meaning that escapes us. Who are they? Their secret resides in the deepest part of life's own secret. They draw near. Life kills them. But the future they have thus awoken with a murmur, sensing them, creates them. Oh labyrinth of utmost love!

—NK

FRONT DE LA ROSE

Malgré la fenêtre ouverte dans la chambre au long congé, l'arôme de la rose reste lié au souffle qui fut là. Nous sommes une fois encore sans expérience antérieure, nouveaux venus, épris. La rose! Le champ de ses allées éventerait même la hardiesse de la mort. Nulle grille qui s'oppose. Le désir resurgit, mal de nos fronts évaporés.

Celui qui marche sur la terre des pluies n'a rien à redouter de l'épine, dans les lieux finis ou hostiles. Mais s'il s'arrête et se recueille, malheur à lui! Blessé au vif, il vole en cendres, archer repris par la beauté.

LE VIPEREAU

Il glisse contre la mousse du caillou comme le jour cligne à travers le volet. Une goutte d'eau pourrait le coiffer, deux brindilles le revêtir. Âme en peine d'un bout de terre et d'un carré de buis, il en est, en même temps, la dent maudite et déclive. Son vis-à-vis, son adversaire, c'est le petit matin qui, après avoir tâté la courte-pointe et avoir souri à la main du dormeur, lâche sa fourche et file au plafond de la chambre. Le soleil, second venu, l'embellit d'une lèvre friande.

Le vipereau restera froid jusqu'à la mort nombreuse, car, n'étant d'aucune paroisse, il est meurtrier devant toutes.

Other Writings

FOREHEAD OF THE ROSE

Despite the open window in the bedroom left so long ago, the rose's fragrance is still bound to the breath that once was there. Again we are without experience, newborn, in love. The rose! The expanse of its pathways would dispel death's boldness. No bars can restrict it. Desire surges back, pain of our foreheads dispersed.

He who walks on the earth of rains has nothing to fear from the thorn, in places long finished or hostile. But if he should pause to gather himself, he is lost! Mortally wounded, he flies to ashes, archer recaptured by beauty.

—MAC & NK

YOUNG VIPER

He slips across the pebble's moss just as the day blinks through the shutter. A drop of water for his cap, two twigs could clothe him. Lost soul of a bit of earth and a boxwood square, he is also their cursed and crooked tooth. His opposite, his adversary, is first light, which after fingering the quilt and smiling at the sleeper's hand, lets go its fork and flees up to the bedroom ceiling. The sun, the second to arrive, embellishes it with a gourmet touch.

The young viper will keep on being cold until the end of time, for, coming from no parish, to all he is a murderer.

—NK

MARMONNEMENT

Pour ne pas me rendre et pour m'y retrouver, je t'offense, mais combien je suis épris de toi, loup, qu'on dit à tort funèbre, pétri des secrets de mon arrière-pays. C'est dans une masse d'amour légendaire que tu laisses la déchaussure vierge, pourchassée de ton ongle. Loup, je t'appelle, mais tu n'as pas de réalité nommable. De plus, tu es inintelligible. Non-comparant, compensateur, que sais-je? Derrière ta course sans crinière, je saigne, je pleure, je m'enserre de terreur, j'oublie, je ris sous les arbres. Traque impitoyable où l'on s'acharne, où tout est mis en action contre la double proie: toi invisible et moi vivace.

Continue, va, nous durons ensemble; et ensemble, bien que séparés, nous bondissons par-dessus le frisson de la suprême déception pour briser la glace des eaux vives et se reconnaître là.

MUMBLING

Not to surrender and so to take my bearings, I offend you, but how in love with you I am, wolf, wrongly called funereal, molded with the secrets of my back country. In a mass of legendary love you leave the trace, virgin, hunted, of your claw. Wolf, I call you, but you have no nameable reality. Moreover, you are unintelligible. By default, compensating, what else could I say? Behind your maneless running, I am bleeding, weeping; I gird myself with terror, I forget, I am laughing under the trees. Pitiless and unending pursuit, where all is set in motion against the double prey: you invisible and I perennial.

Go on, we endure together; and together, although separate, we bound over the tremor of supreme deception to shatter the ice of quick waters and recognize ourselves there.

—MAC

POUR RENOUER

Nous nous sommes soudain trop approchés de quelque chose dont on nous tenait à une distance mystérieusement favorable et mesurée. Depuis lors, c'est le rongement. Notre appuie-tête a disparu.

Il est insupportable de se sentir part solidaire et impuissante d'une beauté en train de mourir par la faute d'autrui. Solidaire dans sa poitrine et impuissant dans le mouvement de son esprit.

Si ce que je te montre et ce que je te donne te semblent moindres que ce que je te cache, ma balance est pauvre, ma glane est sans vertu.

Tu es reposoir d'obscurité sur ma face trop offerte, poème. Ma splendeur et ma souffrance se sont glissées entre les deux.

Jeter bas l'existence laidement accumulée et retrouver le regard qui l'aima assez à son début pour en étaler le fondement. Ce qui me reste à vivre est dans cet assaut, dans ce frisson.

TO RESUME

All at once we've drawn too near to something from which we were kept at a mysteriously favorable and measured distance. Since then, erosion. Our headrest has disappeared.

It is unbearable to feel a helpless and committed part of beauty dying through the fault of others. Committed in your breast and helpless in the movement of your mind.

If what I show you and what I give to you seem less than what I hide from you, my scales are faulty, my gleaning ineffectual.

Poem, you are a wayside altar of darkness on my too freely offered face. My splendor and my suffering have slipped between the two.

To cast away existence hideously hoarded and unearth the gaze that once loved it enough to lay bare its foundation. What is left for me to live will be in this assault, this trembling.

—NK

INVITATION

J'appelle les amours qui roués et suivis par la faulx de l'été, au soir embaument l'air de leur blanche inaction.

Il n'y a plus de cauchemar, douce insomnie perpétuelle. Il n'y a plus d'aversion. Que la pause d'un bal dont l'entrée est partout dans les nuées du ciel.

Je viens avant la rumeur des fontaines, au final du tailleur de pierre.

Sur ma lyre mille ans pèsent moins qu'un mort.

J'appelle les amants.

INVITATION

I summon the loves that, racked and followed by summer's scythe, embalm the evening air with their white inactivity.

No longer nightmare, soft perpetual sleeplessness. No more aversion. Only the pause in a dance whose entrance is everywhere among the sky-drifts.

I come before the murmur of fountains, at the stonecutter's finale.

On my lyre a thousand years weigh less than one dead man.

I summon the lovers.

—MAC

POURQUOI LA JOURNÉE VOLE

Le poète s'appuie, durant le temps de sa vie, à quelque arbre, ou mer, ou talus, ou nuage d'une certaine teinte, un moment, si la circonstance le veut. Il n'est pas soudé à l'égarement d'autrui. Son amour, son saisir, son bonheur ont leur équivalent dans tous les lieux où il n'est pas allé, où jamais il n'ira, chez les étrangers qu'il ne connaîtra pas. Lorsqu'on élève la voix devant lui, qu'on le presse d'accepter des égards qui retiennent, si l'on invoque à son propos les astres, il répond qu'il est du pays d'*à coté*, du ciel qui vient d'être englouti.

Le poète vivifie puis court au dénouement.

Au soir, malgré sur sa joue plusieurs fossettes d'apprenti, c'est un passant courtois qui brusque les adieux pour être là quand le pain sort du four.

WHY THE DAY FLIES

During his lifetime the poet leans against some tree, or sea, or slope, or cloud of a certain tint, for a moment, if circumstance permits. He is not welded to other people's aberrations. His love, his grasp, his happiness have equivalents in all the places he has never been, will never go, in strangers he will never meet. When voices are raised before him, when honors are offered that would bind, if the stars are invoked in relation to him, he responds that he is from the country *next door,* from the sky just now swallowed up.

The poet quickens then races to the outcome.

In the evening, though dimpled like an apprentice, he is a courtly passerby who cuts his farewells short to be there when the bread comes out of the oven.

—NK

LA BIBLIOTHÈQUE EST EN FEU

A Georges Braque.

Par la bouche de ce canon il neige. C'était l'enfer dans notre tête. Au même moment c'est le printemps au bout de nos doigts. C'est la foulée de nouveau permise, la terre en amour, les herbes exubérantes.

L'esprit aussi, comme toute chose, a tremblé. L'aigle est au futur.

Toute action qui engage l'âme, quand bien même celle-ci en serait ignorante, aura pour épilogue un repentir ou un chagrin. Il faut y consentir.

Comment me vint l'écriture? Comme un duvet d'oiseau sur ma vitre, en hiver. Aussitôt s'éleva dans l'âtre une bataille de tisons qui n'a pas, encore à présent, pris fin.

Soyeuses villes du regard quotidien, insérées parmi d'autres villes, aux rues tracées par nous seuls, sous l'aile d'éclairs qui répondent à nos attentions.

Tout en nous ne devrait être qu'une fête joyeuse quand quelque chose que nous n'avons pas prévu, que nous n'éclairons pas, qui va parler à notre coeur, par ses seuls moyens, s'accomplit.

Continuons à jeter nos coups de sonde, à parler à voix égale, par mots groupés, nous finirons par faire taire tous ces chiens, par obtenir qu'ils se confondent avec l'herbage, nous surveillant d'un œil fumeux, tandis que le vent effacera leur dos.

L'éclair me dure.

THE LIBRARY IS ON FIRE

Through the mouth of this cannon, it is snowing. It was hell in our head. At the same moment, it's springtime at the end of our fingers. It's the stride once more allowed, the earth in love, the grasses exuberant.

The spirit also, like everything, has trembled.

The eagle is in the future.

Every act that involves the soul, even if the soul doesn't know about it, will have as an epilogue repentance or chagrin. You have to consent to that.

How did writing come to me? Like bird's down on my window-pane, in winter. Just then there rose in the hearth a struggle of fire-brands, which has, still now, not ended.

Silky towns of the daily gaze, placed between other towns, with the streets traced by us alone, under the wing of lightning, responding to our attention.

Everything in us ought to be just a joyous feast when something we haven't predicted, that we don't shed any light on, that will speak directly to our heart, comes about.

Let's continue to plumb the depths, to speak in even tones, in words grouped together, we shall finally silence all these dogs, having them mingle with the grass, surveying us with a foggy look, while the wind will wipe out their backs.

Lightning lasts me.

René Char

Il n'y a que mon semblable, la compagne ou le compagnon, qui puisse m'éveiller de ma torpeur, déclencher la poésie, me lancer contre les limites du vieux désert afin que j'en triomphe. Aucun autre. Ni cieux, ni terre privilégiée, ni choses dont on tressaille.

Torche, je ne valse qu'avec lui.

On ne peut pas commencer un poème sans une parcelle d'erreur sur soi et sur le monde, sans une paille d'innocence aux premiers mots.

Dans le poème, chaque mot ou presque doit être employé dans son sens originel. Certains, se détachant, deviennent plurivalents. Il en est d'amnésiques. La constellation du Solitaire est tendue.

La poésie me volera ma mort.

Pourquoi *poème pulvérisé*? Parce qu'au terme de son voyage vers le Pays, après l'obscurité pré-natale et la dureté terrestre, la finitude du poème est lumière, apport de l'être à la vie.

Le poète ne retient pas ce qu'il découvre; l'ayant transcrit, le perd bientôt. En cela réside sa nouveauté, son infini et son péril.

Mon métier est un métier de pointe.

On naît avec les hommes, on meurt inconsolé parmi les dieux.

La terre qui reçoit la graine est triste. La graine qui va tant risquer est heureuse.

Il est une malédiction qui ne ressemble à aucune autre. Elle papillote dans une sorte de paresse, a une nature avenante, se compose un visage aux traits rassurants. Mais quel ressort, passée la feinte, quelle course immédiate au but! Probablement, car l'ombre où elle échafaude est maligne, la région parfaitement secrète, elle se

There is only the one like me, the companion man or woman, who can wake me from my torpor, set off the poetry, hurl me against the limits of the old desert for me to triumph over it. No other. Neither sky nor privileged earth, now things which set you to trembling.

Torch, I only waltz with that one.

You can't begin a poem without a bit of error about yourself and the world, without a straw of innocence at the first words.

In the poem, each word or almost should be used in its original meaning. Some of them detach themselves, have many meanings. Some are amnesiac. The constellation of the Solitary is held out.

Poetry will steal my death from me.

Why *pulverized poem*? Because at the end of its voyage towards the Country, after the pre-birth darkness and the earthly harshness, the finitude of the poem is light, a bringing of being to life.

The poet does not retain what he discovers; having transcribed it, he soon loses it. In that resides his novelty, his infinity and his peril.

My métier is a pointed one.

We are born with men, we die unconsoled among gods.

The earth receiving the seed is sad. The seed about to risk so much is happy.

There is a malediction like no other. It twinkles in a kind of laziness, has a comely nature, composes its features in a reassuring fashion. But once passed the deception, what buoyancy, what a rapid rush to the end! Probably, for the shadow wherein it builds is

soustraira à une appellation, s'esquivera toujours à temps. Elle dessine dans le voile du ciel de quelques clairvoyants des paraboles assez effrayantes.

Livres sans mouvement. Mais livres qui s'introduisent avec souplesse dans nos jours, y poussent une plainte, ouvrent des bals.

Comment dire ma liberté, ma surprise, au terme de mille détours: il n'y a pas de fond, il n'y a pas de plafond.

Parfois la silhouette d'un jeune cheval, d'un enfant lointain, s'avance en éclaireur vers mon front et saute la barre de mon souci. Alors sous les arbres reparle la fontaine.

Nous désirons rester inconnus à la curiosité de celles qui nous aiment. Nous les aimons.

La lumière a un âge. La nuit n'en a pas. Mais quel fut l'instant de cette source entière?

Ne pas avoir plusieurs morts suspendues et comme enneigées. N'en avoir qu'une, de bon sable. Et sans résurrection.

Arrêtons-nous près des êtres qui peuvent se couper de leurs ressources, bien qu'il n'existe pour eux que peu ou pas de repli. L'attente leur creuse une insomnie vertigineuse. La beauté leur pose un chapeau de fleurs.

Oiseaux qui confiez votre gracilité, votre sommeil périlleux à un ramas de roseaux, le froid venu, comme nous vous ressemblons!

J'admire les mains qui emplissent, et, pour apparier, pour joindre, le doigt qui refuse le dé.

malicious, the perfectly secret place will shy away from any appellation, will always escape in time. For some clairvoyant ones, it draws in the veil of their sky rather frightening parabolas.

Books without motion. But books which insert themselves easily into our days, utter a lament, open the dances.

How to speak my freedom, my surprise, at the end of a thousand detours: there is no bottom, no ceiling.

Sometimes the silhouette of a young horse, of a distant child, comes scouting toward my forehead and leaps the bar of my concern. Then under the trees the fountain speaks once more.

We wish to remain unknown to the curiosity of those who love us. We love them.

Light has an age. Night has none. But what was the instant of this integral source?

Not to have many deaths hanging and as if snowed up. Not to have but one, of good sand. And without resurrection.

Let's stay near beings who can cut themselves off from their resources, although for them there exist few recesses, or none. Waiting prepares for them a dizzying insomnia. Upon them beauty places a hat of flowers.

Birds confiding your gracefulness, your perilous sleep to a cluster of reeds, once the cold has come, how like you we are!

I admire hands that fill things, and, to match up, to join, the finger refusing the dice.

Je m'avise parfois que le courant de notre existence est peu saisissable, puisque nous subissons non seulement sa faculté capricieuse, mais le facile mouvement des bras et des jambes qui nous ferait aller là où nous serions heureux d'aller, sur la rive convoitée, à la rencontre d'amours dont les différences nous enrichiraient, ce mouvement demeure inaccompli, vite déclinant en image, comme un parfum en boule sur notre pensée.

Désir, désir qui sait, nous ne tirons avantage de nos ténèbres qu'à partir de quelques souverainetés véritables assorties d'invisibles flammes, d'invisibles chaînes, qui, se révélant, pas après pas, nous font briller.

La beauté fait son lit sublime toute seule, étrangement bâtit sa renommée parmi les hommes, à côté d'eux mais à l'écart.
Semons les roseaux et cultivons la vigne sur les coteaux, au bord des plaies de notre esprit. Doigts cruels, mains précautionneuses, ce lieu facétieux est propice.

Celui qui invente, au contraire de celui qui découvre, n'ajoute aux choses, n'apporte aux êtres que des masques, des entre-deux, une bouillie de fer.

Enfin toute la vie, quand j'arrache la douceur de ta vérité amoureuse à ton profond!

Restez près du nuage. Veillez près de l'outil. Toute semence est détestée.

Bienfaisance des hommes certains matins stridents. Dans le fourmillement de l'air en délire, je monte, je m'enferme, insecte indévoré, suivi et poursuivant.

I find sometimes that the current of our existence is difficult to seize, because we endure not only its capricious power, but the easy motion of the arms and legs which would have us go where we would be happy to, on the longed-for shore, toward the meeting of loves whose differences would enrich us, this motion remaining unaccomplished, rapidly declining into just an image, like perfume rolling up upon our thought.

Desire, desire which knows, we draw no advantage from our shadows except from some veritable sovereignties accompanied by invisible flames, invisible chains, which, coming to light, step after step, cause us to shine.

Beauty makes its sublime bed all alone, strangely builds its renown among persons, right by them, but off to one side.
Let's sow the reeds and cultivate the vine on the hills, on the edge of the wounds of our spirit. Cruel fingers, hands full of precautions, this flippant place is propitious.

The one who invents, by contrast with the one who discovers, adds nothing to things, brings to beings only masks, compromises, a stew of iron.

Finally life entire, when I snatch the sweetness of your amorous truth from your deep!

Remain close to the cloud. Keep watch close to the tool. All sowing is detested.

Human benevolence on certain strident mornings. In the swarming of the delirious air, I rise, I close myself in, insect undevoured, followed and following.

René Char

Face à ces eaux, de formes dures, où passent en bouquets éclatés toutes les fleurs de la montagne verte, les Heures épousent des dieux.

Frais soleil dont je suis la liane.

Facing these waters, hard in their form, where all the flowers of the green mountain pass in bouquets burst apart, the Hours espouse gods.

Fresh sun whose liana I am.

—MAC

LES COMPAGNONS DANS LE JARDIN

L'homme n'est qu'une fleur de l'air tenue par la terre, maudite par les astres, respirée par la mort; le souffle et l'ombre de cette coalition, certaines fois, le surélèvent.

Notre amitié est le nuage blanc préféré du soleil.

Notre amitié est une écorce libre. Elle ne se détache pas des prouesses de notre coeur.

Où l'esprit ne déracine plus mais replante et soigne, je nais. Ou commence l'enfance du peuple, j'aime.

xxe siècle : l'homme fut au plus bas. Les femmes s'éclairaient et se déplaçaient vite, sur un surplomb où seuls nos yeux avaient accès.

À une rose je me lie.

Nous sommes ingouvernables. Le seul maître qui nous soit propice, c'est l'Éclair, qui tantôt nous illumine et tantôt nous pourfend.

Éclair et rose, en nous, dans leur fugacité, pour nous accomplir, s'ajoutent.

Je suis d'herbe dans ta main, ma pyramide adolescente. Je t'aime sur tes mille fleurs refermées.

Prête au bourgeon, en lui laissant l'avenir, tout l'éclat de la fleur profonde. Ton dur second regard le peut. De la sorte, le gel ne le détruira pas.

THE COMPANIONS IN THE GARDEN

Man is only a flower of air held by the earth, cursed by the stars, inhaled by death; the breath and the shadow of this coalition, sometimes, raise him up.

Our friendship is the white cloud preferred by the sun.

Our friendship is a free bark. It does not detach itself from the deeds of our heart.

Where the spirit no longer uproots but replants and takes care, I am born. Where the childhood of the people begins, I love.

Twentieth century: Humanity was at its lowest point. Women lit up and moved about quickly, on an overhang to which only our eyes had access.

To a rose I bind myself.

We are ungovernable. The only master propitious to us is Lightning, which now lights us and now again splits us apart.

Lightning and rose, in us, in their fleetingness, add together to accomplish us.

I am grass in your hand, my adolescent pyramid. I love you on your thousand flowers closed up.

Lend to the bud, leaving it the future, all the shine of the deep flower. Your harsh second look can do that. Thus the frost will not destroy it.

René Char

Ne permettons pas qu'on nous enlève la part de la nature que nous renfermons. N'en perdons pas une étamine, n'en cédons pas un gravier d' eau.

Après le départ des moissonneurs, sur les plateaux de l'Ile-de-France, ce menu silex taillé qui sort de terre, à peine dans notre main, fait surgir de notre mémoire un noyau equivalent, noyau d'une aurore dont nous ne verrons pas, croyons-nous, l'altération ni la fin; seulement la rougeur sublime et le visage levé.

Leur crime : un enragé vouloir de nous apprendre à mépriser les dieux que nous avons en nous.

Ce sont les pessimistes que l'avenir élève. Ils voient de leur vivant l'objet de leur appréhension se réaliser. Pourtant la grappe, qui a suivi la moisson, au-dessus de son cep, boucle; et les enfants des saisons, qui ne sont pas selon l'ordinaire réunis, au plus vite affermissent le sable au bord de la vague. Cela, les pessimistes le perçoivent aussi.

Ah! le pouvoir de se lever autrement.

Dites, ce que nous sommes nous fera jaillir en bouquet?

Un poète doit laisser des traces de son passage, non des preuves. Seules les traces font rêver.

Vivre, c'est s'obstiner à achever un souvenir? Mourir, c' est devenir, mais nulle part, vivant?

Le réel quelquefois désaltère l'espérance. C'est pourquoi, contre toute attente, l'espérance survit.

Let's not permit anyone to remove the part of nature we close up in ourselves. Let's not lose one stamen, not give up the gravel of any water.

After the departure of the harvesters, on the plains of the Ile-de-France, this narrow tapered flint protruding from the earth, lightly held, causes an equivalent kernel to come forth from our memory, a kernel of a dawn whose change or end we believe we shall not see; only the sublime blush and the lifted face.

Their crime: a raging will to teach us to scorn the gods we have within us.

These are the pessimists that the future raises. They see the realization, in their lifetime, of the object of their apprehension. Yet the grape cluster, which followed the harvest, above its stem, forms a circle; and the children of the seasons, who aren't gathered in the ordinary way, hasten to firm the sand at the edge of the wave. That, the pessimists see also.

Ah, to be able to rise differently.

Listen, will what we are spring forth in a bouquet?

A poet should leave, not proofs, but traces of his passage. Only traces set us dreaming.

Is living insisting on a finished memory? Is dying becoming, but nowhere at all, alive?

The real sometimes takes away the thirst of hope. That's why, expectation to the contrary, hope survives.

Toucher de son ombre un fumier, tant notre flanc renferme de maux et notre coeur de pensées folles, se peut; mais avoir en soi un sacré.

Lorsque je rêve et que j'avance, lorsque je retiens l'ineffable, m'evéillant, je suis à genoux.

L'Histoire n'est que le revers de la tenue des maîtres. Aussi une terre d'effroi où chasse le lycaon et que racle la vipère. La détresse est dans le regard des sociétes humaines et du Temps, avec des victoires qui montent.

Luire et s'élancer — prompt couteau, lente étoile.

Dans l'éclatement de l'univers que nous éprouvons, prodige! les morceaux qui s'abattent sont vivants.

Ma toute terre, comme un oiseau change en fruit dans un arbre éternel, je suis à toi.

Ce que vos hivers nous demandent, c'est d'enlever dans les airs ce qui ne serait sans cela que limaille et souffre-douleur. Ce que vos hivers nous demandent, c'est de préluder pour vous à la saveur: un saveur égale à celle que cbante sous sa rondeur ailée la civilization du fruit.

Ce qui me console, lorsque je serai mort, c'est que je serai là — disloqué, hideux — pour me vois poème.

I1 ne faut pas que ma lyre me devine, que mon vers se trouve ce que j'aurais pu écrire.

Le merveilleux chez cet être: toute source, en lui, donne le jour à un ruisseau. Avec le moindre de ses dons descend une averse de colombes.

To touch a manure heap with our shadow is possible, so surely do we contain evils in our side, and mad thoughts in our heart; but to hold in ourselves something sacred.

When I dream and move forward, when I retain the ineffable, waking I am on my knees.

History is only the other side of the way rulers comport themselves. Also a frightful land where the lycaon hunts and the viper slithers. Distress is in the gaze of human societies and Time, with victories rising.

Shine and leap forward—ready knife, slow star.

Universe that we suffer, oh marvel! The falling pieces are alive.

My all, my earth, as a bird changed into fruit in an eternal tree, I am yours.

What your winters ask from us, is to take off in the air what would be without that only filings and drudges. What your winters ask from us, is to serve as prelude for your taste: a taste equal to that sung by the civilization of fruit under its winged roundness.

What consoles me, when I will be dead, is that I will be there—dislocated, hideous—to see myself as a poem.

My lyre must not find me out, my verse must not become what I would have been able to write.

The marvelous in this being: every spring, in him, gives birth to a stream. With the slightest of his gifts doves shower down.

René Char

Dans nos jardins se prepare des forêts.

Les oiseaux libres ne souffrent pas qu'on les regarde. Demeurons obscurs, renonçons à nous, près d'eux.

Ô survie encore, toujours meilleure!

In our gardens forests are preparing.

Free birds do not let anyone look at them. Let's remain obscure, let's renounce ourselves, near them.

Oh still surviving, better and better!

—MAC

René Char

NEUF MERCI POUR VIEIRA DA SILVA

I

LES PALAIS ET LES MAISONS

Paris est aujourd'hui achevé. J'y vivrai. Mon bras ne lance plus mon âme au loin. J'appartiens.

II

DANS L'ESPACE

Le soleil volait bas, aussi bas que l'oiseau. La nuit les éteignit tous deux. Je les aimais.

III

C'EST BIEN ELLE

Terre de basse nuit et des harcèlements.

*

Nuit, mon feuillage et ma glèbe.

NINE THANKS FOR VIEIRA DA SILVA

I

PALACES AND HOUSES

Paris is finished today. I'll live here. My arm no longer flings my soul faraway into the distance. I belong.

II

IN SPACE

The sun was flying low, as low as the bird. Night extinguished them both. I loved them.

III

IT IS REALLY SHE

Earth of low night and torments.

*

Night, my foliage and my glebe.

IV

LA GRILLE

Je ne suis pas seul parce que je suis abandonné. Je suis seul parce que je suis seul, amande entre les parois de sa closerie.

V

LES DIEUX SONT DE RETOUR

Les dieux sont de retour, compagnons. Ils viennent à l'instant de pénétrer dans cette vie; mais la parole qui révoque, sous la parole qui déploie, est réapparue, elle aussi, pour ensemble nous faire souffrir.

VI

ARTINE DANS L'ECHO

Notre emmêlement somptueux dans le corps de la voie lactée, chambre au sommet pour notre couple qui dans la nuit ailleurs se glacerait.

VII

BERCEUSE POUR CHAQUE JOUR JUSQU'AU DERNIER

Nombreuses fois, nombre de fois,
L'homme s'endort, son corps l'éveille;
Puis une fois, rien qu'une fois,
L'homme s'endort et perd son corps.

IV

GRILLWORK

    I am not alone because I am abandoned. I am alone because I am alone, almond within the walls of its enclosure.

V

THE GODS HAVE RETURNED

    The gods have returned, companions. They've just now entered this life; but beneath the word that opens, the word that revokes has come back too, in order to torment us together.

VI

ARTINE IN THE ECHO

    Our sumptuous intermingling in the body of the milky way, a bedroom at the summit for the two of us, who elsewhere in the night would freeze.

VII

LULLABY FOR EVERYDAY UNTIL THE LAST

Numerous times, any number of times,
Man falls asleep, he is waked by his body;
Then comes a time, only one time,
Man falls asleep and loses his body.

René Char

VIII

AUX MIENS

Je touche à l'étendue et je peux l'enflammer. Je retiens ma largeur, je sais la déployer. Mais que vaut le désir sans votre essaim jaloux? Terne est le bouton d'or sans le ton des prairies.

Lorsque vous surgirez, ma main vous requerra, ma main, le petit monstre resté vif. Mais, à la réserve de vous, quelle beauté?... quelle beauté?

IX

LA FAUVETTE DES ROSEAUX

L'arbre le plus exposé à l'oeil du fusil n'est pas un arbre pour son aile. La remuante est prévenue: elle se fera muette en le traversant. La perche de saule happée est à l'instant cédée par l'ongle de la fugitive. Mais dans la touffe de roseaux où elle amerrit, quelles cavatines! C'est ici qu'elle chante. Le monde entier le sait.

Été, rivière, espaces, amants dissimulés, toute une lune d'eau, la fauvette répète: "Libre, libre, libre, libre..."

VIII

TO THOSE WHO ARE MINE

I touch on the expanse and I can set it blazing. I retain my breadth, I know how to unfold it. But of what value is desire without your jealous swarm? The buttercup is dulled without the meadows' hue.

When you appear, my hand will summon you, the little monster of my hand, still lively. But, apart from you, what beauty?... what beauty?

—NK

IX

THE WARBLER IN THE REEDS

The tree most exposed to the shotgun's eye is not a tree for her wing. The quicksilver one is forewarned: she will pass through in silence. Her fugitive claw grapples and gives up at once a perch in the willow. But from her landing place in the clustered reeds, what cavatinas! It is here that she sings. As the whole world knows.

Summer, the river, spaces, lovers hidden away, a whole water-moon, the warbler repeats, "Free, free, free, free..."

—PT

René Char   405

SUR UNE NUIT SANS ORNEMENT

Regarder la nuit battue à mort; continuer à nous suffire en elle.

Dans la nuit, le poète, le drame et la nature ne font qu'un, mais en montée et s'aspirant.

La nuit porte nourriture, le soleil affine la partie nourrie.

Dans la nuit se tiennent nos apprentissages en état de servir à d'autres, après nous. Fertile est la fraîcheur de cette gardienne!

L'infini attaque mais un nuage sauve.

La nuit s'affilie à n'importe quelle instance de la vie disposée à finir en printemps, à voler par tempête.

La nuit se colore de rouille quand elle consent à nous entrouvrir les grilles de ses jardins.

Au regard de la nuit vivante, le rêve n'est parfois qu'un lichen spectral.

Il ne fallait pas embraser le cœur de la nuit. Il fallait que l'obscur fût maître où se cisèle la rosée du matin.

La nuit ne succède qu'à elle. Le beffroi solaire n'est qu'une tolérance intéressée de la nuit.

La reconduction de notre mystère, c'est la nuit qui en prend soin; la toilette des élus, c'est la nuit qui l'exécute.

ON A NIGHT WITHOUT ORNAMENT

To look at night almost flogged to death; to keep on finding it sufficient for us.

In the night, the poet, the drama, and nature are one, but rising straight up and breathing it all in.

Night brings nourishment, the sun ripens the nourished portion.

In the night our apprenticeships hold themselves in the state useful to others, after ourselves. How fertile is the freshness of this guardian!

The infinite attacks, but a cloud saves.

Night affiliates itself with no matter what immediacy of a life ready to end in springtime, to fly during a tempest.

Night takes the color of rust when it accepts to open its garden gates for us.

In the eyes of living night, the dream is sometimes only a moss spectre.

The heart of night shouldn't be set alight. Dark must be the master where the morning dew takes form.

Night only succeeds night. The solar belltower is just something it permits.

How our mystery changes places, night takes care of that; the grooming of those selected, night manages it.

René Char

La nuit déniaise notre passé d'homme, incline sa psyché devant le présent, met de l'indécision dans notre avenir.

Je m'emplirai d'une terre céleste.

Nuit plénière où le rêve malgracieux ne clignote plus, garde-moi vivant ce que j'aime.

Night makes intelligent our human past, tilts its mirror before the present, puts indecision in our future.

I shall fill myself with a heavenly earth.

Absolute night where the unfortunate dream no longer blinks, keep alive what I love.

—MAC

"To *see* the night, you have to be awake. It is made to be carried on the back of a man and to fill the eyes that are open before the ones closed. Under a nightly space, we are seeking some light on earth and the beings who reflect it. ...In this struggle, night stretches out infinitely, even where it hasn't yet really arrived. Real night, the one where our past bursts into pieces, where our heart seems indestructible." (Char's commentary in *Le Nouvel Observateur,* March 3, 1980.)   —MAC

LA ROUTE PAR LES SENTIERS

Les sentiers, les entailles qui longent invisiblement la route, sont notre unique route, à nous qui parlons pour vivre, qui dormons, sans nous engourdir, sur le côté.

DÉCLARER SON NOM

J'avais dix ans. La Sorgue m'enchâssait. Le soleil chantait les heures sur le sage cadran des eaux. L'insouciance et la douleur avaient scellé le coq de fer sur le toit des maisons et se supportaient ensemble. Mais quelle roue dans le coeur de l'enfant aux aguets tournait plus fort, tournait plus vite que celle du moulin dans son incendie blanc?

TRAVERSE

La colline qu'il a bien servie descend en torrent dans son dos. Les langues pauvres le saluent; les mulets au pré lui font fête. La face rosé de l'ornière tourne deux fois vers lui l'onde de son miroir. La méchanceté dort. Il est tel qu'il se rêvait.

THE ROAD BESIDE THE PATHS

The paths, the grooves that run invisibly along the side of the road, are the only road for those of us who speak to live, who sleep without growing sluggish, on our sides.

—NK

DECLARING ONE'S NAME

I was ten years old. The Sorgue encircled me. The sun chanted the hours on the wise dial of the waters. Insouciance and sorrow had sealed the iron cocks on the roofs of houses and now tolerated one another. But what wheel in the heart of the watchful child was turning harder, turning faster than the mill wheel in its white conflagration?

—NK

SHORTCUT

The hill he has served so well descends torrential at his back. Poor tongues salute him; the mules in the meadow welcome him. The gulley's rose-hued face turns toward him twice the waters of its mirror. Meanness sleeps. He is as he dreamt himself to be.

—MAC

René Char

411

NOUS TOMBONS

Ma brièveté est sans chaînes.

Baisers d'appui. Tes parcelles dispersées font soudain un corps
sans regard.

Ô mon avalanche à rebours!

Toute liée.

Tel un souper dans le vent.

Toute liée. Rendue à l'air.

Tel un chemin rougi sur le roc. Un animal fuyant.

La profondeur de l'impatience et la verticale patience confondues.

La danse retournée. Le fouet belliqueux.

Tes limpides yeux agrandis.

Ces légers mots immortels jamais endeuillés.

Lierre à son rang silencieux.

Fronde que la mer approchait. Contre-taille du jour.

Abaisse encore ta pesanteur.

La mort nous bat du revers de sa fourche. Jusqu'à un matin sobre
apparu en nous.

WE ARE FALLING

My brevity has no chains.

Braced by kisses. Your dispersed particles suddenly compose one
body without a gaze.

Oh my backward avalanche!

All intertwined.

Like a supper in the wind.

All intertwined. Given back to the air.

Like a reddened road across the rock. A fleeing animal.

The depth of impatience and vertical patience fused.

The dance overturned. The bellicose whip.

Your limpid eyes grown larger.

These light immortal words never plunged into grief.

Ivy in its silent strand.

Frond that the sea was approaching. Crosscut of the day.

Lower your weight again.

Death taps us with the back of his pitchfork. Until one morning
soberly revealed in us.

—NK

René Char

NOUS AVONS

Notre parole, en archipel, vous offre, après la douleur et le désastre, des fraises qu'elle rapporte des landes de la mort, ainsi que ses doigts chauds de les avoir cherchées.

Tyrannies sans delta, que midi jamais n'illumine, pour vous nous sommes le jour vieilli; mais vous ignorez que nous sommes aussi l'oeil vorace, bien que voilé, de l'origine.

Faire un poème, c'est prendre possession d'un au-delà nuptial qui se trouve bien dans cette vie, très rattaché à elle, et cependant à proximité des urnes de la mort.

Il faut s'établir à l'extérieur de soi, au bord des larmes et dans l' orbite des famines, si nous voulons que quelque chose hors du commun se produise, qui n'était que pour nous.

Si l'angoisse qui nous évide abandonnait sa grotte glacée, si l'amante dans notre coeur arrêtait la pluie de fourmis, le Chant reprendrait.

Dans le chaos d'une avalanche, deux pierres s'épousant au bond purent s'aimer nues dans l'espace. L'eau de neige qui les engloutit s'étonna, de leur mousse ardente.

L'homme fut sûrement le voeu le plus fou des ténèbres; c'est pourquoi nous sommes ténébreux, envieux et fous sous le puissant soleil.

Une terre qui était belle à commencé son agonie, sous le regard de ses soeurs voltigeantes, en presence de ses fils insensés.

WE HAVE

Our word, like an archipelago, offers you, after pain and disaster, strawberries it brings back from the countries of death, as well as its fingers warm from having sought them.

Tyrannies without a delta, never lit by noontime, for you we are the day grown aged; but you aren't aware that we are also the voracious eye of the origin, although veiled.

To make a poem is taking possession of a nuptial celebration beyond anything found in this life, very attached to it, and yet in proximity to the urns of death.

We must make our dwelling outside ourselves, at the edge of tears and in the orbit of famines, if we want something uncommon to happen, for us only.

If the anguish which hollows us out were to abandon its icy grotto, if the lover in our heart were to stop the rain of ants, the Song would start up again.

In the chaos of an avalanche, two stones wed in their leap could love each other naked in space. The snowy water swallowing them was astonished at their ardent foam.

Man was surely the maddest vow of the shadows; that's why we are shadowy, envious and mad under the powerful sun.

An earth which was lovely has begun its agony, under the gaze of its sisters flitting about, in the presence of its crazed sons.

Nous avons en nous d'immenses étendues que nous n'arriverons jamais à talonner; mais elles sont utiles à l'âpreté de nos climats, propices à notre éveil comme à nos perditions.

Comment rejeter dans les ténebres notre coeur antérieur et son droit de retour?

La poésie est ce fruit que nous serrons, mûri, avec liesse, dans notre main au même moment qu'il nous apparaît, d'avenir incertain, sur la tige givrée, dans le calice de la fleur.

Poésie, unique montée des hommes, que le soleil des morts ne peut assombrir dans l'infini parfait et burlesque.

*

Un mystère plus fort que leur malediction innocentant leur coeur, ils plantèrent un arbre dans le Temps, s'endormirent au pied, et le Temps se fit aimant.

We have in ourselves immense stretches that we will never manage to traverse; but they are useful to the harshness of our climates, propitious to our waking as to our doom.

How to toss back into the shadows our former heart and its right of return?

Poetry is this fruit that we clasp, ripened, joyful, in our hand at the same moment that it appears to us, with an uncertain future, on the frosted stem, in the chalice of the flower.

Poetry, unique ascent of men, that the sun of the dead can never darken in the infinite perfect and ludicrous.

*

A stronger mystery than their malediction making their heart innocent, they planted a tree in Time, fell asleep at its foot, and Time became affectionate.

—MAC

L'ÉTERNITÉ À LOURMARIN

Albert Camus

Il n'y a plus de ligne droite ni de route éclairée avec un être qui nous a quittés. Où s'étourdit notre affection? Cerne après cerne, s'il approche c'est pour aussitôt s'enfouir. Son visage parfois vient s'appliquer contre la nôtre, ne produisant qu'un éclair glacé. Le jour qui allongeait le bonheur entre lui et nous n'est nulle part. Toutes les parties—presque excessives—d'une présence se sont d'un coup disloqués. Routine de notre vigilance... Pourtant cet être supprimé se tient dans quelque chose de rigide, de désert, d'essentiel en nous, où nos millénaires ensemble font juste l'épaisseur d'une paupière tirée.

Avec celui que nous aimons, nous avons cessé de parler, et ce n'est pas le silence. Qu'en est-il alors? Nous savons, ou croyons savoir. Mais seulement quand le passé qui signifie s'ouvre pour lui livrer passage. Le voici à notre hauteur, puis loin, devant.

A l'heure de nouveau contenue où nous questionnions tout le poids d'énigme, soudain commence la douleur, celle de compagnon à compagnon, que l'archer, cette fois, ne transperce pas.

ETERNITY AT LOURMARIN

Albert Camus

There is no longer a straight line nor lighted path with one who has left us. Where is our affection assuaged? Circle after circle, if he approaches, it is instantly to disappear. Sometimes his face presses against ours, yielding only an icy lightning-bolt. The day that spread out happiness between him and us is nowhere to be found. All the parts of a presence—almost excessive—have suddenly come asunder. The routine of our vigilance… And yet this one, suppressed, remains in something rigid, deserted, essential, within us, where our millennia together are no thicker than a closed eyelid.

With the one we love we have stopped speaking, and it is not silence. What exactly is it? We know, or think we do. But only when the meaningful past opens to let him through. Here he is, beside us, then faraway, ahead.

At the hour, once again calmed, when we question all the weight of the enigma, the pain suddenly begins, companion to companion, which the archer, this time, will not pierce.

—MAC & NK

René Char

LES DENTELLES DE MONTMIRAIL

Au sommet du mont, parmi les cailloux, les trompettes de terre cuite des hommes des vielles gelées blanches pépiaient comme de petits aigles.

Pour une douleur drue, s'il y a douleur.

La poésie vit d'insomnie perpétuelle.

Il semble que ce soit le ciel qui ait le dernier mot. Mais il le prononce a voix si basse que nul ne l'entend jamais.

Il n'y a pas de repli; seulement une patience millénaire sur laquelle nous sommes appuyés.

Dormez, désespérés, c'est bientôt jour, un jour d'hiver.

Nous n'avons qu'une ressource avec la mort: faire de l'art avant elle.

La réalité ne peut être franchie que soulevée.

Aux époques de détresse et d'improvisation, quelques-uns ne sont tués que pour une nuit et les autres pour l'éternité : un chant d'alouette des entrailles.

La quête d'un frère signifie presque toujours recherche d'un être, notre égal, à qui nous désirons offrir des transcendances dont nous finissons à peine de dégauchir les signes.

Le probe tombeau : une meule de blé. Le grain au pain, la paille pour le fumier.

Ne regardez qu'une fois la vague jeter l'ancre dans la mer.

THE DENTELLES OF MONTMIRAIL

At the mountain's summit, among the pebbles, the terracotta trumpets of the men of old hoar frost were chirruping like little eagles.

If there is pain, let it be a harsh pain.

Poetry lives on perpetual insomnia.

The heavens seem to have the last word. But it's said in such a low voice that no one ever hears it.

There's no withdrawal; only a patience of the ages upon which we've been leaning.

Sleep, despairing, soon it's day, a winter day.

We've only one resource with death: to create art before it.

Reality can't be traversed unless lifted up.

At times of distress and improvisation, some are killed only for one night and others for eternity: a lark song of the entrails.

The quest for a brother almost always means the search for a being, our equal, to whom we would like to offer transcendencies whose signs we are scarcely through setting straight.

The honest tomb: a wheat millstone. Seed for bread, straw for the dungheap.

Look only once as the wave casts anchor in the sea.

René Char

L'imaginaire n'est pas pur; il ne fait qu'aller.

Les grands ne se perpétuent que par les grands. On oublie. La mesure seule est blessée.

Qu'est-ce qu'un nageur qui ne saurait se glisser entièrement sous les eaux?

Avec des poings pour frapper, ils firent de pauvres mains pour travailler.

Les pluies sauvages favorisent les passants profonds.

L' essentiel est ce qui nous escorte, en temps voulu, en allongeant la route. C'est aussi une lampe sans regard, dans la fumée.

L' écriture d'un bleu fanal, pressée, dentelée, intrépide, du Ventoux alors enfant, courait toujours sur l'horizon de Montmirail qu'à tout moment notre amour m'apportait, m'enlevait.

Des débris de rois d'une inexpugnable férocité.

Les nuages ont des desseins aussi fermés que ceux des hommes.
Ce n'est pas l'estomac qui réclame la soupe bien chaude, c'est le coeur.

Sommeil sur la plaie pareil à du sel.

Une ingérence innommable a oté aux circonstances, aux êtres, leur hazard d'auréole. Il n'y a pas d'avènement pour nous qu'à partir de cette auréole. Elle n'immunise pas.
Cette neige, nous l'aimions, elle n'avait pas de chemin, découvrait notre faim.

The imaginary is not pure; it just goes along.

The great only perpetuate themselves through the great. We forget. Only measure is wounded.

What kind of swimmer couldn't slip entirely under water?

With fists to strike, they made poor hands to work.

Savage rains favor deep passersby.

The essential is what escorts us, in a given time, alongside the road. It's also a lamp without a gaze, in the smoke.

The writing of a blue lantern, hurried, jagged, intrepid, of the Ventoux still a child, always ran along on the horizon of Montmirail that our love brought to me in every moment, took away from me.

Royal debris of an impregnable ferocity.

The clouds have intentions as impenetrable as those of humans.

It's not the stomach asking for hot soup, it's the heart.

Sleep on the wound like salt.

An unnamable force has taken from things, circumstances, beings, their halo of chance. We've no access except starting from this halo. It does not confer immunity.

This snow, we loved it, it had no path, discovered our hunger.

—MAC

René Char

L'ALLÉGRESSE

Les nuages sont dans les rivières, les torrents parcourent le ciel. Sans saisie les journées montent en graine, meurent en herbe. Le temps de la famine et celui de la moisson, l'un sous l'autre dans l'air haillonneux, ont effacé leur différence. Ils filent ensemble, ils bivaquent! Comment la peur serait-elle distincte de l'espoir, passant raviné? Il n'y a plus de seuil aux maisons, de fumée aux clairières. Est tombé au gouffre le désir de chaleur—et ce peu d'obscurité dans notre dos où s'inquiétait la primevère dès qu'épiait l'avenir.

Pont sur la route des invasions, mentant au vainqueur, ex-orable au défait. Saurons-nous, sous le pied de la mort, si le cœur, ce gerbeur, ne doit pas précéder mais suivre?

JOYOUS

Clouds are in the rivers, torrents course through the sky.
Unpicked, the days run to seed, perish in the green. The time
of famine and the time of harvest, one beneath the other in the
tattered air, have wiped out their difference. They slip by together,
they encamp! How should fear be distinct from hope, furrowed
passerby? No more threshold to the houses, nor smoke to the
clearings. Fallen to the pit, the desire for warmth, and this slight
darkness at our back where the primrose became restless at the
future's peeping.

Bridge on the invader's path, deceptive to the victor, merciful
to the undone. Shall we know, under the heel of death, if the heart,
binder of sheaves, should not precede but follow?

—MAC

LE NU PERDU
(1964–1970)

NAKEDNESS LOST
(1964–1970)

TRACÉ SUR LE GOUFFRE

Dans la plaie chimérique de Vaucluse je vous ai regardé souffrir. Là, bien qu'abaissé, vous étiez une eau verte, et encore une route. Vous traversiez la mort en son désordre. Fleur vallonnée d'un secret continu.

TRACED UPON THE ABYSS

In the chimerical wound of Vaucluse I watched you suffering. There, although subsided, you were green water, and yet a road. You traversed death in its disorder. Flower valleyed by a continuous secret.

—MAC

MIRAGE DES AIGUILLES

Ils prennent pour de la clarté le rire jaune des ténèbres. Ils soupèsent dans leurs mains les restes de la mort et s'écrient: «Ce n'est pas pour nous.» Aucun viatique précieux n'embellit la gueule de leurs serpents déroulés. Leur femme les trompe, leurs enfants les volent, leurs amis les raillent. Ils n'en distinguent rien, par haine de l'obscurité. Le diamant de la création jette-t-il des feux obliques? Promptement un leurre pour le couvrir. Ils ne poussent dans leur four, ils n'introduisent dans la pâte lisse de leur pain qu'une pincée de désespoir fromental. Ils se sont établis et prospèrent dans le berceau d'une mer où l'on s'est rendu maître des glaciers. Tu es prévenu.

Comment, faible écolier, convertir l'avenir et détiser ce feu tant questionné, tant remué, tombé sur ton regard fautif?

Le présent n'est qu'un jeu ou un massacre d'archers.

Dès lors fidèle à son amour comme le ciel l'est au rocher. Fidèle, mèche, mais sans cesse vaguant, dérobant sa course par toute l'étendue montrée du feu, tenue du vent; l'étendue, trésor de boucher, sanglante à un croc.

MIRAGE OF THE PEAKS

They take for clarity the jaundiced laughter of shadows. They weigh in their hands death's remains and exclaim: "This is not for us." No precious viaticum embellishes the mouth of their uncoiled snakes. Their wife betrays them, their children rob them, their friends mock them. They see none of it, through hatred of darkness. Does creation's diamond cast oblique fires? Quickly a decoy to shroud it. They thrust in their oven, they place in the smooth dough of their bread just a small pinch of wheaten despair. They have settled and they prosper in the cradle of a sea where glaciers have been mastered. Be warned.

How, frail schoolchild, to convert the future and rake out this fire so questioned, so stirred up, that has fallen on your offending gaze?

The present is only a game or a massacre of archers.

From then on faithful to his love as is the sky to the rock. Faithful, fused, but ceaselessly wandering, concealing his way through all the sweep revealed by the fire, held by the wind; the sweep, the butcher's hoard, bleeding on a hook.

—MAC

René Char

YVONNE
La soif hospitalière

Qui l'entendit jamais se plaindre?

Nulle autre qu'elle n'aurait pu boire sans mourir les quarante
   fatigues,

Attendre, loin devant, ceux qui viendront après;
De l'éveil au couchant sa manœuvre était mâle.

Qui a creusé le puits et hisse l'eau gisante

Risque son cœur dans l'écart de ses mains.

YVONNE
Bountiful Thirst

Who ever heard her complain?

None other but she could have drunk forty trials and not perished,

Nor awaited, far ahead, those coming after,
From waking to setting her way was a man's.

Whoever has dug the well and raised the sleeping water

Risks her heart in the hollow of her hands.

—MAC

LE NU PERDU

Porteront rameaux ceux dont l'endurance sait user la nuit noueuse qui précède et suit l'éclair. Leur parole reçoit existence du fruit intermittent qui la propage en se dilacérant. Ils sont les fils incestueux de l'entaille et du signe, qui élevèrent aux margelles le cercle en fleurs de la jarre du ralliement. La rage des vents les maintient encore dévêtus. Contre eux vole un duvet de nuit noire.

LUTTEURS

Dans le ciel des hommes, le pain des étoiles me sembla ténébreux et durci, mais dans leurs mains étroites je lus la joute de ces étoiles en invitant d'autres: émigrantes du pont encore rêveuses; j'en recueillis la sueur dorée, et par moi la terre cessa de mourir.

Other Writings

NAKEDNESS LOST

They will bear boughs, those whose endurance can exhaust the gnarled night before and after the lightning flash. Their speech exists through the intermittent fruit that spreads it by tearing itself apart. They are the incestuous sons of the notch and the sign, who raised to the rims the flowering circle of the rallying jar. The rage of winds keeps them still unclothed. Against them flies a comforter of blackest night.

—MAC

WRESTLERS

In the sky of men, the star's bread seemed to me shadowy and hardened, but in their narrow hands I read the joust of these stars calling others: emigrants from below deck still dreaming; I gathered their golden sweat, and through me the earth ceased to die.

—MAC

LE GAUCHER

On ne se console de rien lorsqu'on marche en tenant une main, la périlleuse floraison de la chair d'une main.

L'obscurcissement de la main qui nous presse et nous entraîne, innocente aussi, l'odorante main où nous nous ajoutons et gardons ressource, ne nous évitant pas le ravin et l'épine, le feu prématuré, l'encerclement des hommes, cette main préférée à toutes, nous enlève à la duplication de l'ombre, au jour du soir. Au jour brillant au-dessus du soir, froissé son seuil d'agonie.

LEFT-HANDED

You are not consoled when you walk holding a hand, the perilous flowering of the flesh of a hand.

The obscuring of the hand that presses us and draws us on—innocent, too, the fragrant hand with which we fortify ourselves and safeguard our resources, which does not spare us gully and thorn, premature fire, encirclement by men—, this hand preferred to all others removes us from the shadow's duplication, from the day of evening. From the brilliant day above the evening, its threshold of agony bruised.

—NK

René Char

RÉMANENCE

De quoi souffres-tu? Comme si s'éveillait dans la maison sans bruit l'ascendant d'un visage qu'un aigre miroir semblait avoir figé. Comme si, la haute lampe et son éclat abaissés sur une assiette aveugle, tu soulevais vers ta gorge serrée la table ancienne avec ses fruits. Comme si tu revivais tes fugues dans la vapeur du matin à la rencontre de la révolte tant chérie, elle qui sut, mieux que toute tendresse, te secourir et t'élever. Comme si tu condamnais, tandis que ton amour dort, le portail souverain et le chemin qui y conduit.

De quoi souffres-tu?

De l'irréel intact dans le réel dévasté. De leurs détours aventureux cerclés d'appels et de sang. De ce qui fut choisi et ne fut pas touché, de la rive du bond au rivage gagné, du présent irréfléchi qui disparaît. D'une étoile qui s'est, la folle, rapprochée et qui va mourir avant moi.

PERMANENT INVISIBLE

Permanent invisible aux chasses convoitées,
Proche, proche invisible et si proche à mes doigts,
Ô mon distant gibier la nuit où je m'abaisse
Pour un novice corps à corps.
Boire frileusement, ère brutal répare.
Sur ce double jardin s'arrondit ton couvercle.
Tu as the densité de la rose qui se fera.

REMANENCE

From what do you suffer? As if in the noiseless house there were to awake the ascendancy of a face that an acrid mirror seemed to have fixed. As if, the high lamp and its radiance inclined over a blind plate, you were to lift toward your anguished throat the old table with its fruits. As if you were reliving your escapades in the morning haze toward the beloved revolt, which better than all tenderness, could succor you and raise you. As if condemning, while your love sleeps, the sovereign portal and the path leading toward it.

From what do you suffer?

From the unreal intact in reality laid waste. From their venturesome deviations circled with cries and blood. From that which was chosen and left untouched, from the shore of the leap to the coast attained, from the unreflecting present that disappears. From a star which, foolish, came near and will die before me.

—MAC

PERMANENT INVISIBLE

Permanent invisible of coveted hunting grounds,
Close, close, invisible and almost in my hands,
O my distant quarry, those nights when I sink down
To novice flesh against flesh.
Drinking against the cold, being brutal restores.
Over this double garden you form a rounded dome.
You are solid as the rose which is to be.

—PT

René Char

CONTRE UNE MAISON SÈCHE

S'il te faut repartir, prends appui contre une maison sèche. N'aie point souci de l'arbre grace auquel, de très loin, tu la reconnaîtras. Ses propres fruits le désaltereront.

Leve avant son sens, un mot nous éveille, nous prodigue la clarté du jour, un mot qui n'a pas rêvé.

*

Espace couleur de pomme. Espace, brulant compotier.

Aujourd' hui est un fauve. Demain verra son bond.

*

Mets-toi à la place des dieux et regarde-toi. Une seule fois en naissant échangé, corps sarclé où l'usure échoue, tu es plus invisible qu'eux. Et tu te répètes moins.

La terre a des mains, la lune n'en a pas. La terre est meurtrière, la lune desolée.

*

La liberte c'est ensuite le vide, un vide à déséspérement recenser. Après, chers emmurés émentissimes, c'est la forte odeur de votre dénouement. Comment vous surprendrait-elle?

Faut-il l'aimer, ce nu altérant, luster d'une vérité au coeur sec, au sang convulsif!

AGAINST A DRY HOUSE

If you must leave, lean against a dry house. Don't worry about the tree by which you'll know it from a distance. Its own fruits will quench its thirst.

Raised before its meaning, a word wakes us, bestows on us the day's brightness, a word that has not dreamed.

*

Apple-colored space. Space, burning fruit-bowl.

Today is a wild beast. Tomorrow will see it leap.

*

Put yourself in the place of the gods and behold yourself. Once only, being born exchanged, a body stripped clean where usury fails, you are more invisible than they are. And you repeat yourself less.

The earth has hands, the moon has none. The earth is murderous, the moon devastated.

*

Freedom is emptiness afterwards, emptiness to record in desperation. Afterwards, dear wonderfully eminent walled-in ones, it's the strong smell of your undoing. How would that surprise you?

Must we love him, this naked one, provoking thirst, shining with a dry-hearted truth, with a convulsive blood!

René Char

*

Avenir déjà raturé! Monde plaintif!

*Quand le masque de l'homme s'applique au visage de la terre,
elle a les yeux crevés.*

*

Sommes-nous hors de nos gonds pour toujours? Repeints
d'une beauté sauve?
*J'aurais pu prendre la nature comme partenaire et danser avec
elle à tous les bals. Je l'aimais. Mais deux ne s'épousent pas aux
vendanges.*

*

Mon amour préferait le fruit à son fantôme. J'unissais l'un à
l'autre, insoumis et courbé.
*Trois cent soixante-cinq nuits sans les jours bien massives, c' est
que je souhaite aux haîsseurs de la nuit.*

*

Ils vont nous faire souffrir, mais nous les ferons souffrir. Il
faudrait dire à l'or qui roule: «Venge-toi.» Au temps qui désunit :
«Serai-je avec qui j'aime ? Ô, ne pas qu'entrevoir!»
*Sont venus des tranche-montagnes qui n'ont que ce que leurs
yeux saisissent pour eux. Individus prompts à terroriser.*

*

N' émonde pas la flamme, n' écourte pas la braise en son print-
emps. Les migrations, par les nuits froides, ne s'arrêteraient pas
à ta vue.

We experience the insomnias of the Niagara and are looking for lands that are deeply moved, lands likely to move a nature again enraged.

The painter of Lascaux, Giotto, Van Eyck, Uccello, Fouquet, Mantegna, Cranach, Carpaccio, Tintoretto, Georges de La Tour, Poussin, Rembrandt, strands for my rocky nest.

*

Our storms are essential to us. In the order of pain, society is not necessarily at fault, despite its narrow places, its walls, their crumbling and then again their restoration.

We can't measure ourselves against the image that someone else has of us, soon the analogy would be lost.

*

We shall pass from death imagined to the reeds of death lived nakedly. Life, by abrasion, diverts itself through us.

Death is found neither on this side nor beyond. It is apart, industrious, minute.

*

I was born and grew up among tangible contraries at every moment, despite their wide extortions and the blows they exchanged. I roamed about the train stations.

Shining heart does not illuminate only its own night. It rights the drooping stalk.

*

Il en est qui laissent des poisons, d'autres des remèdes. Difficiles à déchiffrer. Il faut goûter.

Le oui, le non immédiats, c'est salubre en dépit des corrections qui vont suivre.

*

Au séjour supérieur, nul invité, nul partage : l'urne fondamentale. L'éclair trace le présent, en balafre le jardin, poursuit, sans assaillir, son extension, ne cessera de paraître comme d'avoir été.

Les favorisés de l'instant n' ont pas vécu comme nous avons osé vivre, sans crainte du voilement de notre imagination, par tendresse d'imagination.

*

Nous ne sommes tués que par la vie. La mort est l'hôte. Elle délivre la maison de son enclos et la pousse à l'orée du bois.

Soleil jouvenceau, je te vois; mais là où tu n'es plus.

*

Qui croit renouvelable l'énigme, la devient. Escaladant librement l'érosion béante, tantôt lumineux, tantôt obscur, savoir sans fonder sera sa loi. Loi qu'il observera mais qui aura raison de lui; fondation dont il ne voudra mais qu'il mettra en oeuvre.

On doit sans cesse en revenir a l'érosion. La douleur contre la perfection.[1]

*

Other Writings

Some set out poison, others remedies. Difficult to decipher. You have to taste.

Immediate yes and no are healthy despite the corrections afterwards.

*

In the sojourn up there, no guest, no sharing: the fundamental urn. Lightning tracks the present, slashes its garden, pursues, without assaulting, its extension, ceases neither appearing, nor having been.

Those favored by the instant have not lived as we have dared to live, without fear of veiling our imagination, imaginative and tender.

*

We are killed only by life. Death is the host. It delivers the house from its enclosure and shoves it to the edge of the woods.

Sun, young lad, I see you; but where you no longer are.

*

He who believes the enigma renewable, becomes it. Freely climbing the gaping erosion, now luminous, now obscure, to know without founding anything will be his law. A law he will observe but which will win out over him; a foundation he won't want but that he will put in place.

We should ceaselessly come back to erosion. Sorrow against perfection.[1]

*

Tout ce que nous accomplirons d'essentiel à partir d'aujour-d'hui, nous l'accomplirons faute de mieux. Sans contentement ni désespoir. Pour seul soleil : le boeuf écorché de Rembrandt. Mais comment se résigner à la date et à l'odeur sur le gîte affichées, nous qui, sur l'heure, sommes intelligents jusqu'aux conséquences?

Une simplicité s'ébauche : le feu monte, la terre emprunte, la neige vole, la rixe éclate. Les dieux-dits nous déleguent un court temps leur loisir, puis nous prennent en haine de l'avoir accepté. Je vois un tigre. Il voit. Salut. Qui, là, parmi les menthes, est parvenu à naître dont toute chose, demain, se prévaudra ?

---

[1] Ici le mur sollicité de la maison perdue de vue ne renvoie plus de mots clairvoyants.

Other Writings

Everything essential we'll accomplish from today on, we'll accomplish for want of anything better. Without satisfaction[1] or despair. For our only sun: Rembrandt's flayed ox. But how to resign ourselves to the date and the odor pinned up on the dwelling, we who now understand even the consequences?

One simple thing appears: fire rises, earth borrows, snow flies, quarrels break out. The so-called gods delegate their leisure to us for a short time, then detest us for having accepted it. I see a tiger. He sees. Greetings. Who there, among the mint, has managed to be born, over whom everything tomorrow, will prevail?

—MAC

---

[1] Here the wall we've sought, of the house now lost from view, no longer sends back any perspicacious words.

LA NUIT TALISMANIQUE
(1972)

THE TALISMANIC NIGHT
(1972)

VÉTÉRANCE

Maintenant que les apparences trompeuses, les miroirs piquetés se multiplient devant les yeux, nos traces passées deviennent véridiquement les sites où nous nous sommes agenouillés pour boire. Un temps immense, nous n'avons circulé et saigné que pour capter les traits d'une aventure commune. Voici que dans le vent brutal nos signes passagers trouvent, sous l'humus, la réalité de ces poudreuses enjambées qui lèvent un printemps derrière elles.

L'ANNEAU DE LA LICORNE

Il s'était senti bousculé et solitaire à la lisière de sa constellation qui n'était dans l'espace recuit qu'une petite ville frileuse.

A qui lui demanda: «L'avez-vous enfin rencontrée? Etes-vous enfin heureux?» il dédaigna de répondre et déchira une feuille de viorne.

VETERANCE

Now that deceptive appearances, all the pockmarked mirrors, are multiplying before our eyes, our past traces truly become the sites where we have knelt to drink. For an immeasurable time we moved about and bled only to capture the features of a common adventure. And so in the brutal wind our passing signs find the reality, beneath the humus, of those powdery strides which stir up spring behind them.

—NK

THE RING OF THE UNICORN

He had felt jostled and lonely at the border of his constellation, only a little town shivering in tempered space.

To the questioner: "Have you finally met her? Are you happy at last?" he did not deign to reply, and tore a leaf of guelder-rose.

—MAC

ÉPROUVANTE SIMPLICITÉ

Mon lit est un torrent aux plages desséchées. Nulle fougère n'y cherche sa patrie. Où t'es-tu glissé tendre amour?

Je suis parti pour longtemps. Je revins pour partir.

Plus loin, l'une des trois pierres du berceau de la source tarie disait ce seul mot gravé pour le passant: «Amie.»

J'inventai un sommeil et je bus sa verdeur sous l'empire de l'été.

A TRYING SIMPLICITY

My bed is a torrent with dried-up banks. No fern looks for its country there. Where have you hidden, my love?

I left for a long time. I came back to leave.

Farther on, one of three stones cradled in the exhausted spring spoke this single word engraved deeply for the passerby: "Friend."

I invented a sleep and drank its greenness under the sway of summer.

—MAC

AROMATES CHASSEURS
(1972–1975)

AROMATIC HUNTERS
(1972–1975)

RÉCEPTION D'ORION

Qui cherchez-vous brunes abeilles
Dans la lavande qui s'éveille?
Passe votre roi serviteur.
Il est aveugle et s'éparpille.
Chasseur il fuit
Les fleurs qui le poursuivent.
Il tend son arc et chaque bête brille.
Haute est sa nuit; flèches risquez vos chances.

Un météore humain a la terre pour miel.

1974

ÉBRIÉTÉ

Tandis que la moisson achevait de se graver sur le
cuivre du soleil, une alouette chantait dans la faille du
grand vent sa jeunesse qui allait prendre fin. L'aube
d'automne parée de ses miroirs déchirés de coups de
feu, dans trois mois retentirait.

ORION'S RECEPTION

Dark bees, whom are you seeking
In the lavender awaking?
Your servant king is passing by.
Blind, he strays, dispersing.
A hunter, he flees
The flowers pursuing him.
He bends his bow and each creature shines.
High is his night; arrows take your chance.

A human meteor has the earth for honey.

1974

—MAC

INEBRIATION

While the harvest finished etching itself
on the sun's copper, a lark sang in a fault of
the great wind its youth which was to end.
Autumn's dawn, bejeweled with mirrors torn by
gunshot, in three months would resound.

—NK

NOTE SIBÉRIENNE

La neige n'accourait plus dans les mains des enfants. Elle s'amassait et enfantait sur notre nordique visage des confins. Dans cette nuit de plus en plus exigue nous ne distinguons pas qui naissait.

Pourquoi alors cette repetition: nous sommes une étincelle à l'origine inconnue qui incendions toujours plus avant. Ce feu, nous l'entendons râler et crier, à l'instant d'être consumés? Rien, sinon que nous étions souffrants, au point que
le vaste silence, en son centre, se brisait.

A FOOTNOTE FROM SIBERIA

The snow was no longer rushing into the hands of children. It piled up on our Nordic faces, gave birth to boundaries. In that night increasingly narrowed, we couldn't make out who was being born.

So why this repetition: we are a spark of unknown origin endlessly burning onward. This fire, do we hear its death-throes and its cries just as we are being consumed? Nothing, but we were suffering so terribly that the vast silence at its center was breaking apart.

—MAC & PT

CHANTS DE LA BALANDRANE
(1975–1977)

SONGS OF THE BALANDRANE
(1975–1977)

JE ME VOULAIS ÉVÉNEMENT... 1926

Je me voulais événement. Je m'imaginais partition. J'étais gauche. La tête de mort qui contre mon gré remplaçait la pomme que je portais fréquemment à la bouche n'était aperçue que de moi. Je· me mettais à l'écart pour mordre correctement la chose. Comme on ne déambu!e pas, comme on ne peut prétendre à l'amour avec un tel fruit aux dents, je me décidais, quand j' avais faim, à lui donner le nom de pomme. Je ne fus plus inquiété. Ce n'est que plus tard que l'objet de mon embarras m'apparût sous les traits ruisse-lants et tout aussi ambigus de poème.

EN DÉPIT DU FROID GLACIAL

En dépit du froid glacial qui, à tes débuts, t'a traversé, et bien avant ce qui survint, tu n'étais qu'un feu inventé par le feu, détroussé par le temps, et qui, au mieux, périrait faute de feu renouvelé, sinon de la fièvre des cendres inhalées.

I WANTED MYSELF TO BE AN EVENT... 1926

I wanted myself to be an event... I imagined myself a musical score. I was awkward. The death's head which, against my will, replaced the apple that I frequently carried about in my mouth, was seen by no one but myself. I went aside so as to bite the thing correctly. As one doesn't saunter, as one can only claim to love with such a fruit in one's teeth, I decided, when I was hungry, to give it the name of apple. I was no longer bothered. It wasn't until later that the object of my confusion appeared to me under the streaming features, just as ambiguous, as a poem.

—MAC

DESPITE THE GLACIAL COLD

Despite the glacial cold that, at your beginning, traversed you, and well before what came about, you were only a fire invented by the fire, robbed by time, and who, at the best, would perish from the lack of the fire renewed, if not from the fever of the ashes breathed in,

—MAC

LA FLÛTE ET LE BILLOT, II

THE FLUTE AND THE BLOCK

LE SCARABÉE SAUVÉ IN EXTREMIS

L'étoile retardataire vient a son tour d'éclater. Notre double coeur l'a perçu. Son brasier au visage grêle sera le dernier d'une longue carrière. Le rang des ténèbres s'est ouvert. Mais qu'elle doit hésiter, sans son nom, à glisser! La souffrance éparpillée commet peu d'énergie. Moins qu'un soleil. Moins qu'une chatte décidée à mordre. Pour nous, il ne s'agit que de naître et de battre l'air, d'écumer un moment, puis d'enserrer une nuque docile et de rire de l'embarras du coursier. Au bord des belles dents des jours, la part privée du coeur, aiguisée de hantises, devra-t-elle encore être ce bourreau de la nôtre, la libérable, comme c'est la coutume? Les meurtrieurs innocents achètent des bijoux à leurs filles. Nous, non. Ah! Aujourd'hui tout se chante en cendres, l'étoile autant que nous.

THE SCARAB SAVED AT THE LAST MOMENT

The tardy star just shone forth in its turn. Our double heart perceived it. Its fire with a frozen face will be the last of a long line. The row of shadows has opened. But how hesitant it must feel, nameless, slipping into it! Scattered suffering commits very little energy. Less than a sun. Less than a cat determined to bite. For us, it is just a matter of being born and beating the air, skimming off a moment, then squeezing a docile nape, and laughing at the confusion of the messenger. At the edge of the lovely teeth of the days, the private piece of the heart, sharpened with obsessions, must it still be this executioner of ours, the one to be freed, as has been the custom? Innocent murderers buy jewels for their daughters. Not us. Ah, today everything is sung in ashes, the star as well as ourselves.

—MAC

LE RÉVISEUR

Il m'était difficile de faire glisser mon imagination au milieu de
tant de calme. A l' entrée même de ce mot creux où rien de ce qui
nous élève ne retentit plus. C' était si bas, si bas devant mes pieds
et sans une trace d'air … Je parviendrai à m'y étendre. Mais seule
l'irascible Riveraine, au sortir des misères et des splendeurs de
la vie, la courtisane au collier de fer, devait permettre l'accolade
véridique, et peut-être consentirait-elle à me la donner pour autant
que je ne l'aie point déçue, si inapte suis-je à me retourner. Je ne lui
demandais que le viatique vicariant, pas davantage. De frénétiques
délateurs, des bourreaux tranquilles, à l'ouvrage dans l'univers,
s'appliquaient selon des préceptes supérieurs. Une domesticité
savante attachait ses connaissances à les satisfaire, emplissait de
proies leurs calices entrouverts. Sur l'écran de ma veille, face à la
glace diffusante des lunes et des soleils, le monde quotidien de
l'internement, de la filature, de la déportation, des supplices et de
la crémation devenait pyramidal à l'image du haut négoce qui
prospérait sous sa potence en or. Mais j'avais vu grandir, écarlate,
l'arrière-fleur aux doigts du ferronnier, bondir de son berceau l'eau
dédiée à la nuit. Comme un lac de montagne avoisinant la neige et
le hameau, j'avais vécu.

THE EXAMINER

It was hard for me to slide my imagination into the center of such calm. At the very entrance of this hollow word where nothing of what uplifts us resounds any longer. It was so low, so low before my feet and without a trace of air…I will manage to stretch out in it. But only the irascible Dweller, leaving the miseries and the splendors of life, the courtesan with the iron collar, could allow the real accolade, and perhaps she would consent to give me one provided I hadn't disappointed her, so inapt am I to reverse myself. I only asked her for the apostolic viaticum, no more than that. Frenetic informers, tranquil executioners, working in the universe, were applying themselves to the task according to superior precepts. A learned domesticity was using its knowledge to satisfy them, filling their half-open chalices with prey. On the screen of my watchfulness, across from the diffusing mirror of moons and suns, the daily world of imprisonment, of networking, of deportation, of torture and cremation, was taking a pyramid shape in the image of the lofty business which was prospering under its golden gallows. But I had seen, in a scarlet late flowering at the fingertips of the blacksmith, the water dedicated to night spring forth from its cradle. Like a mountain lake neighboring the snow and the hamlet, I had lived.

—MAC

René Char

471

FENÊTRES DORMANTES ET
PORTE SUR LE TOIT
(1973–1979)

DORMER WINDOWS AND
DOOR ON THE ROOF
(1973–1979)

LÉGÈRETÉ DE LA TERRE

Le repos, la planche de vivre? Nous tombons. Je vous écris en cours de chute. C'est ainsi que j'éprouve l'état d'être au monde. L'homme se défait aussi sûrement qu'il fut jadis composé. La roue du destin tourne à l'envers et ses dents nous déchiquettent. Nous prendrons feu bientôt du fait de l'accélération de la chute. L'amour, ce frein sublime, est rompu, hors d'usage.

Rien de cela n'est écrit sur le ciel assigné, ni dans le livre convoité qui se hâte au rythme des battements de notre coeur, puis se brise alors que notre coeur continue à battre.

RÉCIT ÉCOURTÉ

Tout ce qui illuminait à l'intérieur de nous gisait maintenant à nos pieds. Hors d'usage. L'intelligence que nous recevons du monde matériel, avec les multiples formes au-dehors nous comblant de bienfaits, se détournait de nos besoins. Le miroir avait brisé tous ses sujets. On ne frète pas le vent ni ne descend le cours de la tempête. Ne grandit pas la peur, n'augmente pas le courage. Nous allons derechef répéter le projet suivant, jusqu'à la réalité du retour qui délivrera un nouveau départ de concert. Enserre de ta main le poignet de la main qui te tend le plus énigmatique des cadeaux: une riante flamme levée, éprise de sa souche au point de s'en séparer.

LIGHTNESS OF EARTH

A rest, a life raft? We are falling. I'm writing you on the way
down. That's the way I feel the state of being in the world. Man is
undoing himself just as surely as he was built up in former times.
The wheel of fate is turning backwards and its teeth are tearing us
apart. We will catch fire soon, we are falling more and more
quickly. Love, that sublime brake, is broken, unusable.

Nothing of that is written on the heavens assigned to us, nor in
the book so coveted that hastens to the rhythm of our heartbeat,
then shatters while our heart continues to beat.

—MAC

A TALE CUT SHORT

Everything that illuminated us within now lay at our feet.
Beyond repair. The intelligence that we receive from the material
world, its multiple outside forms filling us with blessings, was
turning away from our needs. The mirror had broken all its sub-
jects. We do not charter the wind nor descend the wake of the
storm. Fear does not grow, courage does not augment. We are
yet again going to rehearse the next scheme, until the return that
offers a new concerted departure becomes reality. With your hand,
take the wrist of the hand that holds out to you the most enigmatic
of gifts: a laughing lifted flame, enough in love with its stalk to
leave it.

—NK

René Char

ÉPRISE

Chaque carreau de la fenêtre est un morceau de mur en face, chaque pierre scellée du mur une recluse bienheureuse qui nous éclaire matin, soir, de poudre d'or à ses sables mélangée. Notre logis va son histoire. Le vent aime à y tailler.

L'étroit espace où se volatilise cette fortune est une petite rue au-dessous dont nous n'apercevons pas le pavé. Qui y passe emporte ce qu'il désire.

IN LOVE

Each windowpane is a part of the facing wall, each stone sealed in the wall a blessed recluse lighting our morning, our evening with the gold dust mixed into its sands. Our dwelling lives out its fate. The wind loves to cut into it.

The narrow space where this fortune spins away is a little street below, whose paving we cannot see. Whoever passes there takes from it what he wishes.

—MAC & PT

RECHERCHE DE LA BASE
ET DU SOMMET

SEARCH FOR THE BASE
AND THE SUMMIT

PRIÈRE ROGUE

Gardez-nous la révolte, l'éclair, l'accord illusoire, un rire pour le trophée glissé des mains, même l' entier et long fardeau qui succède, dont la difficulté nous mène à une révolte nouvelle. Gardez-nous la primevère et le destin.

UNBENDING PRAYER

Preserve for us rebellion, lightning, the illusory agreement, a laugh for the trophy slipped from our hands, even the whole lengthy burden that follows, whose difficulty leads us to a new rebellion. Preserve for us fate and the primrose.

1948

—MAC

René Char   481

EN VUE DE GEORGES BRAQUE

LAISSONS-LUI LA TRANQUILLITÉ

Laissons-lui la tranquillité et la nature là où il se fixe, travaille. Nous verrons, à moins d'accident en l'observant, qu'il en va pour ce saisonnier comme pour le platane, comme pour le serpent. Il y aurait bien d'autres modèles à proposer, mais l'écorce tombée est ici immédiatement ressaisie et traitée, la peau légère et vide se remplit d'une pommelé d'un ovipare nouveau. Peintre, il ne produit qu'à partir d'un motif temporal; sa façon d'appeler l'inexplicable donne la survie à ce crystal spirite: l'Art.

WITH A VIEW TO GEORGES BRAQUE

LET'S LEAVE HIM TRANQUILITY...

Let's leave him nature and tranquility right there where he situates himself, working. We will see, unless something goes wrong when observing him, that it's the same for this man of seasons as for the plane tree, as for the snake. There might be many other models we could propose, but the bark fallen here is immediately picked up and treated, the light and empty skin fills with the dappled colors of a new ovipare. Painter, he only produces starting with a timely motif; his way of naming the inexplicable permits the survival of this spiritualist crystal: Art.

—MAC

GEORGES BRAQUE

Les enfants et les génies savent 'qu'il n'existe pas de pont, seulement l'eau qui se laisse traverser. Aussi chez Braque 1a source est-elle inséparable du rocher, le fruit du sol, le nuage de son destin, invisiblement et souverainement. Le va-et-vient incessant de la solitude à l'être et de l'être à la solitude fonde sous nos yeux le plus grand coeur qui soit. Braque pense que nous avons besoin de trop de choses pour nous satisfaire d' *une* chose, par conséquent i1 faut assurer, à tout prix, la continuité de création, même si nous ne devons jamais en beneficier. Dans notre monde concret de résurrection et d'angoisse de non-résurrection, Braque assume le perpétuel. Il n'a pas l'appréhension des quêtes futures bien qu'ayant le souci des formes à naître. Il leur placera toujours un homme dedans !

Oeuvre terrestre comme aucune autre et pourtant combien harcelée du frisson des alchimies !

Au terme du laconisme …

Other Writings

GEORGES BRAQUE

Children and geniuses know there is no bridge, only water letting itself be crossed. So in Braque, the spring is inseparable from the rock, the fruit from the earth, the cloud from its fate, invisibly and supremely. The incessant coming and going from solitude to being and from being to solitude establishes right under our eyes the greatest heart there could be. Braque thinks we need too many things to satisfy ourselves with *one* thing, and so we have to guarantee, at any price, the continuity of creation, even if we will never benefit from it. In our concrete world of resurrection and of the agony of non-resurrection, Braque assumes what is perpetual. He never has any apprehension about future quests even as he always cares about forms yet to be born. He will always place a man within them!

Earthly work, like no other and still how harassed by the shiver of alchemies!

At the very end of laconism...

1947

—MAC

BRAQUE, LORSQU'IL PEIGNAIT

Braque, lorsqu'il peignait à Sorgues en 1912, se plaisait, après le travail, à pousser une pointe jusqu'à Avignon. C'est sur les marches du fol escalier extérieur qui introduisent au palais des Papes que toujours le déposait sa rêverie. Il s' asseyait à même La Pierre, et dévisageait, en la convoitant, la demeure qui n'était solennelle et au passé que pour d'autres que lui. Les murs nus des salles intérieures le fascinaient. (« Un tableau accroché là s'il tient, » pensait-il, « est verifié. ») Il attendit, pour savoir, l'année 1947, année au cours de laquelle ses oeuvres y furent mises en évidence.

GEORGES BRAQUE INTRA-MUROS

Palais des Papes, Avignon

J'ai vu, dans un palais surmonté de la tiare, un homme entrer et regarder les murs. Il parcourut la solitude dolente et se tourna vers la fenêtre. Les eaux proches du fleuve durent au meme instant tournoyer, puis la beauté qui va d'un couple à une pierre, puis la poussière des rebelles dans leur sépulcre de papes.

Les quatre murs majeurs se mirent à porter ses espoirs, le monde qu'il avait forcé et révélé, la vie acquiescent au secret, et ce coeur qui éclate en couleurs, que chacun fait sien pour le meilleur et pour le pire.

J'ai vu, cet hiver, ce même homme sourire à sa maison très basse, tailler un roseau pour dessiner des fleurs. Je l'ai vu, du baton percer l'herbe geleé, être l'oeil qui respire et enflamme la trace.

Other Writings

BRAQUE WHEN HE WAS PAINTING

Braque, when he was painting in Sorgues in 1912, liked, after his work, to come over to Avignon. There, on the steps of the crazy exterior staircase leading to the Palais des Papes, his dreaming always set him down. He sat down right on the stone, and kept looking, with envy, at the dwelling which was in the past and solemn only for others than himself. The bare walls of the inner rooms fascinated him. "A painting that was hung there, if it holds up," he thought, "is verified." He waited, in order to find out, for the year 1947, a year during which his works were displayed there.

1963

—MAC

GEORGES BRAQUE INTRA-MUROS

Palais des Papes, Avignon

I saw, in a palace with a tiara on top, a man enter and look at the walls. He crossed through the sorrowful solitude and turned towards the window. The near waters of the river had to turn at the same instant, then the beauty which goes from a couple to a stone, then the dust of the rebels in their papal sepulchre.

The four main walls began to bear his hopes, the world he had forced and revealed, life acquiesced in the secret, and this heart which bursts in colors, that each one makes his own for the best and the worst.

I saw, this winter, the same man smile at his very low house, carve a reed to draw some flowers. I saw him pierce the frozen grass, saw him become the eye breathing, inflaming the trace.

1947

—MAC

René Char

AVEC BRAQUE, PEUT-ÊTRE, ON S'ÉTAIT DIT.

Quand la neige s'endort, la nuit rappelle ses chiens.

Fruits, vous vous tenez si loin de votre arbre que les étoiles du ciel semblent votre reflet.

Nous nous égarons lorsque la ligne droite, qui s'empresse devant nous, devient le sol sur lequel nous marchons. Nous nous abaissons à une piètre félicité.

Saveur des vagues qui ne retombent pas. Elles rejettent la mer dans son passé.

Le sang demeure dans les plumes de la flèche, non à sa pointe. L'arc l'a voulu ainsi.

L'orage a deux maisons. L'une occupe une brève place sur l'horizon; l'autre, tout un homme suffit à peine à la contenir.

La rosée souffre tôt. Par de bas matins elle se mesure avec l'hypogée de la nuit, avec la rudesse du jour, avec le durable tumulte des fontaines.

Cet homme était couvert des morsures de son imagination. L'imaginaire ne saignait qu'à des cicatrices anciennes.

L'art est une route qui finit en sentier, en tremplin, mais dans un champ à nous.

WITH BRAQUE WE USED PERHAPS TO SAY...

When the snow falls asleep, the night calls back its dogs.

Fruits, you stay so far from your tree that the stars in the sky seem your reflection.

We get lost when the straight line, which hastens before us, becomes the ground on which we are walking. We lower ourselves to a paltry happiness

Savor of the waves that do not fall down. They throw the sea back into its past.

Blood dwells in the feathers of the arrow, not at its point. The bow willed it thus.

The storm has two houses. One occupies a brief place on the horizon; the other, an entire man scarcely suffices to contain it.

Dew suffers soon. On early mornings it measures itself with the hypogeum of the night, with the roughness of the day, with the enduring tumult of fountains.

This man was covered with the bites of his imagination. The imaginary only bled in the ancient scars.

Art is a road that finishes in a path, in a trampoline, but in a field of our own.

1963

—MAC

A ***

Tu es mon amour depuis tant d'années,
Mon vertige devant tant d'attente,
Que rien ne peut vieillir, froidir;
Même ce qui attendait notre mort,
Ou lentement sut nous combattre,
Même ce qui nous est étranger,
Et mes éclipses et mes retours.

Fermée comme un volet de buis,
Une extrême chance compacte
Est notre chaîne de montagnes,
Notre comprimante splendeur.

Je dis chance, ô ma martelée;
Chacun de nous peut recevoir
La part de mystère de l'autre
Sans en répandre le secret;
Et la douleur qui vient d'ailleurs
Trouve enfin sa séparation
Dans la chair de notre unité,
Trouve enfin sa route solaire
Au centre de notre nuée
Qu'elle déchire et recommence.

Je dis chance comme je le sens.
Tu as élevé le sommet
Que devra franchir mon attente
Quand demain disparaîtra.

1948–1950

Other Writings

You have been my love for so many years,
Vertiginous depths of waiting
That nothing can age or cool;
Even what lay in wait for our death,
Or slowly found out how to fight us,
Even the alien things,
And myself in eclipse and coming back.

Closed like a boxwood shutter,
Compressed to the limit, chance
Is our range of mountains,
Our constricting splendor.

I say chance, O my hammered-out love;
Each of us can contain
The other's share of mystery
Without releasing its secret;
And the pain which comes from outside
Finds its separation at last
In the flesh of our unity,
At last finds its solar road
In the center of our cloud
It rends and begins again.

I say chance as it seems to me.
You have lifted up the summit
My waiting will have to cross
When tomorrow disappears.

1948–1950

—PT

René Char

A FAULX CONTENTE

TO YOUR HEART'S CONTENT

QUAND LES CONSÉQUENCES NE SONT PLUS NIÉES...

Quand les conséquences ne sont plus niées, le poème respire, dit qu'il a obtenu son aire. Iris rescapeé de la crue des eaux.

Le souffle levé, descendre à reculons, puis obliquer et suivre le sentier qui ne mène qu'au coeur ensanglanté de soi, source et sépulcre du poème.

L'influx de milliards d'années de toutes parts et circnlairement le chant jamais rendu d'Orphée.

Les dieux sont dans la métaphore. Happée par le brusque écart, la poésie s'augmente d'un au-delà sans tutelle.

Le poème nous couche dans une douleur ajournée sans séparer le froid de l'ardent.

Vint un soir où le Coeur ne se reconnut plus dans les mots qu'il prononçait pour lui seul.

Le poète fait éclater les liens de ce qu'il touche. Il n'enseigne pas la fin des liens.

THE CONSEQUENCES NO LONGER DENIED

The consequences no longer denied, the poem breathes, says it has reached its own domain. Iris escaped from the rising of the waters.

Take a deep breath and climb down backwards, then cut across and follow the path which leads only to the self's bleeding heart. Source and sepulcher of the poem. Billions of years flowing in from everywhere, and circular, the song of Orpheus never at an end.

Gods are in the metaphors. Taken over by the sudden change of direction, poetry gains an unsupported beyond.

The poem poses us in a suffering delayed, not separating cold from burning.

There came an evening when the heart no long recognized itself in the words it was speaking for itself alone.

The poet explodes the connections of what he touches. He does not teach the end of all connections.

—MAC & PT

René Char

LES VOISINAGES DE VAN GOGH

IN THE VICINITY OF VAN GOGH

BESTIAIRE DANS MON TRÈFLE

Soupçonnons que la poésie soit une situation entre les alliages de la vie, l'approche de la douleur, l'élection exhortée, et le baisement en ce moment même. Elle ne se séparerait de son vrai coeur que si le plein découvrait sa fatalité, le combat commencerait alors entre le vide et la communion. Dans ce monde transposé, il nous resterait à faire le court *éloge d'une Soupçonnée,* la seule qui garde force de mots jusqu'au bord des larmes. Sa jeune démence aux douze distances croyant enrichir ses lendemains s'illusionnerait sur la moins frêle aventure despotique qu'un vivant ait vécu en côtoyant les chaos qui passaient pour irrésistibles. Ils ne l'étaient qu'intrinsèquement mais sans une trace de caprice. Venus d'où? D'un calendrier bouleversé bien qu'uni au Temps, sans qu'en soit ressentie l'usure.

Verdeur d'une Soupçonnée…

La fatigue est favorable aux animaux généreux, quand nous nous montrons sensibles à leur existence oppressée.

Nausée après un précipité de rêves. Ensuite un souffle original de terreur et de bonheur. Peu en somme.

Qu'est devenu le loup par ces temps d'abandon? Il s'aligna sur l'homme quand il constata qu'il ne pouvait se plier à celui-ci; et la cage s'ouvrit la première devant l'espace de sa mort, au ras de ses pattes pressées.

BESTIARY IN MY TREFOIL

Let's surmise that poetry is a situation between the relation-ships of life, the approach of pain, the choice exhorted, and union in this very moment. It would not be separated from its true heart unless fullness unveiled its fatality, the battle would then begin between emptiness and communion. In this transposed world, we would still have to make the brief *éloge d'une Soupçonnée,* the only one which retains verbal strength up to the edge of tears. Its young madness with the twelve distances thinking to enrich its tomorrows would have illusions as to the least fragile despotic adventure that a living person had lived next to the forms of chaos seemingly irre-sistible. They were that only intrinsically but without a trace of whim. Where did they come from? From a calendar upset although united to Time, without any sense of usury.

Greenery of One Suspected...

Fatigue is favorable to generous animals, when we show our-selves caring about their oppressed existence.

Nausea after a rush of dreams. Then a primitive gust of terror and happiness. Not much, after all.

What has the wolf become in these times of abandon? He was on the side of humans when he noticed he couldn't adapt to them; and the cage opened for the first time in front of the space of his death, at the level of his hurried paws.

—MAC

René Char

CARTE ROUTIÈRE

Toi qui t'allongeas sur des peines dont j'inventais les occasions
Sans les augmenter à ravir,
Tes réticences de trésor mènent à des maigreurs de tisons;
Tu me regardes tel un sourd;
O mon Amie irréfléchie, où s'est glissé ton enjouement?
Mes vieux danseurs exténués par d'imaginaires nuages, les roseaux
    nous en séparent de tout leur ramage froissé.
Soleil tourne autour du jeune arbre, Le vent ne charme que les
    blés. Meure la distante maison.

DE MOMENT EN MOMENT
(from *La Bâton de Rosier / The Rose-Tree Staff*)

Pourquoi ce chemin plutôt que cet autre? Où mène-t-il pour
nous solliciter si fort? Quels arbres et quels amis sont vivants
derrière l'horizon de ces pierres, dans le lointain miracle de la
chaleur? Nous sommes venus jusqu'ici car là où nous étions ce
n'était plus possible. On nous tourmentait et on allait nous
asservir. Le monde, de nos jours, est hostile aux Transparents.
Une fois de plus, il a fallu partir... Et ce chemin, qui ressemblait
à un long squelette, nous a conduits à un pays qui n'avait que son
souffle pour escalader l'avenir. Comment montrer, sans les trahir,
les choses simples dessinées entre le crépuscule et le ciel? Par la
vertu de la vie obstinée, dans la boucle du Temps artiste, entre la
mort et la beauté.

1949

ROAD MAP

You stretched out on strains I invented,
Without magnifying them to delight,
Your restraints of richness lead to meager firebrands;
You look at me as at a deafman;
O my unreflective Friend, where has your gaiety gone?
My old dancers worn out by imaginary clouds, the reeds separate
us from them with all their crumpled foliage.
Sun turn around the young tree,
The wind charms only the wheat.
Let the distant house perish.

—MAC

FROM MOMENT TO MOMENT

Why this path rather than that other? Where does it lead, that
it calls to us so strongly? What trees and what friends are alive
behind the horizon of these stones, in the distant miracle of heat?
We came this far because where we were was no longer possible.
We were tormented and were going to submit. Nowadays, the
world is hostile to the Transparents. Once again, we had to leave...
And this path, which resembled a long skeleton, led us to a coun-
try that had only its breath with which to climb the future. How
to show, without betraying them, the simple things sketched out
between the twilight and the sky? By virtue of stubborn life, in the
curl of Time the artist, between death and beauty.

1949

—MAC & NK

René Char

La Fontaine de Vaucluse. This photo by René Char was inscribed, *"Dans la plaie chimérique de Vaucluse"* (In the mythic wound of the Vaucluse).

MEETING RENÉ CHAR

Nancy Kline

Sometimes what is real fulfills our hopes.
That is why, against all odds, hope survives.
—René Char[1]

In March 1972, I wrote René Char a letter. I had been reading his poetry for ten years, and now, about to begin my dissertation on his work, I was going to visit the Vaucluse for the first time, to look at the specific geography in which all his poems are rooted. Why not write, to ask if I could meet him for the length of a lightning bolt? I doubted anything would come of it. Char was France's greatest living poet and a towering figure in the page. Besides which, the only address I had for him was the town where he lived. Still, why not? I wrote to

René Char
L'Isle-sur-Sorgue
France.

Three days before my departure, when I got a letter back, it felt as though I had been struck—precisely—by lightning. As though Zeus had responded. "You can meet me in my house, 'Les Busclats,'" the poet wrote, and told me how to get there, and asked that I send a telegram two days before my arrival.

And so we began, in a halting, gendered, love-hate, disciple-master but not altogether, fragmentary fashion, to talk to each other. We wrote letters sporadically for the next eleven years, and I visited him in L'Isle-sur-Sorgue six times during that period.

March 25, 1972

The minute I began to drive through the Vaucluse, that country-side of pointed cypresses and clustered reeds, a water landscape ringed with mountains, images and lines I hadn't understood before came clear. I seemed to be *inside* Char's poetry. That morning I started seeking out the specific places he referred to in his work: I went to Roussillon, whose colors were ocher, yellow, terra cotta, pink, and then to the Fontaine de Vaucluse, beloved of Petrarch. The Sorgue bubbled up from a mountain rock to form a deep green pool. Calcified cliffs rose pockmarked and stark around it. German tourists elbowed each other out of the way. Later, Char was to tell me I'd do better not to look in Provence for the sites he names; rather, look in the poems themselves, he said.

I had taken the overnight train from Paris, and in Avignon I picked up a rental car, a stick-shift that I could hardly drive. In my rearview mirror I could see the slack-mouthed horror on the rental agent's face as I lurched and hiccupped my way out of sight. Then I promptly stalled, in the middle of Avignon. A policeman approached. I said, in French, "I'm not used to this car, I don't know where I am. How do I get out of town?" He laughed and said, "Ah, these Parisians!"

At the hour appointed to meet Char, I overshot my destination by ten kilometers and a mountain, but found my way back to what seemed to be his house and parked in a small space marked *Parking privé*, in front of it. A little gate led into a garden with a fig tree at its center, an enclosed meadow beyond, bordered by dark cypress trees. At the sound of my feet on the pebbly walk, a dog barked, inside the house. A man's voice called, "Is someone there?" I called back, "I'm looking for the house of René Char." "This is it," the voice said. "He's yours in a minute."

Incredulity and terror. Suddenly, here he was, "a great big guy in baggy (and I mean baggy) pants," as I noted later in my journal. "He comes out his front door with a great warm smile on his face—so unlike the convicted felon photos in the Char issue of *L'Herne*—alive—an old man only when seen from above, bending over the pages of a book, so that one notices his bald spot and how sunken his cheeks, which look rouged from that angle." (He was sixty-four at the time; I was very young.) What was so striking about his smile was that it rarely appeared in photographs. He was a mountain of a man, very big, dark and handsome, square-jawed, earnest for the camera, somewhat imperious. A seer, a prophet, frowning as though accusing the viewer of levity in the midst of the general catastrophe. In person, however, Char was as warm and seductive, every bit as courtly as his "debonair snake," once we had broken the ice.

That first day, when he came through his front door like a friendly bear, I nearly burst into tears at his actual presence. As he gestured me into his house, I said, "Really you do me too much honor."

"I don't like that kind of talk," he said.

Mute, I preceded him into his studio.

Inside, we sat down opposite each other, one of us, at least, completely at a loss for words.

After what seemed like a very long silence, I babbled, "There must be many people who come to ask you questions about your poetry."

"I don't like people to ask me questions about my poetry," he said.

I wondered how we would get through the next two minutes. But having effectively shut me up, he took control, he asked me about my family and my writing and where I came from, he floated me along on trivia. Since I was working on my dissertation, we talked about academe; we agreed that the university was covered with dust. I wanted him to know that I had published a novel, I was a writer and a reader, not a professor. A young woman named Anne came in, and we were introduced. She disappeared. I wondered who she was. I didn't know the details of his private life—he was a very private man—although, as I remarked to him, I felt as if I *knew* him, even though we had just met, because I'd read him.

He nodded. The spoken word gets in our way, he said. We never say what we mean, the wrong thing comes out, we correct ourselves, add, qualify, we're covered with refuse [*déchets*]. He gestured toward himself: I hope you can excuse me. You've known me in my Sunday best. Now you're meeting me in my old clothes, all spotted.

We began then, tentatively, to talk about his Sunday best, his poems. We discussed the vulnerability in his poetic universe of everything that can be *seen,* the visible versus the invisible, day versus night. We talked about lightning and *Lost Nakedness,* his most recently published collection. Its title poem begins: "They will bear palms, those whose endurance knows how to wear away the gnarled night that precedes and follows the lightning bolt" (OC 431). Did I understand this verse to be about writer's block, back then? And of course about the intermittence of poetry, of all writing.

Char told me that *Lost Nakedness* had sold better than his previous books. People saw the title, assumed it was a dirty book, and bought it. Imagine their disappointment when they got it home, he said.

Gradually, the two of us began to charm each other, we became allies. I was thirty, and cute, and I could quote the poet his work, verse after verse. And he was charming when he wanted to be. He laughed, he flirted, he told stories, and every now and then pontificated about the state of the world. His was a thoroughly compelling presence, he sounded just like René Char. His hatreds were pronounced, he had a wicked tongue. His loyalties were passionate. Of his friend Camus, to whom the wartime journal *Leaves of Hypnos* was dedicated, Char said, Camus knew that words could demoralize. He realized after the war that *The Stranger* had had a demoralizing effect. That's why he wrote *The Plague.* We were friends because both of us recognized that writing imposes duties, it does not grant rights.

The poet talked about the Resistance, and about how during the Occupation, necessarily, he had killed men, each death leaving a *faille* [a gap, a fault] within him. I told him I was particularly touched by the hunted creatures in his pages and the hunter who is on the lookout for them. But the hunter himself is hunted, he observed, and added that he had hunted as a boy, until the day he shot a kingfisher, which died in the palm of his hand, purely beautiful, one bright red drop of blood at its throat. In the instant before it died, the bird opened its eyes and looked straight into his. He said he never shot another animal. Then instantly he qualified the statement: It wasn't out of pity, you understand.

506

As I noted in my journal, Char "went on to say he suffers greatly now whenever animals are killed, but that's because he's getting closer to his own death. When he was younger, he was faster to form scars. Now everything hurts him, he is all wounds, all bleeding (he really said that). After a silence I said, 'Poetry is a hard profession.' 'Yes, but the joy,' he said. His fingernails were bitten to the quick."

I have to smile now at our exchange. Yet after it there came a flash of eloquence. To hear Char talk about art as *this radium* we bring up from within us, despite our malediction, our shadows—to hear this was a marvelous thing. He spoke with the slightest Provençal accent. He said "*gens*" [people], for example, pronouncing the final "s," so that it rhymed, fittingly, with "chance" (a crucial term in his vocabulary). And you could hear a trace of Provençal in the diphthongs of words like "*pain*" [bread].

In the course of the afternoon, he began to recite and read his poetry to me and, after a while, to answer my questions. By the time I left, he was commenting on specific images, telling the back stories of his poems, explicating texts I didn't know how to read.

I remember asking, for example, about "The Nuptial Countenance," which first appeared in 1938. The poems I loved the most were written later than this. They were radiant with a tenderness that seemed to have come out of the war. To my ear, his pre-war poetry was too often overly violent, obscure, and intellectual. But "The Nuptial Countenance" was a major text, and I thought that if I got a chance, it would be interesting—although I knew that in the classroom intentionality was a sin and an irrelevancy—to ask the man who wrote it just what he thought it was about. There came a moment when Char was showing me the catalogue for an art exhibit associated with his poetry, and suddenly there were the opening lines before us:

> Now let my escort disappear, standing in the distance;
> numbers have just lost their sweetness.
> I give you leave, my allies, my violent ones, my indices.
> Everything summons you away, fawning sorrow.

I am in love.
Water is heavy at a day's flow from the spring.
The crimson foliage crosses its slow branches at your
    forehead, dimension reassured…

trans. Mary Ann Caws

Um? I said. I know it's about being in love. But what does it mean?

The escort dismissed at the outset of the poem, he told me, consisted of all the women he'd previously thought he loved. As soon as he was truly in love, all the others ceased to matter, fell away. Ah, I said. And *the crimson foliage [la parcelle vermeille]? Which crosses its slow branches at your forehead, dimension reassured?* Well, he said, talking very fast, as he was wont to do, so that at first I thought I was mishearing—well, his lover had her period, which interrupted their love-making, a temporary separation that disquieted the poet.

I could hardly believe he was saying this, my abstract genius, my terrible towering intellect! How thoroughly *surprising.* Shocked in my young Puritanism, I felt that I couldn't share this reading during his lifetime (and didn't). Then too, I doubted I had heard right. Until later in the afternoon, when he was talking about having once been blocked: I couldn't write, he said, I had my period. There it was, a recurrent image in his poetics. I felt sure I hadn't misunderstood his commentary on "The Nuptial Countenance."

But how fascinating that Char, the most gender-conscious and male of poets, should see himself, blocked, as menstruating. Throughout his work, the Poet (*le poète*) is masculine, Poetry (*la poésie*) is feminine, and the poem is their offspring. What the image of the menstruating male poet seems to encapsulate is Char's notion that writing is love-making and that both activities are sporadic, characterized by eclipse and return; the wellsprings of fertility must pause to renew themselves periodically, and when they do, it is painful and frightening to the poet.

In "The Nuptial Countenance," however, as he went on to explain to me, the poem's speaker is reassured by looking at his lover's forehead, for there he sees that she is still herself and still loves him, and the threatening distance between them disappears ("dimension reassured").

At this point, he refused to go any further with his explication. He did, however, add that his mother had always asked to see his forehead when she doubted his veracity, and then, scrutinizing it, she would remark, Well I guess you're not lying. Once, he lied to her on purpose, to see if she could really tell. She looked at his forehead, and she knew.

So what about intentionality and the hermetic? For me, the unguessed-at presence of the body and its coarseness in this hermetic verse added to the poem. More important, it kindled my understanding of how this poet worked. Char's comments showed me how rooted in the physical he was, no matter how oracular his voice, and how his art transformed his physicality into image, into language.

Throughout the afternoon, the poet and I traded lines of his poetry. This was our common language and would always be the language in which we wrote our letters. When it was past time for me to go, he invited me to come back the next day. I think we still have things to name, he said, don't you?

Wearing a jaunty cap against the sun, he saw me out and kissed my hand when we said goodbye.

Palm Sunday, March 26, 1972

The next day, the poet showed me original editions of his work, and read his poems aloud. When we came on lines that mystified me, I asked about them. As in "The Figtree's Song" (OC 432: "Lied du figuier"):

> It froze so hard that the milky branches
> Attacked the saw, broke off in the hand.
> Spring did not see the gracious ones grow green.
> The figtree asked the master of the fallen
> For the bush of a new faith.
> But the oriole, its prophet,

In the warm dawn of return,
Alighting on the disaster,
Died, not of hunger, of love.

I could read, as well as another, the religious imagery in the poem, and I knew that prophets usually died misunderstood. But the last line mystified me, and I asked Char about it.

He told the following story: The fig tree now flourishing in his garden froze one winter. To save it, he cut off all the branches, so that new ones would grow in their place. The following spring, the orioles arrived to find their tree cut to pieces—a disaster—and not a thing to eat on it. Char got out a package of dried figs, steeped them in milk, and hung them from the truncated tree. At first, the orioles were suspicious, and resisted, but finally they gave in: they ate preserved figs.

We laughed. I pressed him on the last line. He said, They perished for love of the man who'd taken care of them. But did they perish? I said. It's just an image! he snapped. And we moved on to the next page.

Not all his stories were as lighthearted as the oriole's. We talked about the brutality of the Lubéron, the mountainous region where he was a Resistance fighter during the war. We talked about meteors, snakes, insomnia. When he couldn't sleep, he'd used his nights to illustrate, by candlelight, the book he was about to publish, *The Talismanic Night that shone in its circle.*

Toward noon, a local girl knocked at the door, delivering *L'Humanité-Dimanche,* the French Communist newspaper. She did this every Sunday, said Char, who told me she'd recently given birth to an illegitimate child in one of the tiny puritanical villages nearby and, as if that weren't enough to cause her being ostracized, she was politically militant, as he himself had always been. He was giving her some typing to do these days, to help her out. He was, as he had been during the Resistance, actively involved with the people of his region, and many local characters peopled his poetry (as in "Liege Lord"/ "Suzerain," for example).

When I left, he heaped my arms with inscribed copies of his books. Since it was Palm Sunday, in my copy of *Les Matinaux/The Morning Ones* he wrote: *"Les rameaux sont nus!"* [Palms are naked!]. I thanked him for the encounter.

It was a good encounter, I think—? he said, then told me to come back, so we could name more things.

On the way to the car, he picked a branch of rosemary from beside his garden walk and offered it to me. Then, as I drove off, he called, *A bas l'université!*

A bas l'université! I called. *Vive le poète!*

For all the anti-academic rhetoric, I went home to write my dissertation.

Then, that June (of 1972), my friend Patricia Terry, an extraordinary translator (whose translations will be found in this volume), agreed to collaborate with me on a new bilingual edition of Char's poetry. My editor at William Morrow was interested. In a state of excitation, I wrote to ask the poet's permission. Which Char refused, appending to his letter two pages of line-by-line criticism of the English texts that we had sent him for his approval. Each time the translation deviated from a literal, word-for-word rendering of his work, the English was translated back into French, set beside the original French phrase, and censured for inaccuracy.

Shortly after this, I learned that Char's English was shaky, at best. Evidently, the demolitions contained in his letter were the work of a bilingual friend. It would be seven years before he gave me permission to translate 'anything I liked,' to use any translations I wished in the book I was to publish on his poetry.

His crushing letter of August 1972 ended: "Work well! That is, do not curse the Occupant of your Time too much!"

In response I told him we had given up our project (which broke my heart) and sent him a copy of my novel (which I now assumed he couldn't read). I assured him that I did not curse the Occupant of my Time, although sometimes I did "have an urge to take a particularly hermetic verse and wring its neck." The fact that I was paraphrasing

Paul Verlaine ("Take eloquence and wring its neck") seemed to grant permission for this cry of frustration.

Two months later, Char wrote back:

> Your thought of having me read *The Faithful* [the novel] touched me. I'm late in thanking you, having had several hitches in my health these past few months. That's normal: when one reaches the territories of small stones, the foot slips a little! One cannot really curse the Occupant of [her] Time when one has chosen him; nevertheless, as in marriages based at first on love, then on reason, separate bedrooms protect from detestation... But I'm joking. There are no hermetic verses, you're wrong, there is simply a shutter in front of our windowpane that we haven't yet pushed aside... Au revoir, Nancy. In hopes of welcoming you again at Les Busclats.

June, 1977

In fact it was five years before I saw and heard again the rushing water of the river Sorgue as it flowed through the middle of the poet's village, over waterwheels, beneath footbridges, past whitewashed Provençal houses with red-tiled roofs. The currents pulled green river-grasses back and forth beneath the water's surface, as in Char's lovely poem "The Trout." In the background rose le Mont Ventoux.

This time, I'd been invited to lunch at Les Busclats. The poet greeted me abstractedly—he was clearly in the middle of something else—and left me in his studio for what seemed a long time, although when he returned he proved to be as charming as he'd been five years before, and every bit as voluble. I'd come to talk about a paper I was going to give at the MLA on the effect of grammatical gender in his work, specifically, in "Four Who Fascinate"/"Quatre Fascinants," OC 353–4, a series of brief portraits of four natural creatures. Therein, the two grammatically masculine animals (*le taureau, le serpent*) behaved in pointedly phallic ways, whereas the two grammatically feminine animals (*la truite, l'alouette*) effaced themselves or were effaced.

512

The trout was not even present in the poem named for her: "What has become of your quick one," the poet asked the river, "Among the transparent storms / Into which her heart swept her?" The lark was equally effaced, or about to be. In her poem, she was set into the dawn like a jewel, visible, loud, and therefore doomed. Her poem ended: "She fascinates, to be killed she must be dazzled." (These are Patricia Terry's translations.)

A gendered reading now seems obvious, in the wake of feminist interpretation, gender studies, queer theory. In 1977, it was not so obvious. I had been taught that to the French the grammatically assigned gender of nouns is invisible. Obviously, a bull is masculine, but whereas a trout in the physical world may be a female or a male, a French trout will always be feminine on the page. Nor do the French have a personal pronoun for the neutral "it," so that one has to speak of a trout as "she" (*elle*). In theory, this grammatical fact is empty of meaning.

Not so, in René Char's poetic universe. As the poet agreed, when asked. We were discussing a close textual explication I'd recently read of this poem, in which there was no mention of gender at all. Yet to my mind the poem's creatures were gendered and steeped in the erotic. This critic, I said, left sexuality entirely out!

Well, Char said, men live in a cube, and when they read a poem they interpret it in such a way as to fit it into the cube, but *the poem is not in the cube.*

This became our byword, ever after.

We went in to a long and delightful lunch with Anne, which occupied at least half of my visit that day. She was as charming as the poet and talked, at his urging, about the *Thèse d'état* that she was writing, on the painter Georges de la Tour, whose luminous interiors are present in a number of Char's poems. And indeed, painters and painting proved to be the subtext of the visit. So many twentieth century painters (Braque, Miro, Picasso, among others) had illustrated— or responded to—the poet's work, and he to theirs, with poems or prose texts in exhibition catalogues, that a museum was created a few years later in Isle-sur-Sorgue to house the poet's collections.

In his studio, that afternoon, we looked at these. Char showed me Picasso's cover for *The Transparent Ones* and said Picasso had decided that, since they were transparent, he would put masks on them—so they could be seen. These "luni-solar vagabonds" wandered through the countryside where the poet grew up, they were among the "giants" in his childhood who had since disappeared. The man with the scythe, for instance, who Char said left for work an hour early so he could choose the place where he would eat his lunch. Once he had found it, he would put his bundle there and go off mowing. The poet mimed the act of cutting with a scythe and said the mower would work some, then stop to listen to a bird's song, then continue. These giants cared about *the site,* Char said.

We looked at some of the engravings Giacometti did, as he was dying, for the poet's collection *Return Upland.* It was the artist's intention, Char said, that these pictures appear to have been drawn on slate and then erased, and indeed they shimmered gray and ghostly on the page. The last engraving Giacometti made, which he told Char he wanted to finish before he died, was of a man walking toward the abyss—*just this far from it,* said the poet, his hands held out in front of him, mere inches apart. Giacometti died before he could sign the proofs.

A number of Char's gestures were striking that afternoon. We were discussing his aphorism "Mon métier est un métier de pointe" (OC 378: "La Bibliothèque est en feu"/"The Library Is On Fire"), an untranslatable phrase: *my metier is a pointed metier,* but also a metier *in advance of others,* in the avant-garde, a "prow skill," in Jonathan Griffin's questionable but interesting translation (*Poems,* 179).[2] To demonstrate what the image meant to him, Char abruptly stood and pointed his forefinger straight ahead and marched in a beeline across the room.

And there was another moment when he bounded from his chair. He was talking about how the success of any given poem is unrelated to the difficulty or the ease with which it was composed. He had the grace to look at me and say, You are creative too, you know that there are times when you go like this—and he opened up his arms. Moments when you have wings, he said—and suddenly stood up. When you have feathers instead of buttocks (his hands on his buttocks, fluttering like wings). And then, there are other times… And he mimed laboring up a mountain, puffing and swinging his arms, his fists clenched, working at it.

Before I left, he opened a locked cabinet in his studio and took from it the original manuscript of Miro's phallic, magnificent illustrations of *The Hammer Without a Master*. There, on page after page, the hammer appears as a thick black phallic line, slowly exploring, moving forward horizontally, underground, pursued by other black lines—like fish in some deep aquarium, to use Char's phrase—and surrounded by recurrent spots of bright orange and bright green: "sparks," Miro told Char, which proved that the hammer was at work.

The poet had aged since our first meeting. Despite the liveliness of his gestures, it was hard to shake the feeling, when I left, that I'd exhausted him. As we said goodbye, instead of a branch of rosemary, he plucked an almond from the almond tree outside his house and offered it to me. I remembered his verse, written years before: "I am not alone because I am abandoned. I am alone because I am alone, an almond within the walls of its enclosure" (OC 386: "Neuf merci pour Vieira da Silva"/"Nine Thanks for Vieira da Silva").

When I got home, my six-year-old son was playing with some little colored plastic cubes. I asked if I could have one and sent it to the poet. In an emotional letter, I thanked him for my visit and told him that my son had given me the enclosed cube on the day of my return from France.

Char replied with a warm note that read like poetry. Around its margins, he had written: "The cube will see the last almond on the tree grow blunt before it germinates. (The cube is a seer as is your Child)."

Over the next two years, the two of us corresponded sparsely. "I am recovering from a coronary thrombosis suffered last summer," Char wrote, in February 1979. "The heart! Swept out or pruned? Not even that… Here it is, splitting up the middle! What a logical organ!"

When I told him I would be coming to France that summer and asked if I could see him, as I was finishing a book about his work, he sent a postcard picturing a Provençal stone hut—what he calls in his poetry "a dry house"—surrounded by lavender. He wrote that he would help me with the book in any way he could: "Your questions, your words will always be answered with simplicity." He signed the card "with affection, your René Char."

June 9th, 1979

I arrived at Les Busclats, as directed, between two and three o'-clock in the afternoon and stayed for five hours; the poet wouldn't let me leave. He seemed now a sick old man, obliged to walk with a stick and carry medicine for his heart. This made me terribly sad and emphasized what felt like a seismic shift between us. For the first time, I had something beyond my adulation to offer him, and as though to emphasize that things had changed, my hostess for the afternoon was not Anne—she was nowhere to be seen—but Tina Jolas, whom I'd never met before. That day it seemed the poet and I were friends, at last.

Yet even during that warmest of encounters, my friendship with René Char felt as fragile as a goldfinch. His poetry was all about aban-donment, the intermittences of the heart. And the moral voice of the poems was always present in the room; one never lost the sense of being judged. Which helped to make one feel (and become) a klutz in his presence.

Thus, in the middle of the afternoon there was a brief but blatant fall from grace. The poet was holding forth on something, when I caught sight of a tiny spider climbing up my wineglass. Years before, Char had written: "At the threshold of gravity, the poet like the spider builds his road in the sky. Partly hidden from himself, he appears to others, in the spokes of his extraordinary ruse, mortally visible" (OC 165: "Partage formel"/"Formal Share"). This was one of my favorite Charian images. And now, in the middle of his monologue, I said, *Look! There's a poet on my glass!* My remark was meant as a tribute to him, but it made him lose his place. There was general confusion,

I had to repeat and explain my joke (oh misery!), after which he asked Tina if she could remember what he had been saying. She couldn't. Disarray and embarrassment for all concerned. I'd interrupted René Char. You didn't do that. And then too, the interruption seemed to have exposed his frailty. He looked a feeble old man just then, losing the thread.

We soon got back on track, however, and the question that emerged and came to dominate our dialogue that day was: would I say in my book, as other critics had, that his poetry was obscure, and then attempt to explain away its "obscurity"? The leitmotif of the afternoon was the world's mistaken notion that his work was hermetic, incomprehensible, closed in on itself. How could he, a grandson of Rimbaud, Mallarmé, Scève—how could he be called *hermetic*? he asked. And then, poems *should* be mysterious. He told a story from his Surrealist days. There was a jumping bean, he said, and that imbecile Caillois said, We have to open it to see what's inside. But Breton said, No! Breton was right, for once. Whether the worm inside is eating or changing place or trying to get out, what's interesting about that? What's interesting is that *the bean jumps...*

And he had another bone to pick with critics. The trouble is, he said, that critics want to find a plot in poetry. But poetry has no plot, no continuous development like a novel. Poems are inscriptions made here and there and there, on scattered rocks (he was standing, miming this).

He went on to comment that he didn't like to say it, but every poem had a story behind it, and if a text seemed mysterious to me, that was because I was unfamiliar with the story—a fact that shouldn't stand in the way of my reading. You have to enter into poems, he said, listen to the verses that are mysterious to you as you would listen in a cathedral to Josquin des Pres or Monteverdi, music distant from us but full of hunting horns.

And, of course, he's right. This is the only way to read his poems, whose beauty arises, in part, precisely from their mystery. As Helen Vendler once remarked to me, "One feels Char writes with absolute candor, but in a secret language."[3] Which gives to all his work its characteristic luminosity, and expresses, too, his sense that human beings are destroying the contemporary world by demystifying it. The sacred must not be approached too closely. That afternoon, I thought I understood the difference between *hermetic* (impenetrable) and *mysterious* (inexplicable). As in the following luminous poem, "Anoukis et plus tard Jeanne" (OC 314–15):

Anoukis and Later Jeanne

I will unveil you to those I love, like a long stroke of summer lightning, as inexplicably as you showed yourself to me, Jeanne, on a morning made to your design when you led us from rock to rock up to that end of self we call a summit. Your face half-masked by the arm you bent, the fingers of your hand seeking your shoulder, you offered us at the end of our ascent a city, the sufferings and qualifications of a genius, the scattered surface of a desert, and the circumspect turning of a river, on whose bank some builders stood questioning. But quickly I came back to you, my Reaper, for you were consuming your offering. And neither time nor beauty nor chance which unbridles the heart could compare with you.

It was then I revived my ancient wealth, the wealth of all of us, and dominating what tomorrow will destroy, I remembered you were Anoukis the Clasper, just as incredibly as you were Jeanne, my best friend's sister, and as inexplicably as you were the Foreigner to that miserable bell-ringer whose father always used to say Van Gogh was crazy.

Saint-Rémy-les-Alpilles, September 18, 1949

What moves me particularly in this text is the beautiful and inexplicable divinity of the other—which is suspiciously foreign to the uncomprehending. If you are the poet, or fortunate enough to find yourself behind the poet's eyes, you see what is timeless and fertile in the other's mystery; if you are the miserable bell-ringer, you dismiss the mystery and genius of the other as insanity.

No back-story is needed to understand this. Indeed, Char told me toward the end of this fourth visit, you can no more look directly at a poem in order to see it than at the setting sun. The latter is best seen by turning your back (he mimed the action) and looking at the backdrop against which its reddish reflection plays. This, he said, is poetry as it is reflected against the reader's mind.

No real-life anecdote is needed to experience "Anoukis and Later Jeanne," although it helps to know who Anoukis the Clasper is; but as it happens, the poet provided me with such an anecdote—he even offered to introduce me to the woman in the poem. She was the widow of the painter Nicolas de Staël, he said, and de Staël fell in love with her because of Char's poem. The painter read it and asked, Does this woman exist? Char introduced them, it was love at first sight. She always held her arm across her body, reaching for her opposite shoulder, like Anoukis, Char said. It was a tic, it was *attendrissant* [touching]. And what about the bell-ringer, was he real? I asked. Oh yes, the poet said. He rang his bells every which way. Bells are nice when rung right, but this fellow just went at it. And then he told us that his father, a bell-ringer before him, had known the crazy painter in the hospital at the monastery.

I enjoyed this story, but it didn't undo the inexplicable in Char's text. It illustrated how art comes out of life and leads back to life, how poetry and the day-to-day are interwoven, but it left untouched—essentially mysterious—the poem's beauty and the poet's gift. This is as it should be, and it is entirely characteristic of Char who like his "marginal snake" allows us to see him in the page, then suddenly flees—or *pretends* to flee—"along the line uniting light and fear" (OC 354: "Quatre Fascinants"/"Four Who Fascinate"). In his work, transparency alternates with camouflage, eclipse with return. This fluctuation, this elusiveness has always been my experience of reading Char, as it was of knowing him.

And it seems to have been his own experience of Poetry, which in his work is a woman (as noted above, *la Poésie* is feminine in French, and in Char's work). *La poésie m'est hostile* [poetry is hostile to me], he said that afternoon. *La littérature ne m'a jamais consolé de rien.* [Literature (also feminine) has never consoled me for anything.] Throughout his life, Char's work reflected upon this adversarial, spasmodic relationship between the poet and poetry, their "guerilla warfare above reproach" (OC 339ff: "Lettera Amorosa"). In *Leaves of Hypnos,* he wrote, "There are two ages for the poet: the age when poetry mistreats him in every respect, and the other, when she allows herself to be madly embraced. But neither is clearly defined. And the second is not supreme" (OC 223). Poetry is hostile to me, he said, but that's good, it's how I produce.

He told me a story from his earliest childhood. I've done my own psychoanalysis, he remarked, and went on to describe the beautiful Italian nursemaid he'd had until the age of four, whose breast he yearned to take long after he'd been weaned. All the men in the household were in love with her—the baby Char, his father, his grandfather—and she really liked her charge, as witness the fact that she stayed to tend him for so long. This nursemaid used to take him for walks in his stroller, out beside the railroad tracks. In one spot, a narrow tunnel passed beneath the tracks, and she would wait until a freight was coming, then give his carriage a push into the passageway, so that the train was thundering directly over his head. He would burst out crying, and she would take him in her arms, to comfort him.

I got to like it, he said. Then, as was usual after he'd told a story, he shrugged it off.

I was amused but hardly surprised by Char's sado-masochistic reminiscences. I knew from his poetry that he had a taste for pain: "being brutal repairs [us]," he'd written in "Permanent Invisible" (OC 459) in a clearly sexual context. And I was always aware, when I was with him, of his free-floating rage, the violence of which he was capable, his tendency to turn on people. He was not an easy man—but he could be, too, generous, tender, vulnerable. As in the poem "Windowpane" (OC 310, "Le Carreau"):

Pure rains, awaited women,
The face you graze,
Of glass doomed to torment,
Is the rebel's face;
The other, the happy windowpane,
Shivers before the wood fire.

I love you, twin mysteries,
I touch upon each of you;
I hurt and I am weightless.

He himself brought up his own duality during that fourth visit, when he told me that his birth sign was Gemini, the twins, and explained that everything comes in pairs, if you're a Gemini. You have two loves, you have two great sufferings, and so forth. It's complicated, he said, and showed me an astrological chart confirming this, which another writer (Yves de Bayser) had cast for him before they'd even met.

He asked me if my book would be published before the end of the year. I said I seriously doubted it, given how long the process took. It felt to me as though he were pressed for time. But since he had brought up the book, I asked one of the questions I'd come over specifically to ask: Could I use translations other than those already published in the United States? Use any translations you want, said Char, as blithely as if he'd never squelched the translation project with Patricia Terry. Translate the poems yourself, he said. Tell Gallimard I've already seen them and approved!

He gave me cherries from his cherry tree, when I left, and filled my arms with books.

Back home at my own desk, I took another look at a particularly beautiful picture postcard I'd admired amongst the papers on Char's worktable, which he had added, without comment, to the heap of parting gifts he'd given me. The postcard reproduced one small segment of a wall in the pope's bedroom at the palace in Avignon: suspended against a bluish greenish background hung two empty golden birdcages. I wrote to him, "Like the pope, I look every day at the two birdcages you gave me—from which the birds are absent—and I think, Of course! The bird isn't in the cage any more than the poem is in the cube..." (June 18, 1979)

By return mail, I received a second postcard from the pope's bedroom. This one showed the detail of a wall painting, in which a blue gray bird with a yellow breast perched on the curlicue of a pale yellow vine, against a pullulating background of brown and blue leaves. The shape of the vine's curlicue was the letter "C." On the back of the card Char had written:

> Rest assured, the pope's bedroom is full of surprises... The victorious thrush sings here on the initial of my name! And forgive the bird without religion! Aren't the cages the deserted confessionals where the bird-poem didn't belong? Its word rises from the green obscurity of the leaves all the way to you, Friend... (25 June '79)

That fall, he sent me his new book, *Dormer Windows and Door on the Roof,* and as my own book neared publication we exchanged increasingly warm letters. He wrote of "the pitfalls of Time and the grumpy health which plagues [me]" (23 April 1980). He now signed his letters to me "I embrace you." When I was finally able to send him *Lightning: The Poetry of René Char,* he replied with a lovely letter and an invitation to return to Les Busclats. I told him I would come over at Thanksgiving of that year, and he sent me his phone number. He had had no phone when we first met; I understood its presence now to be a function of his failing health. He signed his note to me, thrillingly, "your friend and reader, René Char."

November 30, 1981

The morning of the day I was to lunch with him, "in the simplicity of the trees denuded of their leaves, but beside a good wood fire" (his letter of 15 November 1981), I rented a car as usual and headed toward Les Busclats. I no longer hiccupped my way out of the garage, but I was nervous, excited, going to celebrate, and in my pocket there was a letter from the eminent French scholar Henri Peyre, who'd written to say that in his opinion Char deserved the Nobel Prize, if only he would accept it. I bore this message with me.

In the narrow country road outside the poet's house, I turned my car around, so I could park facing the right direction: I wanted to make a graceful exit when I left. In the middle of my U-turn, as I reversed, I felt a sudden lurching bump. I seemed to have backed into a ditch. I put the car into first, stepped on the pedal, and heard the blood-curdling, unmistakable, heart-stopping screech-and-crumple of automobile metal tearing itself across an alien object. And there was the sudden smell of gas. Could I have punctured the gas tank? I looked, as best I could, underneath. I didn't see a leak. So I pulled into René Char's *parking privé*.

The poet came bounding out of his house, beaming, with his arms wide open, and kissed me on both cheeks, and ushered me into his studio.

But after a few moments, I said: Um? I *hate* to have to say this. But I think I may have put a hole in the thingummy (I didn't know the French word for gas tank)—with the gas in it? In my car? I think— it's just possible—that a little gas may be leaking on your parking space.

One frozen moment of horror, and Char was out of his chair, shouting for Anne, and the two of them were out the door at a dead run.

Anne moved the car away from the front of the house, Anne called Avis, Avis towed the car, Anne drove me to pick up a replacement, Char cleaned out his parking space as best he could, and we three finally sat down to lunch, two hours later than planned.

"Lightning!" the poet said, in English, and raised his glass, laughing, and we all toasted each other.

It was a hilarious meal. I was as funny as I could possibly manage. Thank God we're friends, I thought, thank God he likes the book.

After a while, I brought up Henri Peyre's letter, which read, in part:

I have long been an admirer of Char. We were at the same high school (in Avignon), where he had been a student of my father's; and although born in Paris, my origins are in a village in the Vaucluse, 15 kilometers from L'Isle sur Sorgue, where I used to go by bicycle during my vacations. I have tried several different times, and in the face of his reluctance, to get him the Nobel Prize—we should try again before he dies. (August 3, 1981)

I didn't mention the part about dying, but I did say that, according to Peyre, Char himself hadn't wanted to be nominated. Did he still feel this way? Would he object to my urging Peyre to proceed?

I remember that the poet was standing at the diningroom table, holding a square wooden coffee grinder in his hands. Well, why not?! he said. And violently ground the coffee beans, round and round and round, a great burst of energy. If only for the money, he said. One would like to be able to leave something. I've never forgotten this burst of joy on his part. I said I would write to Peyre the minute I got home.

There wasn't much talk about Char's poetry during our (alas) abbreviated celebration, even though I had another paper to give at the MLA just one month later, on the interrelationship of internal and external geographies in the poet's work. We didn't have much time, but I did tell Char that the paper I would be presenting in December revolved around his lovely prose poem, "Le Thor" (OC 239):

In the path of numbed grasses where we were astonished as children that night risked going past, wasps no longer went to brambles nor birds to branches. The air opened to the morning's guests its turbulent immensity. There were only filaments of wings, the temptation to shout, a vaulting between light and transparency. Le Thor exalted on the lyre of its stones. Mont Ventoux, mirror to eagles, was in sight.

In the path of numbed grasses, the chimera of a lost age smiled at our young tears.

I loved the transparency of this text and its luminous joy. For once, I had no questions. But Char pointed out the confluence in its title of locality—Le Thor was an actual place, just down the road—and myth, Thor being the Norse god of thunder. And in this connection, the mythic as it is expressed in the quotidien, the poet told me about the shepherd who had lived next door until his recent death. He talked in images, said Char. But how else could a totally uneducated man express himself and the complexities of his experience except through metaphor? You look for words you don't even know, and then to evoke or explain what something is, you compare it to something else.

The poet and I parted friends.

Immediately upon my return, I sent him a rueful letter of thanks, and he replied:

> Despite the parsimony of our Time of friendship, due
> to the rut that finished off your radiator and inundated,
> more with worry than with gasoline, the sweet moment
> spent with you, what does it matter! As we are affection-
> ately attached to you, we derived happiness from your visit
> and the words spoken. You…know how to navigate on
> poetry like a cupid in the paintings of Poussin. (7-12-81)

This, presumably, in contrast to my navigational skills on the roads of Provence. Nevertheless, Char signed his letter "Love," in English.

I wrote to Henri Peyre, and sent Peyre's reply on to the poet. Then, in the wake of my MLA paper on "Le Thor," I wrote to ask Char if I'd misinterpreted a crucial image: "Le Thor exalted on the lyre of its stones." Did the line refer to the path named in the poem, as I thought, or as an audience member had suggested, to an abbey located in the vicinity?

The poet responded (1/29/82):

> ...I answer your question with tenderness. Thouzon [the abbey in question], in my mental gaze, is not Le Thor. Yes, the *path* for lovers is the only lyre in Le Thor for me, along with several meters of ruined ramparts, doubtless romanesque—the church is romanesque "on the exterior." Your respiration was right. Other ruins will come to place themselves in a later poem, those of Thouzon, which are 14th century (a castle-abbey,* the whole unreadable, except by me!) All the countryside of Le Thor resounded to the lyre in question: I was in love and the individual and the living earth were intermingled. The blue-blood Ventoux was smiling...

> *The Cathars had their eye on this.

In France, meanwhile, suspense built all that year toward the awarding of the Nobel Prize in Literature, which was to be announced in October. In September, *Le Nouvel Observateur* devoted a full page to the opening of the René Char Museum in Isle-sur-Sorgue. The article was entitled "The Poet's Dwelling" and subtitled: "René Char's spiritual royalty has at last found its palace on the Sorgue."[4] Finally, he was Pope! Everyone who counted in "Saint-Lubéron-des-Prés" had attended the museum's opening, along with representatives of the Paris publishing world and many local inhabitants. The *Nouvel Obs* celebrated Char and noted that his complete works were about to come out in the Pléiade Edition. This was impressive. Only great writers appear in this edition, and they are usually long dead when they do. The article went on to say that the poet "[was] being talked about for the next Nobel Prize, the last French poet laureate [having been] Saint-Jean Perse (in 1960)." Char was at his zenith.

That October, the 1982 Nobel Prize was awarded to Gabriel Garcia Marquez.

Of course I wrote Char a letter, which I doubt consoled him. Nor, I suspect, did my suddenly showing up in France that December, for what turned out to be the last time we would see each other.

December 1982

The poet greeted me and led me into his studio, where he and Anne were in the midst of correcting the Pléiade galleys, an enormous proofreading job. Months later, I received a copy of *Oeuvres complètes,* and saw that in the bibliography he had included *Lightning,* although he'd told me when I visited that nothing written about his poetry would be mentioned, only his own work and translations of it. It was understood that that excluded my book. But by attributing to it "numerous unpublished translations" (unpublished because he had forbidden their publication), he was able to name it. The irony was not lost on me, nor the generosity of his gesture.

At Les Busclats, we discussed our mutual disappointment about the Nobel Prize, his obviously greater than mine and intensified by the fact that Gallimard had called him on the day before the prize was announced to tell him that he'd won it. Anne confirmed this, in response to my horrified incredulity. Don't leave the house, his publisher had said, and told him to prepare himself for all the television crews who would arrive at dawn.

I still can't bear to think of what that morning must have felt like to him. Although I've since read an alternate version of the story, which ends with Char's greeting the news that he hadn't won with unfeigned indifference.[5] Whatever the case, by December equanimity reigned

During that last visit, we discussed, aptly enough, a wonderful text about encounter and leave-taking. At first tender and accessible, then abruptly difficult, but always rich in texture and image, "Biens égaux" (OC 251) embodies for me—as it did the first time that I read it—the experience of meeting, on the page and in the flesh, René Char:

Equal Shares

I am in love with this tender patch of countryside, with its armrest of solitude, at whose edge storms come gently undone, on whose mast a lost face for an instant lights up and reaches me again. As far back as I can remember, I see myself bent over the plants in my father's disorderly garden, attentive to sap, my eyes embracing forms and colors that the faint nocturnal wind watered better than the feeble hand of man. Marvel of a return that no fortune offends. Noon tribunals, I keep watch. I who have the privilege of feeling at once uncertainty and confidence, defection and courage. I have held on to no one except the fusing angle of an Encounter.

On a road of lavender and wine, we walked side by side in a childhood setting of bramble-throated dust, knowing we were loved by one another. It is not a man with a head of fable that you kissed later behind the mists of your constant bed. Here you are, naked and of all the others the best, only today as you find your way out of a rough-hewn hymn. Is space forever this absolute and sparkling leave-taking, this frail about-face? But predicting that, I affirm that you live; the furrow lights up between your blessing and my pain. Heat will come back with silence as I lift you, Inanimate.

trans. Mary Ann Caws & Nancy Kline ⸱

The speaker returns to the garden of his childhood, his father's garden. How not to hear beneath the sensuous detail (*attentive to sap!*) a biblical reference, an Edenic—or Vauclusian—innocence permeating the first stanza, in which the lost father is found again? The speaker is in love, and in love with a *site;* he feels contradictory emotions that one might expect to be at odds with one another, yet they coexist within the poet, precisely because he is a poet. Or perhaps he is a poet because he is the site of these contradictions. They accompany him, in any case, as he creates. Then, most Charian of all, comes the first stanza's final line: "I have held on to no one except the fusing angle of an Encounter." Here is his relinquishment of the other, as it occurs throughout his work. He and the other meet and fuse in the encounter, and that fusion is all that he retains.

As though to show us what he means, he takes us by the hand into his second stanza, where he and his lover walk through the childhood setting he has just evoked. Later, they make love in her constant bed. But what is the "rough-hewn hymn" she finds her way out of? Here I begin to stumble. And then the beautiful but mysterious line: "Is space forever this absolute and sparkling leave-taking, this frail about-face?"

This was the line that I asked Char about, and he said: There always comes the moment when you have to separate from your poem. And I suddenly understood his text. *That's* who he's making love to, *that's* what he's doing throughout: he's writing a poem and then letting go of it.

You have to make an about-face and leave the poem, he said to me, and this you must do in the moment of deepest emotion, when you belong to it most entirely and you are at your weakest. Yet the turning-away is unavoidable, and you must find the strength to accomplish it. Then, when you come back the next day, it is not the same, it's never the same, not possibly, because when you were most deeply involved you used your strength of will to separate from it.

His comment gave me the text, at least his version of it, which I found—and find—deeply moving. And it influences the translation of the perplexing penultimate phrase, "le sillon s'éclaire entre ton bien et mon mal," which might be rendered as "the furrow lights up between your good and my evil." This biblical translation, however, does not speak (to my ear) of the poet's wrenching himself away from his poem. Thus the above translation: "The furrow lights up between your blessing and my pain."

How formal I sound here, taking my leave of René Char and his text and mine. But he was less than formal when he said goodbye to me. It was raining, and he walked me to the front gate of Les Busclats under his umbrella. When we got there, he said, "Nancy, thank you for your fidelity," and kissed me once on each cheek. Then he paused, and suddenly got pensive. He looked at me, and in a pensive tone he said, "If we never see each other again…" and he leaned forward under his umbrella and kissed me on the mouth—once, twice, three times. A pause. And once more.

He turned and was gone.

***

[1] René Char, *Oeuvres complètes.* Gallimard: Bibliothèque de la Pléiade, 1983, p. 382: "Les Compagnons dans le jardin" ("Companions in the Garden"). Subsequent references to this edition will be designated OC; they will appear in the text, accompanied by poem titles. All unattributed translations in this essay are my own. Other people's translations will be so marked.

[2] *Poems of René Char,* translated and annotated by Mary Ann Caws and Jonathan Griffin. Princeton University Press, 1976.

[3] Private conversation, July 15, 1979.

[4] *Le Nouvel Observateur,* September 9, 1982: 52.

[5] Laurent Greilsamer, *L'Éclair au front: la vie de René Char.* Fayard, 2004: 430.

RENÉ CHAR: RESISTANCE AND GRANDEUR

Mary Ann Caws

In my country, we say thank you.
« Qu'il vive ! »

1.   The Person in the Poems

What René Char stands for, as person and poet, is clear. This is more true for him than for many other poets, and this difference is particularly visible in two forms. First, and most obviously, in his notes kept during the time of the Resistance, those *Leaves of Hypnos* which appear here in a brand-new translation. Second, in his series of aphorisms published over the years, from early to late in his writing. They read like a diary of moral thinking, in its variousness and frequently ambiguous resolutions—or non-resolutions. And third, in those prose poems, often aphoristic in themselves, that lay out a territory mined with explosive possibilities.

To go into Char territory is to venture into another land from our own as readers. I suspect this is, paradoxically, most apparent for those of us who actually live parts of our lives in his land itself. How to phrase this: it is as if the very landscape, the very earthscape and mountainscape—so locally named and felt—were to be the most universal of all. As if this geography, moral as much as physical, were to give the greatest possible scope to our daily and yearly and lifelong stretching toward something other, beyond ourselves and our private mindscape.

My first book on René Char was dedicated to "A Vaucluse of the mind…" and in a sense, all my writings on him and his poems have been dedicated, devoted, determined to be concerned with just that.[1] Char as a person and as a poet required an utter devotion: otherwise, nothing. That was clear from the start, no doubt about it, to anyone reading and writing or wishing to write on him and his work. Those, it is as clear as his moral fiber, were never to be two separate things. There were no fabrications lurking about in the fabric of his being, which was his writing.

That is not to say—the warning signs were up everywhere, posted by his friends, his texts, his demeanor always—that being his friend, translating and commenting upon his texts, interpreting his demeanor, were ever to be simple. Otherwise, it would not have been worthwhile devoting so much time and effort and love and fidelity to working with him and his self and writings. And it was never not worth while. For him, I like to think, as well as for us.

Us in this case contains those of us participating in this volume of homage to him, as well as all his readers, commentators, and translators. I speak here, and gladly, as representative of all three modes.

2. The Person in the Translator

Full disclosure. I am writing here as one of the numerous persons to whom René Char has given a reason for so many things, moral, psychological, and creative. For at least thirty-six years now, I have lived in the Vaucluse every summer, originally because of him. After meeting him in his Paris apartment on the rue des Chenalailles, where he had invited me after my first essay on him, I moved my family to live near him in the summers, in a more-than-rustic field house, a "cabanon" whose memoir I have made into a book on Provençal cooking, explicitly under the aegis of his poetry and his welcome. It is more the place's memoir than my own.

I and my husband live there surrounded by the books and photographs that he has given us, along with postcards of his texts to stick on the walls we plastered with such effort, so long ago. Our children used to send their drawings to their "renéchar," and he kept their photographs in his glassed-in bookshelves. In the winter, at the Graduate School of the City University of New York, where I teach, I speak a great deal about his texts and his life, and the Resistance, remembering so strongly his comrades of that time I would meet in his home.

What I remember with most clarity is his own presence in the Vaucluse or at our "Cabanon Biska" in nearby Mormoiron—"bisquer" for the Provençal "to complain," because one of the former owners was given to doing just that. The cabanon reminded René Char of the Resistance and the *maquis,* he said, as he sat on a wine crate so as not to break our only chair, in a fragile canvas cloth. His eyes became as damp on this occasion as mine were, often, in our work together. Or just in my work on his work, alone. We would usually meet at Les Busclats, his house in L'Isle-sur-Sorgue, where we would discuss his poems I was translating, or whatever commentary I was writing on him, sometimes in French, more often in English. I persevered, over the years, in doing this out of enthusiasm, or rather, with an ongoing consciousness of how important was this task, of which he said: "You are giving a universal interpretation of my work." Ah, how I would like to hope he was right.

Year after year I would go to work with Char in January, between semesters of teaching. In the summer too, of course, and over the years, we would discuss his poems and my translations and commentaries, but the Januaries were different indeed. I would arrive in Paris, take the TGV to Avignon, spend a wakeful night in some hotel there, and take a bus to L'Isle-sur-Sorgue the next day. There I would rent a motorbike, since I do not drive, would put my papers and books in the basket, and maneuver it, rather clumsily, up the road (formerly the Route de Saumane, now called the Route des Busclats), to Les Busclats, Char's hard-to-find house. I was terrified of the traffic on the main road, of the dogs on the minor roads, and mostly, of seeing him. Going alone to speak with him was in any case always serious, professional, and emotionally scary. This was each time like a brand-new fright about something I couldn't live up to, but wanted to more than anything I could think of at the moment. Or, in fact, right now.

In those bygone days, there was no phone at Les Busclats: you had to cable. Having said when I would arrive, I would come up in the early afternoon, leaving my bike outside his wooden gate, on which the name René Char was written faintly. Then I would walk down the gravel path toward the house under the tall trees. To my left, the large field of lavender basked in the sunlight. Char's dog Tigron would bark to let him know I was arriving, and he would meet me at his door with a large smile, his arms open.

About my independence as a translator, I should have known right off, pragmatically and symbolically, that there was going to be somewhat of a problem. One day, when I had, as usual, left my motorbike (my small "*vélomoteur*") in the small road outside the gateway to his house, Char simply picked it up and carried it to his back yard, right by his door. Any transport, clearly, was to be on his ground and his terms. Of course, and equally clearly, that was the exalting as well as the troubling point.

Outside, at the white table in the winter, the chairs were usually empty. In the summer, there were quite often a number of visitors waiting, and I would have to talk to them, of course, this being France, but I always hoped we would be alone, and we were, after the others left. We would drink cool water or the sweet golden Beaumes de Venise muscat wine, and talk about poetry. He would make lunch for me at the fireplace in his workroom, and we would talk and talk. The pale sun outside would go paler, and his green lamp would shine down on his desk. In the corner, his bench had always three hats waiting upon it, each for walking in a different mood, I supposed.

Everything had the colors of his thought for me in those times. Even on the days when I was not working with him, when I would explore the region, through the little towns with the stone fountains and the street markets, the words of his poems rang in my ears. Or I would read them in a field with mint or buttercups. The books he gave me had—still have—their pages full of mint and buttercups. So do the pages of my many memories of the Vaucluse, where we still live our summers.

Until his death, unless we went as a family in our 2CV to see René Char, I continued to go on my bike to Les Busclats, even afraid as I was of the dogs that would bark after me on the long twilight ride home. It always seemed worth it, and the fright was, I knew, part of what I was giving, in return for what he gave me. I would pick up a round loaf of bread hot from the oven in the neighboring town where they still baked it in a wood-burning stove, *au feu de bois.* I'd also buy a little pot of lavender honey to go with it, snatch a handful of twigs from the rosemary growing by my door, and a blue flower or two— the kind that would open in a few hours—and place them on the rear of my bike, held down by a bright-colored elastic band. If it was the cherry season, I would pick a good quantity, tie them up in a plastic bag, put them on the back of the bike where they wouldn't squish, and rev up the motor as if I had a larger beast to carry me. (Sadly, when Albert Camus' daughter was visiting, and René offered her some cherries, I promptly sat on the rest, disgracing myself and my white slacks.)

Sometimes, exhilarated by our discussions, with my basket full of lavender from his garden and a book or two, I would make my way home up the mountain road by Saumane, over the ridge with the scrubby bushes. I would stop from time to time just to sit and breathe in the herb-filled air. Unforgettable.

I have never stopped knowing how fortunate I was, to have René Char as a friend. My father always warned me that I would know more about books than about life; I am not convinced, still now, that knowledge of one gets in the way of the other. It seemed not to matter with Char that my spoken French was never to be perfect. We would work hour after hour, until the poet would rub his eyes with fatigue. Then he might look over with a smile and exclaim:

-How your face lights up when you work.

Perhaps it does. I suppose if you get that light in your eye, you can be trusted.

I'd very much like to think of that light suffusing these pages.

3. Resistance in Every Way[2]

It's of René Char's life as a *résistant* that I'd like to think for a moment. He was not only a resistance fighter in the war—to which the *Leaves of Hypnos,* so masterfully translated by Nancy Kline here, bears witness, as well as Sandra Bermann's essay in this book—but a fighter all along on the moral plane, his whole life long. The combats in which he was involved, though the most famous were certainly those about which he wrote those texts, were not in any way to be reduced to those, which is my point here. To be sure, this gravity of speech, these sudden bursts of knowledge traversed by lightning flashes in *Leaves of Hypnos* as in all his aphoristic work, are unequaled. But what he learned there, and teaches us here and always in his texts he left— as in the conversations any of us had with him over the years—was to sustain his writing and thinking throughout his lifetime (and, by extension, those of his friends and commentators throughout theirs). These historic and exterior events left their traces on the inside.

I remember his telling me about first having to kill—how it haunted him. How great was his respect for Louis Curel de la Sorgue, striding out on his land and refusing to bear witness against those he knew who had collaborated with the enemies. This was the first text he insisted I translate. It had not crossed my mind as crucial to the extent to which it was, for him.

How his moral combats continued, over the years and events and places. We have only to think of his manifestations against the pollu- tion of the Sorgue river, against the factories dumping their chemicals into the water and killing the fish… about which he wrote a play, and about which he spoke at length. And his protest, with Picasso, in *Pro- vence Point Omega,* against the nuclear installations on the Plateau d'Albion, against everything the heartless modern world represented for him, and against which many of his texts stand so firmly. These are the real combats, as he used to say, this is the real thing: "*Ceci est le vrai.*"

What he taught me, among so many other things over the years, was the way you always have to fight against everything morally hate- ful, whether that is major or minor. It's the principle that we maintain, he used to say, and not the public aspect of it. The present and not just the historic truth, so much more obvious.

4. Interrogative Space

The kind of space Char dwells in, and invites us into, is entirely other from ordinary expectation. As the writer Alfred Kazin put it once in a letter to me of December 22, 1977, in response to my first book of translations of Char: "The trouble with this kind of dense utterly transporting kind of poetry is that is locks you (sic) into another world, so that you have to rub your eyes to look at *this* one...What a lapidary style indeed. With poetry in German and English the 'otherness' is in the words; here, somehow, it is in the intervals of thought and resolution between the words." Kazin adds, in this letter, that his friend Hannah Arendt, "who was an exile in France during the first Hitler years, owed a good deal of resolution to her reading of Char's *Feuillets d'Hypnos.* There is a beautiful passage in her *On Revolution* (Viking, 1963) on Char," and Kazin reminded me of it:

> His book of aphorisms was written during the last year of the war in a frankly apprehensive anticipation of liberation; for he knew that as far as they (writers and artists) were concerned there would be not only the welcome liberation from German occupation but liberation from the 'burden' of public business as well. Back they would have to go to the *épaisseur triste* of their private lives and pursuits...' If I survive, I know that I shall have to break with the aroma *(sic)* of these essential years, silently reject (not repress) my treasure.'

Now, even now, to read René Char is necessarily to accept entrance into another space. I am calling this an interrogative one, believing this form of reading to require acceptance of the question as form and as a clue to something far more profound than it might seem at first glance. It calls for participation in the ongoing process of creation, never at an end in Char's poetics.

In Char's work, even the image itself is often subjected to questioning. Caught in the net of a certain phrase, it acquires an emotive complexity it would not otherwise have had to that degree. For many years, what has been most easily visible is the side of Char as Resistance fighter, the mountainous spirit, the respected and outspoken sage who manifested with Picasso, who protested against the dumping of chemical products in the river Sorgue, poisoning the fish: see, in particular, his play *Le Soleil des Eaux* (*The Sun of the Waters*). This was the man who, as Le Capitaine Alexandre, fighting in the maquis, stood for the courage and integrity of humans against the worst sides of their nature.

I think the great poetry that will endure has a quite other kind of complication. So I shall be emphasizing here the ambivalent side of these major texts for whose extraordinary breadth and depth exactly this radical and primary *questioning* is often responsible. The texts are open to challenge, and are otherwise engaging for us through this openness.

Unlike the prose statements with a political bent, these interrogative passages I am interrogating rarely pose their questions in a way that might provoke or even invite a literal response. Their tone, their questioning color suffices unto itself. Already one of the militant poems of *Le Marteau sans maître* indicates in its title, "Versant," that we should look at the text as if it were on a slope, possibly difficult of access. The principal image upon which the poem finishes neither asks for a response nor holds out any promise of a solution:

> Quel carreau apparu en larmes
> Va nous river
> Coeurs partisans?[3]
>
> (What tear-streaked windowpane
> Will hold us fixed,
> Partisan hearts?)

That suggests emotion and fidelity but guarantees nothing. Compare it with an unquestioning passage there might have been, such as:

> Un carreau apparu en larmes
> Va nous river
> Coeur partisans.

Without the interrogation, the poem would have fallen flat, or at least into prose. The implied suggestion in a questioning form opens the text toward many possibles.

This same effect turns at the heart of the brief poem both celebrated and celebratory: *"J'avais dix ans. La Sorgue m'enchassait... Mais quelle roue dans le coeur de l'enfant aux aguets tournait plus fort, tournait plus vite que celle du moulin dans son incendie blanc?"* ("I was ten years old. The Sorgue encircled me... But what wheel in the heart of the watchful child was turning harder, turning faster than the mill wheel in its white conflagration?" ["To Announce One's Name"])[4] The child and the wheel are set at the center of the formal, psychological, and metapoetical ring of the poem—not spelled out, but set spinning in the mind. The emotive force is immense, precisely because nothing is more certain than the presence of this water wheel, turning with its moss-laden dark wood in the sparkle of the river Sorgue in Char's town, L'Isle-sur-Sorgue.

For the second edition of *Le Marteau sans maître,* the liminary prose poem has at its center another question, this time answered, and concerned with a reality foreseen—that of the terrible years 1937–44. The rhetorical question at the outset frames the initial image so strikingly that it is precisely toward this "enraged sea" that the other images flow, in the radiant light or the enigmatic twilight. The central force of the text appears to alter according to the water's current:

> Towards what enraged sea, unknown even to the poets,
> around 1930, could this river—hardly noticed—be flowing

as it ran along in the lands where the agreements of fertility were already dying, where the allegory of horror was taking on a solid shape, this radiant enigmatic river baptized *The Hammer without a Master*? Towards the hallucinating experience of the man knotted up with Evil, massacred and yet victorious.[5]

All the liquid vocabulary: river, tears, sea, is linked here, near the Sorgue, to the water wheel's motion. This wheel slowly revolving in the Provençal sun seems to turn for the single watching figure:

Ce soir, la grande roue errante si grave du désir peut bien être de moi seul visible … Ferai-je ailleurs jamais naufrage?

(Tonight, the great wandering wheel of desire, so grave, may well be visible to myself alone… Shall I ever be shipwrecked anywhere else?)

The unanswered question remains all the more resonant in the mind.

In these poems, the unique twist given to the text comes from uncertainty on one side and a very sure sense of self on the other. The moral plane characteristic of Char's writing—at once deeply sensual and deeply metaphysical—has to do with this imbalance. It is as if the questioning were to bestow value upon the effort, as well as substantiating the identity of the questioner. The intense concentration required lends its energy to the very structure of the work, rendered more dynamic than rhetorical:

Pourquoi changer la pente du chemin qui conduit du bas jusqu'au sommet et que nous n'avons pas le temps ni la force de parcourir en entier?[6]

(Why change the slope of the path leading from the bottom to the summit, which we have neither time nor strength to follow the whole way?)

540

The questioning mode is precisely what leaves the work open to our reading, as it changes, and to alternative readings. Each builds upon the ground of the actual, insofar as it can be known—and yet the ultimate mysteriousness of the whole, past the part or the source of creation, is intact. And must be left so, as integrity demands. Jean Starobinski puts it like this, declaring Char the poet of openness, who is able "while giving to the present and to presence all their possible brightness, to safeguard the integrity of the faraway and the absent."[7] We fill in as we can, from our own lives and thoughts, and what we know of his, even if only by suggestion. It is never simple, never obvious or clichéd.

The texts of each of the series of aphorisms, several of which are translated here, manifest the kind of interrogative space created around the work by a question suddenly sweeping clear the margins, cutting short any trivial possibility of the kind we might have been predicting: "But who can reestablish around us this immensity, this density really made for us, bathing us on every side...?"[8] It won't be anything expected, for the "diagonal" breathing Char attributes to himself in no way conforms to any received ideas. Only those persons who have chosen to adopt his oblique form of being, that "slope" always on the difficult way uphill to the top of something, like his *Recherche de la base et du sommet (Search for the Base and the Summit)*, are endowed with the kind of breath proper to inhabitants of this interrogative space—shifting, sloped, radiant. "Toute respiration propose un règne..." (Every breathing proposes some reign...)

Char's last collection, *Eloge d'une soupçonnée (In Praise of Someone Suspected)* includes many such interrogations, not always noticeable at first glance. "Riche de larmes" (Rich in tears), the very first text, excerpted from one of the poet's notebooks, asks a question about the clarity and the experience of melancholy. In the middle of the dark night of the soul, when "il fait nuit sur soi," what is the use of any even poetic illumination? The response seems implicitly to be that our midposition between birth and death enlightens us sufficiently. So even the end of this poem is lit from the inside:

What a marvelous moment, that in which man needed no
silex, nor any twigs to call fire to himself, but in which the
silex simply raised itself up upon his path, making of this
man a light forever, an interrogative torch.[9]

The image seen as a probing light retains its ambivalence while per-
mitting that oblique, diagonal, non-conformist breath. The way in
which the text turns around itself towards the total lighting up by fire
is reminiscent of that eternally desiring wheel seen in Char's earliest
youth, turning and questioning.

It is also always a question of that slope on which the poet and
reader will find themselves morally engaged. Every question we had,
we keep; each simply finds itself suspended on some higher level. The
questions explicit or implicit in earlier poems find some response
here, or lead toward another question, such as that relating to the
mysterious wolf in the "Marmonnement" or "Mumbling," whose nails
marked a circle around the young boy upon the Ventoux, terrified all
night. Speaking of this poem and this experience, Char breathed
harder. Here, in this poem and in his remembering it with me, he was
once more "incomparable, compensating"—and Char asks: "What
has the wolf become in all this time of abandon?"[10] In such a universe,
nothing, however mysterious, can simply be dropped.

The image of the rose had served in an early volume to open to-
wards the future: "Une rose pour qu'il pleuve!" (A rose for it to rain!),
where the watering of the earth is phonetically suggested in the rose
itself: "arroser" or to water. It had also served to elicit the Greek
philosopher Zeno's enigma about movement, in which the arrow
touching all the points in the trajectory may be seen only as stable
within them, never really moving. "Front de la rose" links the smell
of the rose to the breath in the room: the wide wind of a future desire
mortally wounds the lover of beauty, who calls at once for death and
the end of sterility, in calling "La rose!" What is watered here is the
thorny poem.

Celui qui marche sur la terre des pluies n'a rien à redouter de l'épine, dans les lieux finis ou hostiles. Mais s'il s'arrête et se receuille, malheur à lui! Blessé au vif, il vole en cendres, archer repris par la beauté.[11]

(He who walks on the earth of rains has nothing to fear from the thorn, in places long finished or hostile. But if he should pause to gather himself, he is lost! Mortally wounded, he flies to ashes, archer recaptured by beauty.)

When this rose returns, it is fully and finally linked with death, in the "Regard à terre"—that glance towards earth:

Les pétales s'ouvrent et s'étendent, sortent de la ronde, escortées par la mort, adjoints un instant au coeur révoquant de la rose.[12]

(The petals open and spread out, going beyond the circle, escorted by death, joined for an instant to the heart of the rose, revoking.)

But this rose will finally see the end of the oral jousting: "Effeuillaison de la rose. Dissipation de l'Etoile." ("Depetaling of the rose. Dissipation of the star.") Everything has to end now between these pages, within the natural space of the image, that would go past mere "literature" in order to prove itself in what we may choose to call the real.

5. Where to Live

René Char used to speak of what Mallarmé's swan longed for, "a region in which to live," and it strangely resembled the landscape glimpsed in these profound *Voisinages de Van Gogh (In the Vicinity of Van Gogh)*. Here he found the stars close, calling them by the most intimate of pronouns: "nos tutoyeuses," affirming their "frightening familiarity." They in fact formed part of his workmanship: "Une étincelle a brûlé mon tablier de cuir. Qu'y pouvais-je? Cuir et cendre!" ("A spark burned my leather apron. What could I do? Leather and ashes!") This spark falling on the artisans' apron reminds us of the strength of vertical relations, of the correspondences at the heart of the myth wth which Char identifies himself, that of Orion the Hunter fallen to earth, his face blackened by the darkness of space, and of the other sparks in the *Chants de la Balandrane,* where they fall upon that same leather apron:

> Dans le foyer de ma nuit noire
> Une étincelle provocante
> Heurta le tablier de cuir...[13]

> (In the hearth of my dark night
> A provoking spark
> Struck my leather apron...)

The artisanal stuff of these star-texts burns, provokes, shocks. And just that fire teaches the poet and readers to depart "en longue partance," ferociously:

> Nous faisons nos chemins comme le feu ses étincelles, sans plan cadastral. Nos vergers sont transhumants.[14]

> (We make our paths as the fire, its sparks, without any territorial map. Our orchards go from meadow to meadow.)

And in one of these last texts, the reader becomes finally aware of space opening towards a red sun we can only approach with a question:

> Quand saurons-nous vivre conversant avec toi, rouge soleil trop filial...?[15]

(When shall we finally know how to live, conversing with you, red sun too much a son...?

This collection, ending with the life of France's most mountainous poet, links desire, question, and courage:

A nos mains un désir d'outre destin, quelle crainte à nos lèvres demain?[16]

(for our hands, a desire beyond fate, what fear for our lips tomorrow?)

The question goes so far, accompanied by its image, that there is no necessity to respond: "No reason, no fear. " We already know this, and the answer is itself absorbed by the question—such is the final profundity of the interrogative image.

La seule liberté, le seul état de liberté que j'ai éprouvé sans réserve, c'est dans la poésie que je l'ai atteint...[17]

(The only freedom, the only state of freedom that I ever experienced without reserve, was in poetry.)

Just as the reading of each of Char's texts necessarily brings one more element of knowledge, through its interrogation of the world and the self, a passive reading that does not question the very act of reading would find no vital point in his universe. "What comes into the world to disturb nothing is worth neither consideration nor patience."

6. The Aphoristic Mode

To manifest his basic moral stance, Char chose the literary form we know as the aphorism, from long ago the form most suited to the moral dictum: La Rochefoucauld, and on and on. Now even this form is a rebellion against rules, as if, exactly as if, he had chosen it as a refusal of what might have seemed the most logical, for instance a poem, long or short, or then an essay. I believe that choosing this form indicates—in the strongest possible fashion—his choice of poetic path. It already indicates a revolt against literary and social norms. For the aphorism is often colored by the idea of moralizing, of indications about the way we should live.

Jean Starobinski says of Char's aphorisms, that they form "the perfect example of the amorous and bellicose commerce between contraries… we see in them, little by little, the answer becoming questioning; absence, the future, distance, taking place in the heart of this apparently closed form, breaking its shell; the definition placed at the service of the indefinable, and the precept only enjoining in order to liberate. Having chosen, among all the modes of expression the one supposing the greatest constraint, Char makes it the key of freedom."[18]

Now, re-reading these aphorisms, I see nothing sermonizing about them, rather a condensation of form and thought, a struggle against more usual forms—a struggle for the life of the spirit as it is allied with the life of form itself. Of course, no one ever exploded a train station with an aphorism. No, but the appeal issued by this form in all its tension becomes dangerous for those whom Rimbaud called "les assis," the comfortably seated ones in their smug ease. An incitation to act in a way that has no polite equivalent.

Several characteristics of the aphorism are in perfect accord with Char's aesthetics, as if the mode had always been chosen with that aesthetic mind, and of course it was. Brevity, which we feel from the beginning, a certain tension, a close-up view, and a feeling of the imperative—as well as a space for meditation and in some cases, interrogation. In René Char's aphorisms, there is a luminosity which affects all the rest of his texts. The aphorism knows how to specify the localization of thought and vision, and is thus perfectly adapted to Char's texts, so often based on the nearby places he loved and we may or may not know. Localising is a fight against a neutralising globalism, so frequently responsible for statements somewhat given to blah-dom, which are so beloved of our politicians. For Char, "Le poème est toujours marié à quelqu'un."[19] "The poem is always married to someone." And, frequently also, to some place.

What I have found in re-reading these aphorisms Char wrote during the length of his life is that they change, according to their time of writing, far less than his other texts. I think there is perhaps in them a kind of wisdom that isn't vulnerable to events.

Over the years, we had quite a few discussions about the words "souffle" and "respiration" or breath. Char, emphasizing his "diagonal breath," allied with a robust temperament.[20] He had been tempted to call the volume now entitled *Fureur et mystère* something entirely other: "Trois Respirations," or "Three Breaths," a title he would then have liked me to use as the title of one of my books on his work. Somehow in English it didn't seem to me to work, one of the great trials of all of us who spend much of our lives translating those poets we have loved. "Never," says the poet Yves Bonnefoy, "never translate a poet you do not love." And indeed, I have not done so, nor shall I ever.

The impression of gravity, of deep sadness that could be felt in René Char from time to time is explained in this small text from *L'Age cassant*, a collection from the years 1963–65.

> Je suis né comme le rocher, avec mes blessures.
> …
> J'ai de naissance la respiration agressive.[21]
>
> (I was born like the rock, with my wounds.
> ….
> From birth I have had an aggressive breathing.)

Which marks the fact that it isn't experience only that has taught him to suffer, breathe, grow, but that he comes to all that by his very nature. He was born René Char; he did not just become that name. And I have been wondering recently to what extent the aphorism is and is not linked with the legend. Both affirm things you cannot prove, but which have a kind of sense of probability larger than life. "Larger than life," like the stature of René Char, whom William Carlos Williams compared to a mountain. Char was definitely outside of the norm, to be sure, on all fronts.

I have taken great pleasure in translating many of his aphorisms, especially those in series. And an even great joy in meditating on their wise concision. They never say too much. Take number 42 of *Partage formel (Formal Share)*:

> Etre poète, c'est avoir de l'appétit pour un malaise dont la consommation, parmi les tourbillons de la totalité des choses existantes et pressenties, provoque, au moment de se clore, la félicité.[22]

> To be a poet is to have an appetite for a discomfort whose consummation, among the whirlwinds of totality of things existing and foreseen, provokes, at the moment of closure, happiness.

While waiting for this final word "félicité," we notice, as almost everywhere in his aphorisms, the two contraries which are finally resolved. Aphoristic condensation, like this, is such that thought is resolved only under tension, while in a poem or an essay the tension can drag itself out at greater length. Here, the unquiet and the tornadoes lead, at the last moment, to a supreme joy.

In the aphoristic series, the poet's mission shines forth: which is not to equate it with a clarity that would stifle suggestion at its very source: "Un poète doit laisser des traces de son passage, non des preuves. Seules les traces font rêver."[23] (A poet should leave, not proofs, but traces of his passage. Only traces set us dreaming.) And again, this poet reflects, for himself and every other poet, upon a poet's duty. Things are to be seen close up, not to be judged from far off. "Penchez-vous, penchez-vous davantage." (Lean over, lean over further.) And then he reflects on, and within, the poet's precarity and final knowledge: "Il ne sort pas toujours indemne de sa page, mais comme le pauvre il sait tirer parti de l'éternité d'une olive."[24] (He won't always emerge unscathed from his page, but like the poor man, he knows how to use the eternity of an olive.)

Here's one of the texts Char gave me to stick on my walls of the cabanon Biska, which he loved:

> "Ce qui vient au monde pour ne rien troubler ne
> mérite ni égards ni patience." [25]

> "What comes into the world to disturb nothing
> deserves neither attention or patience."

This comes from the aphoristic series which itself leans over and bends itself so closely toward the animal kingdom to which Char always felt himself so close: *"A la santé du serpent" (Here's to the Snake).* It's certainly true that he, René Char, came into his and our world to upset things, to disquiet, to undo what was too simple, in the surroundings and in the persons surrounded by any landscape whatsoever, not just that of the Vaucluse. A good conscience was never his, would never have been his, and should never have been—nor has it ever been—ours.

Never was he willing to be part of the collective public conscience reassuring itself: in 1962, in *La Parole en archipel (The Word as Archipelago),* he makes this clear:

> Obéissez à vos porcs qui existent. Je me soumets
> à mes dieux qui n'existent pas.
> Nous restons gens d'inclémence.

> (Obey your swine who exist. I submit to my gods
> who do not.
> We remain men for inclemency.) [26]

In 1983, he continued to express, in his paradoxical fashion, this disturbance he spread everywhere:

Le poète fait éclater les liens de ce qu'il touche. Il
n'enseigne pas la fin des liens.[27]

(The poet bursts the bonds of what he touches. He
does not teach the end of the bonds.

7. Translation/Interpretation

Many of Char's greatest texts turn in circle form, like a great
wheel, including "Le Martinet," about the fragility of the bird, like the
poet or anyone in love—the swift who will be felled by a single narrow
gunbarrel. This is deeply true of the particular and famous poem
called "Allégeance," which appears here in two translations, that of
Patricia Terry, whose translation of "Le Martinet" we are including
here, and my own. About "Allégeance," I had an ongoing conversation
with René Char. The first time I published it, in the volume I edited
for the Princeton University Press, I had rendered the "il" of the poem
as "he," for what I thought were obvious reasons, as I had done for
"Le Martinet" in the New Directions volume of René Char.[28] And,
secondly, there was René Char himself, and I am convinced that every
translator and writer who knew him would instinctively read that "al-
legiance" as owing to him, pledging fidelity to his voice. So I first
wrote "he," and published it then, like that.

However, a few years later, I finally understood, after our conver-
sation, that it had to be "she." How, after all, could Char be writing
about a "he," but more importantly, as he explained to me, the "il" re-
fers to "mon amour," the Elizabethan way of referring to "my beloved."
The central personality in question, called simply "mon amour" or
"my beloved" takes this term from the Elizabethan vocabulary, close
to which Char remained, and which he wanted me to emphasize. We
hear: "Where'er she goes…" Indeed, one of the most illuminating ways
in which to regard his poetry is that of the English poetry of that era,
with its deeply sensual reverberations, its serious intertwining of
thought and emotion.

The poem remains as one of the most characteristic and moving of all Char's love poems. I take it as representative of his deeply abiding respect for the other, his profound feeling, and his instinctive closeness to the poetry of another time and another nation—his bearing, consciously, of the tradition of Elizabethan love poetry into the present poetry of France. It is a noble and grave statement of giving, light, and terrible loss.

The manuscript reproduced in Marie-Claude Char's edition of Char's works shows the poem as originally called "La main et les étoiles" (The hand and the stars), at the bottom of which appears "Pour Marie-Claude à qui ce manuscript 'pensait'" (for Marie-Claude, about whom this manuscript 'was thinking').[29] The different renderings of this poem seem to me to be, in their own way, homages to our allegiance to his form of writing. Like our readings of the poet, our translations of the poetry change over time, and are, in a sense, continuous with each other. So in this volume, we have included both translations, Patricia Terry's, and my own, as a double homage and allegiance, and as exemplifying an issue in translation as interpretation. Like our readings of the poet, our translations of the poetry, regardless of the change, and deeper through it, are, in a sense, continuous with each other.

In any and each case, the quite exceptional stature of the poet and lover here includes both genders in one: so must, it is clear, the translator, the reader, and the critic. No reader of either gender is excluded from the voice of this text, nor any beloved. An epic poem in a small space, this text does indeed take its own soaring high and free, unfaltering, even past sadness and loss, illuminated past contradiction, into a greater and deeper place.

8. Problematic Passages

A few disturbing problems arose, as I suppose they were bound to, during the very long time we worked together on co-operative translations and read together my commentary on his work, as it appeared in different places. Chief among them all was a translational attitude. My criteria for translation included the following major one: I had to be able to read the English aloud and have it sound right. Now that "right" was, naturally for me, what mattered to my ears, and to my notion of "right." The latter is, of course, every translator's primary issue. But here was René Char, very much alive and very much caring about the English translation. In order to "keep the poem face to the wave," as he said, I had to use words I found too heavy in English for his Provençal subtlety: I remember, for example, the French word "bivouaquer" in the poem "Congé au vent" ("In the Absence of Wind") as it had been translated by Denis Devlin and Jackson Matthews.[30] Oof, I said, thinking of the translation, how can we use the word "bivouac" in English? The translators, in that edition, settled for the rendering "Camped." Me, I struggled along, convinced, then unconvinced, altering the result every time.

In some cases, I would write an essay on one of his newest poems, only to have him add a stanza at the end, thus effectively writing in poetry what I had anticipated beyond the actual text. My prose, obviously, would fall flat at such a confrontation. Above all, the personal reactions on both sides seemed, at times, uncomfortable: one day, unable to translate the word "grège," I asked for a clue to its meaning.

-Ah, said Char. You see, if you and I had a child

together, that is what it would be called.

I didn't really see, and in fact, the response did not seem a great help to me. The whole enterprise seemed freighted with a great deal of emotional charge. So it was, in the long run, a surprise that it worked at all. Unless, as it may well be, such personal involvement gives a kind of strength to the translation. I cannot say. In any case, in English, either I was to make reference back to the original meaning (a "Greek fire," that is, a bonfire), or I could play on the sense of color: gray and beige, as in: "greige," as in fact I translated it, the first time around. The rest went by the wayside, as it were.

In any case, the compromises that had to be made were not all in one direction, not all from the predominance of the French to the subordinate English. In translating Char's long poem, "The Nuptial Countenance," or "Le Visage nuptial" (I used "Countenance" instead of "Face," since I found "nuptial" instead of the possible "wedding" so very formal). And in that poem I found what so many others before me must have: that the word "plaisir" in French could yield only a far milder English expression.

> -So, said Char, we will change the French to "joie"...
> Just put a footnote that I have changed my poem so
> that you could translate it.

The footnote I felt I could not possibly add had also to do with a change of color, to the "murmure de dot noire" (Murmur of black dowry), and an "obscure plantation," appearing to concern a brunette, from the person to whom the poem was originally addressed, Greta Knutson, very much a blonde. Was I to bring this up, or not? I did bring it up.[31] "Poetic license," said the poet.

But this was not Char's only change of text or mind. When he was reading my commentaries on his work, some of his past references he wanted to undo, as in the dedication to "Compagnons dans le jardin" (Companions in the Garden):

> -You see, he said loudly one day when I had gone
> with the children just to say hello, to have had a
> friend is not necessarily always to keep that friend.

The children quaked visibly, perhaps worrying that he was speaking of our friendship: he wasn't. We remained friends until his death.

9. Participatory Poetics

Char insisted always on what he would call an "anterior echo," one of those paradoxes which carry their fruit both conceptual and poetic, like the idea of a rose existing in order for it to rain: "une rose pour qu'il pleuve." In the *Chants de la Balandrane* (named after a nearby place), he speaks of "nos sèches paroles d'avant-dire"—our dry words of before-speaking, what prepares the speech itself. This preparatory poetics makes and marks the path before and behind, in this work founded on the real sense of the real, of the tools of labor and the effort of decision. That is where the reader comes in. And where the translator is forced to plunge in, decide, and allow, in turn.

Things are not always super-clear in this universe, nor meant to be. This psychological truth, occasionally phrased as a warning, is graspable in the text of some of the greatest of his poems, where the gap between one word and another, one idea and another, is clear. We have to go across the divide, participating in the process of the poem as it makes and remakes itself, marking the path, with some kind of unknownness... This is the mystery in the poet's deepest being, to be cherished: even the statement, in the *Rougeur des Matinaux,* is set between parentheses, as if to protect it: ("J'aime qui m'éblouit puis accentue l'obscur à l'intérieur de moi." I love whatever dazzles me and then accentuates the obscurity in my interior.) It leads to what some critics have thought of as the hermetic—but I would not describe it like that—rather a kind of writing and living and seeing that allow a sense of mystery, always, in the margin of the poem. Not only allow, but require.

And precisely here is the point of an image constantly recurring in Char's work and thought: that the mystery at the heart of the rose must be kept intact, must not be disturbed. Everything is not to be unfolded—the dignity of the poem requires a kind of withholding. Of not making explicit all the terms included in what is said. Leaving room...

There is often an undercurrent half-understood, if not entirely grasped, behind another. Just as "the poem is always married to someone," the *arrière-histoire* of a work, precisely as it is not stated, not spelled out in any prosaic manner, lends—or rather, gives—depth to the reading. Behind the words, other words silenced. So, for example, the strong poem "Living with Such Men," plays itself out against an entire backdrop of military or naval imagery. In true resistance mode, the poet does mental battle against evil, all the way to exhaustion:

J'ai voyage jusqu'à l'épuisement, le front sur le séchoir
noueux. Afin que le mal demeure sans relève, j'ai étouffé ses

engagements. J'ai effacé son chiffre de la gaucherie de mon étrave. J'ai répliqué aux coups. On tuait de si près que le monde s'est voulu meilleur. Brumaire de mon âme jamais escaladée, qui fait feu dans la bergerie déserte?

(I have traveled to exhaustion, my forehead on the knotted towel-rail. Lest evil be relieved on its watch, I stifled its undertakings. I rubbed out its number from the awkwardness of my prow. I responded to the gunshots. Killing was at such close range that the world willed itself better. Foggy November of my soul never mounted, who is firing in the deserted sheep pen?)

The terms "relève," "engagements," "coups," "tuer," "escalader," "faire feu"—all are part of the battalion of skirmish vocabulary, with an aura of Napoleonic zeal—in the "Brumaire" context. And yet, of course, the text can be translated through metaphor, skirting the battle. This sort of decision, made, as it were, under the fire of publication, and our solutions, will be visible in the pages of this volume. Nothing is fixed in the land of René Char, where the olive tree glitters in the sun and the clouds form over the Roman walls and the lavender...

But it is often a lonely land. As solitude remains solitude, distance remains distance, and absence mingles with presence only when called upon to do so. Poet and reader accept a certain gap between themselves also, like the gap between parts of the poem, or the elements in a series of aphorisms. The reader understands when permitted to do so, as does the translator. We cannot be sure.

What is certain is the individuality of these ways of going we choose. "Tu tiens de toi tes chemins" (Your paths depend on yourself), he says in the *Chants de la Balandrane*... "Go your own way, Marianne," I can hear him saying. "It is a good way." There are not faulty ways of reading such a poet: there are only rich readings and richer, fuller ones.

I like the way William Carlos Williams encountered Char—a really good way:

René Char
　　you are a poet who believes
in the power of beauty
　　　　to right all wrongs.
　　I believe it also.[32]

10. Against a Dry House

In the Vaucluse, the ancient stone heaps from Ligurian times—
"les bories"—stood, and still stand, miraculously. They were erected,
like the equally ancient stone walls visible here and there, dry because
they were erected with no mortar. They serve even now as images of
what used to be dwellable in, modest, just enough for the human
body and life. René Char's group of texts, *Contre une Maison sèche
(Against a Dry House),* is formed as statement and echo, as a mani-
festo of courage and loss, free of the nostalgia that an empty senti-
mentality would excuse. The villages of *bories* are no more, and yet
these texts stand firm.

Finally, these dry heaps of stone, in whatever shape we encounter
them, and against which he would have us all lean—the only shelter
we could or should afford ourselves in these times of his and ours—
have nothing comforting about them. They have everything of the
uncomfortable, the explosive, the miraculous. And so these construc-
tions from long ago, continuing as best they and we can, even now,
will have no end.

---

[1]　*The Presence of René Char.* Princeton: Princeton University Press, 1976.

[2]　Part of this text was written, in French, for the celebration of René Char's cente-
nary celebration in Avignon, August, 2007; I have translated it here. The personal
geography based on the Cabanon Biska is the basis of my *Provençal Cooking:
Savoring the Simple Life in France.* (New York: Pegasus Books, 2008.)

[3]　René Char, *Oeuvres complètes.* Paris: Pléiade, 1983, p. 45.

4   *Ibid*, p. 401.

5   *Ibid*, p. 3.

6   René Char, *Eloge d'une soupçonnée.* Paris: Gallimard, 1988, p. 9.

7   Jean Starobinski, in *René Char: Exposition au Palais des Papes.* Avignon, 1990, p. 305.

8   *Oeuvres*, p. 759.

9   *Eloge d'une soupçonnée.* Paris: Gallimard, 1988, p. 175.

10 From *Oeuvres,* p. 369.

11 *Ibid,* p. 364.

12 *Eloge d'une soupçonnée.* Paris: Gallimard, 1988, p. 180.

13 *Oeuvres,* p. 562. This is an example of the kind of "mortal partners" poet and translator become. When I translated this poem for the special issue of *World Literature Today,* devoted to Char, it had one less stanza. I had written a commentary on the first version, showed it to the poet, and he incorporated some of my remarks into the last stanza of the poem as printed, added in proof.

14 *Eloge,* first edition, p. 27.

15 *Ibid,* p. 22.

16 *Eloge d'une soupçonnée.* Paris: Gallimard, 1988, p. 195.

17 *Ibid,* p. 177.

18 Jean Starobinski, *op cit,* p. 305.

19 *Oeuvres,* p. 159.

20 *Oeuvres,* p. 540, and conversations at Le Barroux.

21 *Oeuvres,* p. 765.

22 *Oeuvres,* p. 164-5.

23 *Ibid,* p. 382.

24 *Ibid,* p. 167.

25 *Oeuvres,* p. 263.

26 *Oeuvres,* p. 413.

27 *Oeuvres,* p. 783.

28 Originally in *Poems of René Char,* ed. Mary Ann Caws, co-trans. with Jonathan Griffin. Princeton, NJ: Princeton University Press, 1976. I had rendered the "il" of the poem as "he," for what I thought were obvious reasons, which turned out to be the wrong ones. The later version of "Allegeance" appears on pp. 94–95 of *René Char: Selected Poems,* ed. Mary Ann Caws and Tina Jolas. New York: New Directions, 1992, pp. 58–9.

29 *Ibid*, p. 278. Manuscript reproduced in *René Char: Faire du chemin avec,* ed. Marie-Claude Char. Paris: Gallimard, 1992, p. 272. the bottom of which appears, "Pour Marie-Claude à qui ce manuscript 'pensait'" (for Marie-Claude, about whom this manuscript 'was thinking').

30 *Selected Poems,* p. 15–16.

31 *Ibid*, p. 31–32. A problem discussed in my *Surprised in Translation.* Chicago: University of Chicago Press, 2006, p. 14.

32 William Carlos Williams. *Pictures from Brueghel and Other Poems.* New York: New Directions, 1955, pp. 86–88. The same quotation appears as an epigraph in the New Directions volume, *René Char: Selected Poems.*

SELECTED WORKS BY RENÉ CHAR

Le Marteau sans maître / The Hammer with No Master (1934)

Placard pour un chemin des écoliers / Notice for a Schoolchild's Path (1937)

Dehors la nuit est gouvernée / Outside the Night is Ruled (1938)

Fureur et mystère / Furor and Mystery (1948)

Les Matinaux / The Dawn Breakers (1950)

Recherche de la base et du sommet / Search for the Base and the Summit (1955)

La Parole en archipel / The Word as Archipelago (1962)

Le Nu perdu / Nakedness Lost (1971)

La Nuit talismanique / Talismanic Night (1972)

A Faulx contente / To Your Heart's Content (1972)

Aromates chasseurs / Hunting Herbs (1975)

Chants de la Balandrane/ Songs of the Balandrane (1977)

Fenêtres dormantes et porte sur le toit / Dormer Windows and Door on the Roof (1979)

Les Voisinages de Van Gogh / In the Vicinity of Van Gogh (1985)

Éloge d'une Soupçonnée / In Praise of One Suspected (1988)

MAJOR TRANSLATIONS OF RENÉ CHAR

Hypnos Waking: Poetry and Prose by René Char. New York: Random House, 1956. Translations by Jackson Mathews, William Carlos Williams, Richard Wilbur, William Jay Smith, Barbara Howes, W.S. Merwin, and James Wright.

Leaves of Hypnos. Translation by Cid Corman. New York: Grossman, 1973.

Stone Lyre: Poems of René Char. Translated by Nancy Naomi Carlson, and Ilya Kaminsky. Tupelo Press, 2010.

The Dawn Breakers / Les Matinaux. Ed. and tr. Michael Worton. Newcastle-on-Tyne: Bloodaxe Contemporary French Poets, 1993.

The Smoke That Carried Us: Selected Poems by René Char, Susanne Dubroff, and Christopher Merrill. Buffalo: White Pine Press, 2004.

The Word as Archipelago, by René Char, translated by Robert Baker. Richmond, CA: Omnidawn Publishing, 2011.

TRANSLATIONS AND CRITICAL WORKS
ON RENÉ CHAR BY THE EDITORS

Sandra Bermann:

"La traduction de l'histoire: la poésie de René Char," *René Char et ses alliés sub-
stantiels,* ed. Marie-Claude Char, Association Campredon Art et Culture, Maison
René Char, 2003, pp. 79–97.

"Translating History," in *Nation, Language, and the Ethics of Translation,* ed. Sandra
Bermann and Michael Wood, Princeton: Princeton University Press, 2005, pp.
257–73.

Mary Ann Caws:

Poems of René Char, co-trans. with Jonathan Griffin. Princeton, NJ: Princeton Uni-
versity Press, 1976.

The Presence of René Char. Princeton, NJ: Princeton University Press, 1976.

"On René Char," in *World Literature Today.*

L'Oeuvre filante de René Char. Paris: Nizet, 1981.

Visage nuptial and *Le Marteau sans maître* trans. for the BBC and the program, Bar-
bican Centre, London, 1991.

Translations of René Char in *Against Forgetting: Twentieth-Century Poetry of Wit-
ness,* ed. Carolyn Forché, Norton, 1992.

Selected Poems of René Char. Ed. with Tina Jolas and trans. New York: New Direc-
tions, 1992.

Translations of René Char in *The Yale Anthology of Twentieth-Century French Poetry,*
ed. Mary Ann Caws. New Haven, CT: Yale University Press, 2004.

René Char: The Summons of Becoming, trans., with lithographs by Ed Colker, 2007.

Nancy Kline (Piore):

"The Sexualized Poetic Universe of René Char," *Stanford French Review*, Spring 1978.

Lightning: The Poetry of René Char. Boston: Northeastern University Press, 1981.

Translations of René Char in *Selected Poems,* eds. Mary Ann Caws and Tina Jolas. New York: New Directions, 1992.

"Le Mortel partenaire," trans. in *The Yale Anthology of Twentieth Century French Poetry,* ed. Mary Ann Caws. New Haven, CT: Yale University Press, 2004.

"Leaves of Hypnos" (excerpts) and "Hypnos Moon" trans. in *Brooklyn Rail,* December–January, 2007–2008.

CRITICAL WORKS IN ENGLISH BY OTHER AUTHORS

Cranston, Mechthild, "Orion resurgent: René Char : poet of presence," Studia humanitatis, 1983.

La Charité, Virginia. "The Poetics and the Poetry of René Char," *Studies in the Romance Languages and Literatures 75,* 1968.

Lawler, James. *René Char: The Myth and the Poem* (Princeton NJ: Princeton University Press, 1978).

Sobin, Gustaf, trans., *The Brittle Age and Returning Upland.* Denver: Counterpath Press, 2009. Preface by Mary Ann Caws.

Wright, Franz, trans. *No Siege is Absolute: Versions of René Char.* Providence, RI: Lost Roads Publishers, 1984.

©Mary Ann Caws

MARY ANN CAWS is Distinguished Professor of English, French, and Comparative Literature at the Graduate Center of the City University of New York, and has taught at The School of Visual Arts, Princeton University, and the Université de Paris (Paris VII). She is the recipient of Guggenheim, National Endowment for the Humanities, Getty, and Rockefeller fellowships, past president of the Modern Language Association, the American Comparative Literature Association, the Association for the Study of Dada and Surrealism, the Academy of Literary Studies, and has served on many editorial boards and national committees.

She is the author of *The Eye in the Text: Essays on Perception from Mannerism to Modern; André Breton; Yves Bonnefoy; Reading Frames in Modern Fiction; The Surrealist Voice of Robert Desnos; The Inner Theater of Recent French Poetry; The Art of Interference: Stressed Readings in Verbal and Visual Texts; The Metapoetics of the Passage: Architextures in Surrealism and After; La Main de Pierre Reverdy; L'oeuvre filante de René Char; The Surrealist Look: An Erotics of Encounter; Women of Bloomsbury: Virginia, Vanessa, and Carrington; Robert Motherwell: What Art Holds; Picasso's Weeping Woman: The Life and Art of Dora Maar; Robert Motherwell with Pen and Brush; Virginia Woolf; Marcel Proust; To the Boathouse: A Memoir; Pablo Picasso; Henry James; Glorious Eccentrics: Modernist Women Painting and Writing; Surprised in Translation; Salvador Dalí;* and *Provençal Cooking: Savoring the Simple Life in France.* She is the editor of *Textual Analysis: Some Readers Reading; Surrealist Painters and Poets; Surrealist Love Poems; Surrealism; the Harper Collins World Reader; the Yale Anthology of Twentieth-Century French Poetry; Selected Poems and Prose of Stéphane Mallarmé; Mallarmé in Prose; The Essential Poems and Texts of Robert Desnos.* She is the translator of *Approximate Man and Other Writings* by Tristan Tzara, *Mad Love* by André Breton, *The Secret Art of Antonin Artaud* by Jacques Derrida and Paule Thévenin, *Robert Motherwell,* by Marcelin Pleynet; *Ostinato* by Louis-René des Forêts, the co-editor of *Bloomsbury and France: Art and Friends,* and the co-editor and co-translator of volumes by André Breton, Paul Eluard, and Pierre Reverdy. She is a member of Phi Beta Kappa, an Officier in the Ordre des Palmes Académiques, a life member of Clare Hall, Cambridge, a fellow of the New York Humanities Institute, a member of the Century Association, and was elected to the American Academy of Arts and Sciences. She lives in New York with her husband, Dr. Boyce Bennett.

Further information can be obtained at her website:
www.maryanncaws.com

NANCY KLINE's short stories, memoirs, essays, translations, and reviews have appeared widely. She has published six books: a novel (*The Faithful*); a critical study of the poetry of René Char (*Lightning*); a biography of Elizabeth Blackwell, M.D. (*A Doctor's Triumph*); an annotated translation of Claudine Herrmann's *Les Voleuses de langue (The Tongue Snatchers)*; a collection of essays on the teaching of writing (*How Writers Teach Writing*, as editor and contributor); and a new translation of Paul Eluard's *Capital of Pain* (with Mary Ann Caws and Patricia Terry). She has been awarded a National Endowment for the Arts Creative Writing Grant and First Prize in the Minnesota Review Fiction Contest, as well as numerous fellowships at artists colonies, among them, Yaddo, MacDowell, and the Virginia Center for the Creative Arts. Her current projects include a book of creative nonfiction entitled *Other Geographies,* a translation of Jules Supervielle's *Selected Prose and Poetry* (introduction and translations of prose texts by Nancy Kline; poems translated by Patricia Terry and Kathleen Micklow) and a co-translation with Patricia Terry of Jules Laforgue's *Legends and Morals.* From 1989 through July 2007, she taught in the English and French Departments at Barnard College, where she was founding director of the Writing Program. She has also taught full-time at Harvard, UCLA, the University of Massachusetts–Boston, and Wellesley. She is now an Associate at the Bard Institute for Writing & Thinking and teaches creative writing under the auspices of *Poets & Writers.*

TITLES FROM BLACK WIDOW PRESS

TRANSLATION SERIES

A Life of Poems, Poems of a Life
by Anna de Noailles. Translated by Norman
R. Shapiro. Introduction by Catherine Perry.

Approximate Man and Other Writings
by Tristan Tzara. Translated and edited by
Mary Ann Caws.

Art Poétique
by Guillevic. Translated by Maureen Smith.

The Big Game
by Benjamin Péret. Translated with an
introduction by Marilyn Kallet.

Capital of Pain
by Paul Eluard. Translated by Mary Ann
Caws, Patricia Terry, and Nancy Kline.

Chanson Dada: Selected Poems
by Tristan Tzara. Translated with an
introduction and essay by Lee Harwood.

*Essential Poems and Writings of
Joyce Mansour: A Bilingual Anthology*
Translated with an introduction by
Serge Gavronsky.

Essential Poems and Prose of Jules Laforgue
Translated and edited by Patricia Terry.

*Essential Poems and Writings of
Robert Desnos: A Bilingual Anthology*
Edited with an introduction and essay by
Mary Ann Caws.

EyeSeas (Les Ziaux)
by Raymond Queneau. Translated with an
introduction by Daniela Hurezanu and
Stephen Kessler.

Furor and Mystery & Other Writings
by René Char. Edited and translated by
Mary Ann Caws and Nancy Kline.

The Inventor of Love & Other Writings
by Gherasim Luca. Translated by Julian &
Laura Semilian. Introduction by Andrei
Codrescu. Essay by Petre Răileanu.

La Fontaine's Bawdy
by Jean de La Fontaine. Translated with an
introduction by Norman R. Shapiro.

Last Love Poems of Paul Eluard
Translated with an introduction by
Marilyn Kallet.

Love, Poetry (L'amour la poésie)
by Paul Eluard. Translated with an essay by
Stuart Kendall.

*Poems of André Breton:
A Bilingual Anthology*
Translated with essays by
Jean-Pierre Cauvin and Mary Ann Caws.

Poems of A.O. Barnabooth
by Valéry Larbaud. Translated by Ron Padgett
and Bill Zavatsky.

Poems of Consummation
by Vicente Aleixandre. Translated by Stephen
Kessler

Préversities: A Jacques Prévert Sampler
Translated and edited by Norman R. Shapiro.

The Sea and Other Poems by Guillevic.
Translated by Patricia Terry. Introduction by
Monique Chefdor.

To Speak, to Tell You?
Poems by Sabine Sicaud. Translated by
Norman R. Shapiro. Introduction and notes
by Odile Ayral-Clause.

FORTHCOMING

*Guarding the Air: Selected Poems of
Gunnar Harding*
Translated and edited by Roger Greenwald.

Pierre Reverdy: Poems Early to Late
Translated by Mary Ann Caws and
Patricia Terry.

Jules Supervielle: Selected Poems
Translated by Nancy Kline and Patricia Terry.

*Boris Vian Invents Boris Vian:
A Boris Vian Reader*
Edited and translated by Julia Older.

MODERN POETRY SERIES

ABC of Translation by Willis Barnstone

An Alchemist with One Eye on Fire
by Clayton Eshleman

Anticline by Clayton Eshleman

Archaic Design by Clayton Eshleman

Backscatter: New and Selected Poems
by John Olson

The Caveat Onus by Dave Brinks

City Without People: The Katrina Poems
by Niyi Osundare

Concealments and Caprichos
by Jerome Rothenberg

Crusader-Woman by Ruxandra Cesereanu.
Translated by Adam J. Sorkin. Introduction
by Andrei Codrescu.

Curdled Skulls: Poems of Bernard Bador
Translated by the author with
Clayton Eshleman.

Endure: Poems by Bei Dao. Translated by
Clayton Eshleman and Lucas Klein.

Eye of Witness: A Jerome Rothenberg Reader
Edited with commentaries by
Heriberto Yepez & Jerome Rothenberg

Exile is My Trade: A Habib Tengour Reader
Translated by Pierre Joris.

Fire Exit by Robert Kelly

Forgiven Submarine by Ruxandra Cesereanu
and Andrei Codrescu

from stone this running by Heller Levinson

The Grindstone of Rapport:
A Clayton Eshleman Reader

Larynx Galaxy by John Olson

The Love That Moves Me by Marilyn Kallet

Memory Wing by Bill Lavender

Packing Light: New and Selected Poems
by Marilyn Kallet

The Present Tense of the World: Poems 2000–
2009 by Amina Saïd. Translated with an
introduction by Marilyn Hacker.

The Price of Experience by Clayton Eshleman

The Secret Brain: Selected Poems 1995–2012
by Dave Brinks

Signal from Draco: New and Selected Poems
by Mebane Robertson

FORTHCOMING

An American Unconscious
by Mebane Robertson

Memory by Bernadette Mayer

LITERARY THEORY /
BIOGRAPHY SERIES

Revolution of the Mind:
The Life of André Breton
by Mark Polizzotti

Clayton Eshleman: The Whole Art
Edited by Stuart Kendall. (forthcoming)

LOUISIANA HERITAGE SERIES
Second Line Press imprint

Jules Choppin: New Orleans Poems in Creole
and French
Translated by Norman R. Shapiro. Intro-
duction by M. Lynn Weiss.

Dinner at Antoine's
by Francis Parkinson Keyes

WWW.BLACKWIDOWPRESS.COM

This book was set in Warnock Pro, a typeface that looks to the past as well as to the future. Designed by Robert Slimbach in 2000, it is a highly readable font. Warnock Pro was built upon sound principles of classic design while being centered in our time. Its structure is both rational and dynamic, striking a balance between innovation and restraint.

The secondary font is Futura, a geometric typeface designed in 1927 by Paul Renner.